The First
Agraristas

The First Agraristas

AN ORAL HISTORY
OF A MEXICAN
AGRARIAN REFORM
MOVEMENT

ANN L. CRAIG

University of California Press
Berkeley · Los Angeles · London

University of California Press
Berkeley and Los Angeles, California
University of California Press, Ltd.
London, England
©1983 by
The Regents of the University of California
Printed in the United States of America

1   2   3   4   5   6   7   8   9

Library of Congress Cataloging in Publication Data

Craig, Ann L.
    The first agraristas.

    1. Land reform—Mexico—Lagos de Moreno.   2. Ejidos—
Mexico—Lagos de Moreno.   I. Title.
HD1333.M6C7 1983   333.3'1'7235   82-10978
ISBN 0-520-04708-7

To the first agraristas,
and to my mother and father

Contents

Figures and Tables

Figures

Tables

Appendix B

Preface

This study began with an interest in rural inequalities, and the attempts that had been made to address this problem in Mexico. I was struck by the fact that very little had been written about land reform and campesino activism in Mexico from the vantage point of the participants in these political movements. While there had been numerous studies of the national politics of land reform, its symbolic and practical objectives, and obstacles to implementing the laws, we knew almost nothing about the foot-soldiers of the land reform movement in Mexico: the people who actually brought about land redistribution in the smaller communities of central Mexico during the 1920s and 1930s. As a political scientist, I was interested in discovering how rural political activists defined their ideas and objectives, how they explained their entry into the reform movement, and why they persisted in the face of intense opposition.

In the field, I became a student of local political history, committed to recording the experiences of this generation of peasant activists before their deaths erased the memory of these events. (In fact, several of my informants have died since the fieldwork was completed.) Thus a study of land reform and peasant activism necessarily also became an oral history. The principal interviewing and archival research were completed during sixteen months of residence in the municipio of Lagos de Moreno, in the state of Jalisco, between January 1975 and December 1976, and during another brief trip to Lagos in August 1980.

The agraristas of Lagos de Moreno delved as deeply as they could into their individual and collective pasts in order for me to write this history. Their trust, friendship, and interest made the research professionally exciting and personally rewarding. I am especially indebted to José Romero Gómez for entrusting me with his personal archives as well as for his frankness. I am similarly grateful to Arcadio Amézquita (now deceased), Cipriano Barbosa, Nicolás Domínguez, Salvador Martínez (deceased), Francisco Navia, Juan Oliva, Víctor Reyes, and Ernesto Rodríguez (also deceased), whose political life histories are recounted in Chapter 6, and to all of the other agraristas who also shared their experiences but whose stories could not be fully reported due to space constraints. Juan Oliva and his wife, Doña Trinidad, and Sra. Elvira Hernández added special warmth to my Lagos sojourns through the many pleasant hours they spent reminiscing with me.

Many other Laguenses freely shared their remembrances and observations of local events. I am particularly grateful to Leoncio Gutiérrez Lechuga for expanding my understanding of Alteño politics; to Pepe and Nena Gutiérrez, who added insight to hospitality; and to Professor José Villagrán, for helping me to locate José Romero in Mexico City. Alfredo Hernández Terres kindly gave me access to his local press archive. Lic. Alfonso de Alba Martín provided useful historical background and introductions to fellow Laguenses which greatly eased my entry into local circles. Rosa de Lima Mancilla became a good friend who helped enormously with the practicalities of fieldwork.

Special appreciation is due Roberto Moreno Herrera and his staff in the local Delegación de Hacienda for permitting me to examine their historical archives. The staff of the archives of the Secretaría de Reforma Agraria in Mexico City assisted my research there with efficiency and courtesy.

Maps, graphs, and original artwork were expertly prepared by Thomas Casmer. The originals of some of the photographs reproduced here were provided by José Romero, the family of Salvador Martínez, José Villagrán, Elvira Hernández, Francisco Navia, Alfredo Hernández Terres, and María Concepción Salas Aguirre. Their generosity in sharing these materials is most appreciated. Photographs of the agraristas and Lagos de Moreno in 1975–76 are by the author and Wayne A. Cornelius.

Friends and colleagues in Mexico City have also contributed to this study. From the beginning, when they suggested I consider Lagos as a research site, Carlos Salinas and Cecilia Ocelli de Salinas provided invaluable encouragement, contacts, and essential comforts when they were most needed. Guillermo de la Peña, Andrés Fábregas, Luis González y González, and Wigberto Jiménez Moreno all shared important data on regional and state politics.

Thoughtful comments on earlier drafts by Lyle Brown, Wayne A. Cornelius, Martin Diskin, Merilee S. Grindle, Harold R. Isaacs, David Laitin, Brian Loveman, Samuel Popkin, Lucian W. Pye, David Ronfeldt, Tracy Strong, John Womack, and an anonymous reviewer all helped to clarify my arguments. My field research in Mexico was made possible by a fellowship from the Joint Committee on Latin American Studies of the Social Science Research Council and the American Council of Learned Societies. The University of California, San Diego, supported the revision of the manuscript through a grant from the Academic Senate Committee on Research and a Junior Faculty Summer Fellowship. Elizabeth Burford demonstrated exceptional skill and patience in preparing the final manuscript. The assistance of all of these persons and institutions is gratefully acknowledged; none bears responsibility for the facts and interpretations presented in this work.

My family has lived with this book as long as I have. It is for them: for my parents, Harriett and Norman, whose interest in Latin America kindled my own and whose support has always been invaluable; for Wayne, for his enduring faith and fortitude from the first days of fieldwork; and for our son Craig, for more joy than any parent can describe.

Ann L. Craig

La Jolla, California
September 1981

Glossary of
Spanish Words
And Acronyms

Spanish Words

agrarismo–the movement for land reform, nationally and locally applied.

agrarista–used originally to refer to activists in the agrarian reform movement, now applied more generally in Lagos to beneficiaries of the land reform.

Alteño–a native of the Los Altos de Jalisco region.

ayuntamiento–the elected governing council of a municipio.

campesino–"person of the fields," rural dweller with an agricultural occupation, a tiller of the soil.

compañero–companion, associate, colleague, fellow-member (in the group pursuing labor and agrarian reform).

Cristero–a supporter of or participant in the popular Catholic rebellion against the federal government which occurred (primarily) in 1927–29.

ejidatario–a beneficiary of the government land reform program who is entitled to cultivate land in an ejido.

ejido–agricultural land restored or granted by the government to a community under the terms of the Agrarian Reform Law, title to which resides in the community. Also used to refer to the community possessing such title.

hacendado–owner of a large landholding (hacienda).

Laguense–resident of the municipio of Lagos de Moreno, Jalisco.

mestizo–a Mexican of mixed Spanish and Indian ancestry.

municipio–the political-administrative unit of a state, roughly equivalent in size and function to a county in the United States.

norteño–used in Los Altos to refer to a person who has been to the United States to work or live.

peón–a day laborer in agriculture.

peón acasillado–an hacienda employee who occupies rent-free housing provided by the hacienda owner and who is assured of permanent employment regardless of the agricultural cycle.

rancho–a small rural community (usually less than 500 inhabitants); also, a small landholding.

Acronyms

CAM–Comisión Agraria Mixta

CCM–Confederación Campesina Mexicana

CNC–Confederación Nacional Campesina

CROM–Confederación Regional Obrera Mexicana

CTM–Confederación de Trabajadores Mexicanos

PAN–Partido de Acción Nacional

PNA–Partido Nacional Agrarista

PNR–Partido Nacional Revolucionario

PRI–Partido Revolucionario Institucional

PRM–Partido de la Revolución Mexicana

SOV–Sindicato de Oficios Varios

SRA–Secretaría de Reforma Agraria

UOL–Unión de Obreros Libertarios

1

Introduction

Lagos de Moreno

Lagos de Moreno, Jalisco, is not special, except as each town is special to its own residents; nor is it representative of all Mexican towns, as none could really be. Its history, politics, economics, and society resemble those of the Los Altos region, the state of Jalisco, and Mexico. Yet Laguenses say there is no other like it.

Anyone traveling in Mexico between San Luis Potosí and Guadalajara, or from Aguascalientes to León, has passed through the town. The night traveler arriving before ten o'clock hears taped music played through loudspeakers in the central plaza—everything from Vivaldi to Tom Jones, but only rarely Mexican music—as young boys and girls walk around in concentric circles moving in opposite directions. At night, the main church and the principal streets are brightly illuminated by electric fixtures reminiscent of turn-of-the century gas lamps. Near the central plaza, the visitor passes streets lined by the large homes of *"las familias de abolengo"*—the blue-blood families—with their colonial-style architecture, façades of pale pink or beige stone adorned with iron grillwork, shuttered six-foot windows, and heavy wooden doors.

The main highway, now diverted from the narrow center streets, skirts the periphery of the most populous residential areas. The traffic moves rapidly past children, cyclists, and animals. Only the most intrepid traveler takes his eyes from the road to look up the hill, past the small brick or adobe homes fronting on dirt roads, to the pseudo-Grecian Templo del Calvario at the crest, or to the new residential construction scattered on the adjoining hillsides. Spreading out below is the town of about 40,000 people, neatly laid out in perpendicular streets extending

The town of Lagos de Moreno in 1976, as seen from the highway to Guadalajara.

Along Calle Pedro Moreno—formerly one of Lagos' most elegant residential streets—some of the houses have been divided into smaller residences often occupied by members of an extended family.

from the main plaza, except where the river breaks the pattern. From the highway, the town is dominated by the main church, which dwarfs all other structures, including its twelve sister churches.

Frequent travelers to the region note seasonal changes as the summer months of rain swell the river, dress the fields in green, and bring clouds that cut the bright sunlight with their shadows. In the winter the fields are parched and brown, except for occasional patches of irrigated winter fodder crops. When the river through the town dries up in the winter and spring months, the air at midday carries the odor of sewage and in the evening the hum of mosquitoes. In late July and early August, the town is bedecked with crepe streamers and banners, awakened by early-rising religious pilgrims, and enlivened by the municipal fair—all for the annual local fiesta. On national holidays, schoolchildren or labor union members turn out for the requisite parades and ceremonies. At election time, there are political posters and wall slogans—but only the minimum necessary for a candidate's appearance and campaign rallies. On Sundays and religious holidays, peasants from the surrounding area pour into town to go to market and church services, riding on the flatbeds of milk trucks and private pickups that are given over to taxi service for the day.

This book is about the town of Lagos de Moreno, and the *municipio*[1] it dominates as *cabecera* (municipio seat). It is a history of agrarian reform in one municipio of Mexico: how, with whom, and why it began; what obstacles or assistance the participants in the movement encountered; how it was consummated; and why it declined. It examines the work and ideas of those Laguenses who sought between 1924 and 1940 to bring radical social, economic, and political changes to their communities by advocating the implementation of national agrarian and labor reform laws, and the consequences of this movement for them person-

---

[1]*Municipios* in Mexico are the rough equivalent of counties in the United States. They are the basic political-administrative units of each state. In Jalisco, each municipio has an elected governing council (*ayuntamiento*) and a president (*presidente municipal*) who presides over the ayuntamiento as chief executive officer of the local government and serves as liaison with state and federal government authorities. The municipio government is responsible for maintaining the civil registries and disbursing limited tax revenues returned to it by state and federal governments, primarily for urban service maintenance, road improvements, and salaries of local government employees. Lagos de Moreno is one of the largest municipios in the state of Jalisco, covering roughly 2,570 square kilometers with a total population in 1970 of 65,950. About half of that population is dispersed in 324 rural localities.

ally and for their communities. It is the story of a generation of local agrarian activists—the first *agraristas*.[2]

The Laguenses' story is more than a compelling local drama enacted, with variations, on hundreds of stages throughout Mexico during the third and fourth decades of the twentieth century. The gradual rise and precipitous decline of agrarian activism in the municipio of Lagos de Moreno reveal some of the basic difficulties and incentives for the political organization of rural dwellers, past and present. This case also sheds light on a rarely studied but significant part of Mexico's experience with land reform and peasant organization: the role of urban laborers and small-town tradesmen in "peasant" movements.

Studies of Agrarian Reform and Peasant Movements in Mexico

Mexico is one of the few countries in Latin America which has implemented an extensive national program of land reform. Of these few, Mexico's program has the longest history and thus has been extensively studied.[3] Most of these studies have been written from a national perspective, exploring a variety of political and economic questions designed to evaluate the success or failure of national land reform. Thus there are studies of the politically stabilizing impact of land grants, the potentially destabilizing impact of a termination of land redistribution, and the political control of *campesinos*[4] by the state in the wake of the

[2]Originally, in Lagos, *agraristas* referred to activists in the agrarian reform movement; the term is now applied more generally to beneficiaries of the land reform (*ejidatarios*).

[3]Jorge Martínez Ríos (1970) has compiled a useful annotated bibliography of the literature on land tenure patterns and rural development in Mexico published between 1522 and 1968. A shorter, more selective annotated bibliography has also been published by the Land Tenure Center at the University of Wisconsin (Land Tenure Center Library Staff, 1974: vol. 2, 368–431). Among the classical national studies of land reform and agrarian problems are Simpson (1937), Tannenbaum (1956), and Whetten (1948). More recent studies include: Chevalier (1967), de Appendini and Almeida Salles (1975), Eckstein (1966), Gutelman (1974), Karst and Clement (1969), Montes de Oca (1977), Restrepo and Sánchez Cortés (1972), Reyes Osorio et al. (1974), Stavenhagen (1970b, 1975, 1977), Stavenhagen, et al. (1975), Tello (1968), Whiting (1977), and Yates (1981).

[4]In general I prefer to use *"campesinos"*— "people of the fields"—rather than the term "peasants." Nonetheless, both terms are used interchangeably in the text for stylistic convenience and to facilitate comparisons with the literature on peasant movements and peasant organizations. These terms are used as occupational labels to identify men and women whose work is in agriculture and who are (usually) rural residents; they include a broader population than either the beneficiaries of land reform (*ejidatarios*) or the proponents of agrarian reform (*agraristas*).

land reform program. Economists have often examined the impact on agricultural production of private versus *ejido*[5] land tenure, and the effects of technological changes on ejido productivity. Some studies have carefully dissected the implementation of land reform. More recent scholarship has focused increasingly on the role of international capitalism and external economic dependence as constraints on agrarian development. A few studies have examined the development of national peasant organizations.[6] The literature also includes a slowly growing number of studies of agrarian reform in specific regions or communities where important national politicians and peasant leaders made significant contributions to the local movement.[7]

These studies clearly have expanded our understanding of agrarian politics and economics in Mexico. Yet we still know relatively little about local agrarian reform movements which did not achieve national notoriety, particularly those in regions characterized in pre-reform days by medium-sized haciendas, now converted into subsistence plots, individually cultivated by *ejidatarios*, rather than collective ejidos. Very little is known about the community leaders and early participants in local agrarian reform movements—the first agraristas.

How has this omission in the literature influenced our assumptions about campesino political organization and land reform in Mexico? From the literature, we learn of the Mexican Revolution as a bourgeois political movement and a popular uprising which led to the significant redistribution of land (among other changes) but not, in the long run, to resolution of the problems of political and economic inequality in rural areas.

The redistribution of land was accomplished in the earliest period (roughly 1912 to 1930) and in a limited number of regions (parts of the states of Morelos, Chihuahua, Veracruz, Tamaulipas, and Yucatán) as the result of the armed rebellion and the persistence of campesinos who had been dispossessed of ancient rights by the encroachments of commercial

[5]An *ejido* is an expanse of land, title to which resides in a community of beneficiaries of the agrarian reform (ejidatarios). Some ejidos are collectively or cooperatively farmed and the crops are also marketed collectively. In the majority of the ejidos in Mexico—and in all of them in Lagos de Moreno—the property is collectively owned, and some lands (woodlands, pastures) are for collective use, but the arable land is divided into individually cultivated ejido parcels or plots (*parcelas*).

[6]See especially Falcón (1978), [Fowler] Salamini (1978), Gómez-Jara (1970), González Navarro (1968), Huizer (1968–69), Huizer and Stavenhagen (1974).

[7]See, for example, Brading, ed. (1980), Falcón (1978), [Fowler] Salamini (1976, 1978), Friedrich (1970), White (1969), and Womack (1968).

agriculture, and whose very survival was threatened by the absence of alternatives for subsistence livelihoods. These campesinos were supported in their demands by sympathetic regional or state-level officials. The second, much more extensive wave of land redistribution occurred between 1934 and 1940 under President Lázaro Cárdenas as a result of that administration's commitment to resolve a multitude of petitions left pending by prior administrations. Cárdenas' administration was also determined to impose land reform in regions where redistribution served the short-term political and economic interests of the state as much as or more than the needs of disadvantaged campesinos—regions where the Cárdenas regime and the campesinos often faced the same enemies.

This book does not dispute the conclusions of Mexicanists about the course of the Mexican Revolution and land reform when viewed from the national center. It does, however, seek to clarify the nature of campesino participation in that process, in regions that were neither convulsed by popular insurrection nor key targets of state intervention during the first two decades of the Mexican Revolution. The campesinos in Lagos de Moreno did not take up arms against the pre-Revolutionary oligarchy. Were they, then, conservative, individualistic, low-risk-takers? Did they simply not face a subsistence crisis? How then do we explain their capacity to sustain collective political action throughout nearly ten years of struggle, when such action involved taking considerable risks in exchange for delayed payoffs? If they were politically naive, how did that change? How do we explain the success of an eminently legalistic-bureaucratic organization, sustained by local leaders, which secured from the state its desired political outcomes—at least in the short term? Most of the petitions for ejido land in Lagos de Moreno were granted by President Cárdenas. Were the agraristas mere pawns of the state in this process? Or did they form a mutually beneficial alliance (however unequally balanced) with the state? Did they win more from the state than they surrendered to it?

Some elements of the local process of agrarian reform in Lagos were also encountered in Mexican communities studied by González y González (1974), Friedrich (1970), Ronfeldt (1973), and Schryer (1980), but there are important contextual differences. Two of those communities had experienced agrarian revolts, inspired by the Revolution, involving at least limited armed confrontations between peasants and landholders. By contrast, the agrarian reform in Lagos de Moreno had its roots in nonviolent politics and the work experiences of those who petitioned the government for land. There is no record of any strikes, land seizures, or peasant revolts in the municipio of Lagos. Ronfeldt's study of Atencingo focuses on a large-scale sugar-cane hacienda and the attached refinery, an enterprise unmatched in Lagos de Moreno in terms of scale, economic importance, and the public attention it later received. Paul Friedrich's study of Naranja deals with an Indian community with a history of communal landholding and a native son who rose to become a peasant leader in his state. None of the 40 ejidos which exist today in Lagos de Moreno were granted as the restitution of communal lands, nor were any of them established as collective ejidos. Frans Schryer's study of an aborted land reform movement in the municipio of Pisaflores, Hidalgo, was conducted in an area dominated politically and economically by a "peasant bourgeoisie" of small private landowners, an area which had no large-scale latifundism prior to 1920. San José de Gracia, the community studied by Luis González y González, is most similar in political and social ambience to the communities in Lagos de Moreno, but the land reform which occurred there was much more limited, in both scope and participants.

Agrarian Activism in Lagos

The agrarian reform movement in Lagos de Moreno took place in a region of relatively infertile, underexploited landholdings, of which only a handful employed machinery or were of any substantial commercial value. The large landholdings in the municipio were owned by Mexican citizens, most of whom resided in the town of Lagos de Moreno and, seasonally, on their haciendas. The cultural tradition and service amenities in the town, and the political conservatism of the landholding class, all served to reinforce an insular oligarchy informed about but removed from developments outside its domain. The local economic structure and the conservative Catholicism of all classes in the region of Los Altos tended to create an environment hostile to political and social reform.

Thus it was in an overwhelmingly antagonistic environment that a few individuals in the second decade of this century dared to consider implementing in their local area the "social justice" articles of Mexico's Constitution of 1917. While the vast majority of the municipio's residents were engaged in agricultural activities, the municipio seat provided some alternative sources of employment. Most of the *earliest* participants in the agrarian and labor reform movements had either been employed in the skilled trades or in the local textile mill, or had worked for a period of time in the United States. While the surrounding region of Los Altos had been largely insulated from the winds of change that swept some parts of Mexico during the first three decades of this century, the reform leaders in Lagos had not been part of a self-contained community. Local social and economic structures may have been stable, but workers were in and out, collecting new ideas, capital, skills, and contacts with non-local politicians.

My research began with several very concrete questions about agrarian activism in Lagos de Moreno: How did the communities and individuals who petitioned for ejido lands know that this choice was open to them? Who decided to petition for land? What social, political, or economic arguments were used to justify petitions for agrarian reform— and to oppose them? How elaborate was the ideology of local movement participants, and how extensive were their goals for reform? What factors contributed to delays or obstruction of land redistribution efforts? What factors contributed to successful outcomes? How much awareness was there at the local level of national events, leadership, and ideology? What kinds of men were among the first in their communities to participate in the movement for agrarian reform? Why and how did they decide to join, and how did they participate? Finally, what do these surviving foot-soldiers of the agrarian reform movement have to say about what they did and what was accomplished? How were their lives and thoughts about political action transformed by participation in the movement and its aftermath?

The answers to these questions help to illuminate three issues of general interest to students of peasant movements and collective political action: the participant's motivations or justifications for joining the movement, the conditions under which political organization withers or flourishes, and the conditions under which peasant organizations may be manipulated to serve the state's objectives of mass political control and cooptation of peasant leaders.

The agraristas in Lagos emerge as purposive political actors whose participation in the local reform movement is an instrumental act. The movement in Lagos did not spring from rage or anguish over a subsistence crisis or the violation of an historic right (cf. Scott, 1976; Moore, 1966). This is not to say that the agraristas were without ideals or that their objectives were exclusively material. The rank-and-file of the movement shared a simple ideology linked to the defense of human dignity and moral rights which was only weakly influenced by any structured political theory.

The community leaders who initiated the local petitions for land reform and who became leaders in the local peasant and labor movement
did so as the result of individual or, at most, family decisions. They were
rarely chosen as leaders by community consensus (cf. Womack, 1968).
Their personal decision to struggle to secure the redistribution of land
was not taken primarily in deference to community norms nor out of a
general concern for community welfare. The agraristas did recognize
that collective benefits would accrue to the landless and poor as a result
of their leadership and their petitioning efforts. Some hoped for that
outcome; all recognized that many campesinos who had not joined the
movement would also benefit from the reforms. But the reformists' participation was based first and foremost on anticipated benefits (land,
improved working conditions, higher wages for urban worker collaborators, greater control over their own lives) for themselves, for their families, and for the group of agrarista leaders of which they were a part.
Because of local politics and features of local agriculture, these benefits
were very unlikely to be realized in the absence of persistent local initiative.

Both individual decisions to join the reform movement and collective
decisions by community leaders about political strategies were affected
by carefully reasoned assessments of alternatives and risks. It is this
deliberate assessment of risks in defining objectives and choosing strategies which makes the agraristas' behavior instrumental. Their decisions (and the decisions of those who did *not* join) took account of the
economic, cultural, moral, physical, and political risks. Among the economic hazards, the most notable included the loss of jobs or the reduc-
tion of income (through boycotts) to known advocates of land reform,
and the possible unavailability of credits, seeds, and other essentials for
farming after the agraristas received land and became independent
cultivators. Among the cultural and religious risks, the most important
were social isolation (in those communities where most residents ardently opposed land reform) and denial of Catholic Church rites and
threats of eternal damnation from priests who portrayed participation
in land reform as a capital sin. The physical risks included death, and
severe beatings. The political risks were more collective than individual
(except in the case of the topmost local leadership). Communities had to
gamble on building alliances with a potentially losing political coalition
at the state and national levels, risking future reprisals or denials of
benefits. The specific weight of each of these elements of the decision to
participate varied over time, as local and national political contexts
changed.

Some decisions to join the land reform movement in Lagos were rooted in a sense of loss or deprivation attributable to concrete local changes: the economic ravages of the Revolution, population pressure on the productive capacity of the land, changed terms of employment on the haciendas, and declining employment opportunities. For some participants, the sense of deprivation was heightened by changing individual standards of acceptable working conditions, resulting from new information they acquired by word of mouth, through education, or as the result of personal experiences in nontraditional job situations (e.g., working in the United States). These experiences helped to define their personal economic need as access to land, and the only viable solution as land reform.

But the agraristas' definition of the problem and its solution did not suffice to change their circumstances. At the same time that the needs-and-risk calculations of a critical core of Lagos' campesinos changed to accommodate agrarian activism, changes in the official structure of support for peasant organizations and land reform reduced the risks and increased the benefits which activism might yield. These changes in the structure of support were accompanied by local decisions to take advantage of the new situation. After 1917, a new political and economic opportunity was created nationally by the popular demand for land reform arising during the Revolution and by the enactment of enabling legislation for national land reform. Later, the risks to participants were reduced by the willingness of certain national, state, and local political figures and of organized interest groups affiliated with the state to encourage and protect communities which petitioned for access to land.

These alliances with mostly non-local political officeholders enabled the agraristas in Lagos to survive, to strengthen the local peasant league, to expand recruitment, and to press more aggressively for land reform. The agraristas established clientelist relationships with personalistic political parties in Jalisco, with organizers affiliated with national labor unions and national political parties, with governors and gubernatorial candidates in Jalisco and other states, with national peasant leagues and their leaders and affiliates in other states, and with political campaign organizers for presidential candidates.

Even if these contacts originated with outside agents who "penetrated" the region, there is no evidence to suggest that they were alliances forced upon the Laguenses or into which they entered naively. In fact, the local leadership consciously pursued a variety of alliances reflecting diverse and even contradictory political philosophies and programs. Until 1938, the relationship with outside agents was sustained by mutual consent, with both parties in the alliance benefiting from it. The local strategy to secure land and labor reform (and, for the top leadership, a redistribution of political power) can be characterized as peaceful, legalistic appeals to the state pursued through and reinforced by a network of political alliances. The group claims asserted in that manner were appeals to the state to intercede, to enforce new rights and privileges already granted in principle to the landless campesino class.

This was a strategy arrived at by local consensus, encouraged by the official and semi-official agencies with which the local group was affiliated. It is true that the alliances forged during this period were used by the state after 1938 to reduce the political independence of local peasant organizations. But to say this is not to detract from the accomplishment of this group of campesinos, who maneuvered within the system so successfully that by the later years of Lázaro Cárdenas' presidency they had received the rewards they sought. Clearly this is not a case where independent peasants succeeded in forcing an outcome to which the state was opposed. What we see is a group of campesinos who retained their objectives and a degree of group integrity throughout a period of vacillating support from political officeholders—a group which held out long enough to support the election of officeholders who shared their objectives. Once successful, however, the local reform movement did not develop new goals and greater independence; rather, it became an arm of the Mexican state.

The history of agrarian activism in Lagos is principally a chronicle of campesino political power growing in tandem with the expansion of state power, and then declining with the consolidation of the state's power and the satisfaction of the agraristas' demands for land. It illustrates the process by which meeting and containing limited demands served to expand the domain of state control.[8] The two most critical factors explaining the capacity of the local agrarian organization to survive were the extent of support received by the local group of reformists from state and federal officials, and the skill and persistence of the local group in securing that external support. In the late 1920s and early 1930s, the strength of the local movement and its ability to secure favorable government decisions on its behalf were severely limited by the absence of external support and protection. This support was provided

---

[8]For a general discussion of the Mexican regime's success in satisfying and manipulating local-level demands to enhance its control over the poor, see Craig and Cornelius (1980), esp. pp. 369-371.

consistently only during the presidency of Lázaro Cárdenas, from 1934 to 1940. Other local land reform movements in Mexico during this period failed because local agrarian leaders established political connections with the *wrong set* of state-level officials (see, for example, Schryer, 1980: chap. 5).

Nevertheless, the Lagos case also suggests that strong commitment to land reform on the part of state and national leaders may not be sufficient—particularly in regions which are neither politically nor economically critical to the central government—without equally committed and persistent local mobilization to secure the implementation of laws originating at the national level. While some outside political figures encouraged the reform movement in Lagos, the achievement of land reform would have taken much longer—and perhaps would not have occurred at all—without the determined pursuit of land reform by local actors.

The beneficiaries of land reform have been incorporated into a national peasant union, the Confederación Nacional Campesina (CNC), which is now a major bulwark of the Mexican state. For the generation of agraristas in Lagos de Moreno who managed to benefit from the land redistribution, this was, and is, regarded as an acceptable price to pay for benefits received. Later generations of landless campesinos and many scholars would disagree.

Site Selection and Methodology

I chose to study Lagos de Moreno for several reasons. The Los Altos de Jalisco region, and Lagos de Moreno in particular, offered important contrasts with other regions or communities in which local studies of agrarian reform have been completed. Most of these studies have been conducted in the regions of Mexico characterized in the past by vast haciendas, often owned by foreigners, engaged in large-scale commercial agriculture, which were expropriated to form collective ejidos. However, by 1970 only 14 percent of all ejidatarios in Mexico lived in collective ejidos. Precisely because of those features which make them more interesting research subjects (high government investment, complex internal organization, high economic productivity), collective ejidos are not representative of the economic or political problems of ejidos generally, nor of the pattern of their creation, nor of the relationships of ejidos with the state and federal government.[9]

This study is set in an area that is, in many ways, more typical of the conditions under which most of Mexico's ejidatarios live today. Located in north-central Mexico, with a relatively dense settlement pattern, the Los Altos region of Jalisco is characterized by poor soil and highly variable rainfall, an overwhelmingly *mestizo* population, a pattern of small landholdings, devout Catholicism, conservative politics, and an economy based on dairy farming and small-scale cultivation of maize, beans, and chiles.

A substantial number of properties (rather than a single huge hacienda) were affected by the agrarian reform movement based in Lagos. Unlike the rest of the region, where very small properties were the rule, the municipio of Lagos de Moreno still had numerous large landholdings (according to the local tax records for 1930, 74 individuals owned properties ranging in size from 500 to 30,000 hectares). As a result, 40 ejidos were established in Lagos—more than in any other municipio in the Los Altos region. The haciendas from which these ejidos were formed were all owned by resident Mexican citizens who farmed or grazed animals on part of their land. The remainder of the arable hacienda lands were let out in share-cropping arrangements. This pattern of land tenure and land use contrasted sharply with haciendas in northern and south-central (for example, Puebla and Morelos) Mexico, which were often characterized by absentee foreign ownership or large-scale commercial agriculture.

I was also drawn to Lagos by the lure of the undiscovered. When my fieldwork began, there were very few published studies based on fieldwork completed in the region.[10] It had been almost totally neglected by

[9]Collective ejidos have received the most extensive federal government investments in irrigation, credit, and mechanization. In general, these ejidos have also maintained higher productivity and grow important national staples (sugar) and export crops (cotton, tomatoes, citrus fruits). In addition to their economic importance, collective ejidos are also more complex than individually cultivated ejidos because they usually include credit societies or collective work groups. Studies of these ejidos and surrounding regions include Alcántara (1977), Carlos (1974), Friedrich (1970), Glantz (1974), Hewitt de Alcántara (1976), Landsberger and Hewitt de Alcántara (1973), Mares (1981), Martínez Saldaña (1980), Restrepo and Eckstein (1975), Ronfeldt (1973), Sanderson (1981), Senior (1940), Warman (1976, 1980), and R. Wilkie (1971).

[10]They included a volume of folktales (Robe, 1970), a study of an agricultural community with a history of heavy migration to the United States (Taylor, 1933), a series of essays

anthropologists—both Mexican and North American—probably because it lacked the substantial Indian population which has attracted generations of anthropologists to such states as Oaxaca and Michoacán. A team of students from the Centro de Investigaciones Superiores del Instituto Nacional de Antropología e Historia (CISINAH, now CIESAS) completed a series of community studies in the region in 1974–75, the results of which have now been published.[11] Three works (D. Bailey, 1974; J. Meyer, 1973–74, 1976; Tuck, 1982) have called new attention to the Los Altos region in Jalisco, but only with regard to its role in conflicts between the Catholic Church and the Mexican state during the 1920s and early 1930s. My study adds to our understanding of the Church-state conflict in the Los Altos region by focusing on the convergence between that conflict and the struggle for agrarian reform.

The fundamental difficulty in researching a local political history such as the one undertaken here is that small communities and ordinary people do not keep a detailed written record of their lives and of local events, much less of changing political ideas. Documentary sources are scarce in the absence of the skills or incentives for generating and preserving them: among non-elites, where literacy skills are minimal, and above all, where possession or creation of documents involves increasing personal risk of association with an incriminating activity. The researcher finds, therefore, that the richest source of data is oral history. Here the rubric of "oral history" encompasses two kinds of information: collective, community history to which the informant has been a witness, and individual life histories. My interviews with the first agraristas in Lagos yielded both kinds of data. They confirmed, as one agrarista exclaimed, that "Life is a history."

Primary reliance on oral history is a relatively recent phenomenon in the study of Mexican political history.[12] Initially the method was used to

---

published by a group of French scholars interested in Guadalajara and its hinterland (Demyck, 1973; Institut des Hautes Études de l'Amérique Latine, 1973; Rivière d'Arc, 1973a, 1973b), and a survey of the water problem in the Los Altos region (Alvarez, 1958, 1964).

[11]See Espín and de Leonardo (1978), del Castillo (1979), Díaz and Rodríguez (1979), Fábregas (1975), and Martínez Saldaña and Gándara Mendoza (1977).

[12]The importance of historical information preserved in oral tradition has been recognized by other community researchers in Mexico, who have often relied upon it for "background" or to interpret data gathered from other sources. Historical interview data have been an important part of village studies of agrarian reform (Friedrich, 1970; Landsberger and Hewitt de Alcántara, 1973; Ronfeldt, 1973; R. Wilkie, 1971); of village histories (Gil, 1975; González y González, 1974); of regional studies of peasant politics (e.g., Warman, 1976, 1980); and of studies of local politics (Cornelius, 1975; Fagen and Tuohy,

document the life histories and ideas of elites whose contributions to national history were important.[13] Increasingly, non-elite oral sources are also being tapped. Jean Meyer (1973–74) relied heavily on oral history in his exhaustive study of the Cristero rebellion. Eugenia Meyer (1977) and her colleagues have undertaken a revision of the history of the Villistas in the Mexican Revolution based on oral history interviews with the followers of Pancho Villa. Other scholars have begun to record national experiences of social change as reflected in small communities and the lives of individual residents.[14] This study represents an effort to develop the richness of Mexican oral sources in a new direction: the interlacing of life histories of non-elites with national and community political changes.

The oral history materials focus upon the survivors of the most critical phase of the agrarian reform movement in Lagos: the community leaders and first beneficiaries of the ejidos established before or during the presidency of Lázaro Cárdenas (i.e., prior to 1941). Current ejido leaders and key informants in Lagos, Guadalajara, Zacatecas, and Mexico City were used to identify all individuals who had been active in securing land reform in the municipio. I interviewed every surviving agrarista who was mentioned, as well as the relatives of reform leaders who are now deceased. These interviews were conducted in communities throughout the municipio of Lagos de Moreno and in Guadalajara, Zacatecas, and Mexico City. In all, more than 100 hours of taped interviews were completed, with 42 men and women who had direct, personal experience in the Lagos agrarian reform movement. Detailed community and life-history interviews were conducted over two to six

---

1972; Graham, 1968). However, in all of these cases, primary or equal attention was accorded to documentary sources, survey data, or other non-historical interview materials.

[13]See, for example, J. Wilkie (1973), J. Wilkie and Monzón de Wilkie (1969), and the research conducted by the Archivo de la Palabra at the Instituto Nacional de Antropología e Historia. The Archivo de la Palabra (formerly the Programa de Historia Oral) is compiling an oral history archive based on the recollections of important national political figures, labor leaders, and Revolutionary heroes; folkloric music of the Revolution; and interviews with leaders and participants in mass movements such as Pancho Villa's army of the Revolution, Emiliano Zapata's peasant army and agrarian reform movement, and the Cristero rebellion.

[14]See Pozas Arciénega (1968), Elmendorf (1976), Horcasitas (1974), and Schryer (1980). The best known of all life history materials collected in Mexico are those used in the works of Oscar Lewis (1959, 1961, 1964, 1974). These are not, however, strictly comparable to the historical research cited here. Lewis collected complete individual and family histories for the purpose of family and cultural analysis. While of compelling interest, his work is not particularly useful to the political historian.

sessions (depending on the individual subject's health, facility of recol-
lection, and place of residence) with 20 agraristas, the only locatable
surviving regional and community leaders. The resulting material has
been used primarily in Chapters 4 and 5, but it is also an important
source of the historical data presented in Chapters 2 and 3.

In addition to the life histories and community history interviews with
the first agraristas, interviews were conducted with other ejidatarios,
landless campesinos, local newspapermen, politicians, party functionaries, government administrators, private landowners, and merchants
who have lived in Lagos or have taken an amateur historian's interest in
the town and region. For the most part these interviews—conducted in
Lagos, the adjacent municipio of Unión de San Antonio, and Guadalajara—were not tape-recorded.

Wherever possible, documentary sources were consulted to check or
supplement materials from oral sources.[15] There is, however, very little
written documentation of local events, and even less that deals with non-
elites. The documents that do exist reflect an assumption that the only
truly important and interesting things that have happened in Lagos have
involved the educated, the wealthy, and the socially prominent. One finds
little awareness that the political history of a community includes all of
its people, or that the success and prominence of some residents is intimately connected to the way of life of the anonymous majority. My experience was that for a local history focusing on non-elites, traditional
documentary sources provide at best a general outline of events. They
can also be useful for fixing dates (which fade in memory) and for describing procedural relations between ejido communities and government agencies. Although one can collect data on non-elites as a group
and on ejido communities through traditional documentary sources, it is

---

[15]Locally, I was granted access to the minutes of the meetings of the municipal government from 1900 to 1940 (*Libros de Actas del Ayuntamiento*); archives of newspapers and
literary magazines published in Lagos during this century; property records in the state
tax office (*Libros de Catastro*, Secretaria de Hacienda del Estado); and all ejido documentation still held by the men on whom case materials were collected. Despite repeated efforts,
I was not permitted to study Catholic Church records (see Appendix C). The most useful
federal government documents were in the Archives of the Agrarian Reform Ministry
(Secretaría de Reforma Agraria) in Mexico City. I consulted copies of the principal newspapers published in Guadalajara during the period of intense agrarian reform activities
between 1929 and 1938 and scattered issues for other years, but found that there were
few useful reports on activities outside of the state capital. I also consulted agrarian and
population censuses in the federal government's General Office of Statistics (Dirección
General de Estadística). The quality, utility, and contents of these archives and other
documentary sources are discussed in detail in Appendix C.

very difficult to trace specific individuals or to link them to events. For the latter purposes, I relied heavily on private archives (mainly disordered file folders of a few letters) rather than on publicly available documents.[16]

Organization of This Book

Chapter 2 describes the local social, economic, and political context from which the reform movement in Lagos emerged. This chapter begins with a contemporary (mid-1970s) description of the municipio of Lagos de Moreno and the Los Altos de Jalisco region of which it is a part. The remainder of the chapter traces the history of Lagos from the Spanish colonial period through the Revolution of 1910–17, with particular attention to the ways in which the municipio of Lagos de Moreno reflects— and departs from—the development patterns of the Los Altos region.

Chapters 3 and 4 focus on the movement for agrarian reform and its leaders at the municipio level. Chapter 3 provides a description of the local land-tenure system and labor conditions as the reform movement began. Both chapters address some of the general concerns outlined above: the arguments used to justify land reform; the allies, obstacles, and assistance encountered by the movement; and the risks confronted by the participants.

In Chapters 5 and 6, attention shifts to individual leaders of the movement. Detailed profiles of 8 key participants in the formation of ejido communities in the municipio of Lagos are developed, largely from personal interview data. The focus here is on the leaders' reasons for joining the movement, the nature of their participation, the impact the movement had on their lives, and their retrospective evaluations of the agrarian reform. Chapter 6 also provides a general description of the first generation of ejido community leaders and their patterns of political participation at the community and municipal levels since the decline of the agrarian reform movement.

The concluding chapter examines the social, economic, and political legacy of *agrarismo* in Lagos, and its implications for future relations between campesinos and the Mexican state. Appendix A provides a detailed description of the legal-bureaucratic process for securing ejido lands which had to be followed by the agraristas in Lagos and elsewhere

---

[16]The most important of these private archives are the documents which had been preserved by José Romero Gómez, whose political life history is recounted in Chapter 5. This archive is referred to in the text as AJRG.

in Mexico. Appendix B consists of supplementary tables of data on land tenure and ejido grants in the municipio of Lagos de Moreno. Finally, Appendix C elaborates on the advantages of oral history as a research methodology, and describes in detail the archives which were used for written documentation of the history of agrarian activism in Lagos de Moreno.

2

The Burden
Of Tradition

The municipio of Lagos de Moreno is one of a score of municipios which together comprise the region known as Los Altos, in the northeastern section of the state of Jalisco (see Figure 1). Climate and natural resources have limited the options for regional agriculture and for economic expansion in general. Historically evolved political arrangements and social values are also heavy legacies which continue to influence the local acceptability of alternatives for economic and political organization. The nature and outcome of the struggle for agrarian reform in Lagos de Moreno can be understood only in this context.

Los Altos de Jalisco: "Region of Poor Soil and Industrious People"

Comprised of approximately 24 municipios, the Los Altos region is a small plateau, bounded by Guadalajara's Valle de Atemajac on the southwest, the states of Aguascalientes and Zacatecas on the north, and the states of San Luis Potosí and Guanajuato to the east and southeast. Most of the region lies at about 1800 meters above sea level. Rolling plains are broken by small hills, occasional low mountains, depressions, gullies, and narrow ravines.

As described in a promotional booklet published by the municipio of Lagos, this is a "region of poor soil and industrious people." Peasants say that the land is "tired"; even the untrained eye can detect extensive erosion and deforestation. Thin topsoil, poor in nutrients, has been further depleted by overplanting, overgrazing, and little attention to erosion

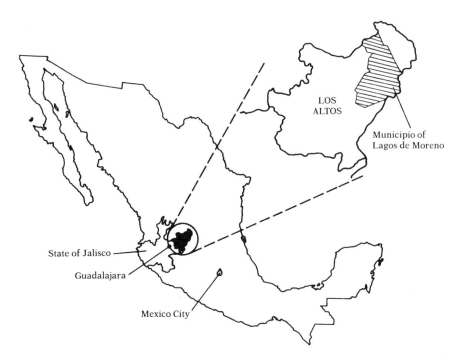

Figure 1. State of Jalisco, Los Altos region, and municipio of Lagos de Moreno.

control, so that it currently measures only 10 to 20 centimeters. Natural vegetation is sparse—low grasses, cacti, huizache and mesquite trees. There is little wildlife, with the exception of rodents, some snakes, and birds; even rabbits are rare. Climatically the region is semi-dry, with a clearly defined dry winter season in which minimum temperatures can drop below freezing. Rainfall, which ranges from 400 millimeters per year in the east to 800 millimeters per year in the south, is concentrated in a short June-to-October season. It is also highly erratic: droughts alternate with floods, in rapid succession. But even if all of the rainfall in Los Altos did not flow away, or evaporate, and remained where it was needed, it would still be insufficient to satisfy the region's agricultural needs.[1]

There are marked seasonal changes in the appearance of the land, changes which accentuate the vital importance of water. In the winter,

[1]D.P.E.S. (1968: 4). On the importance of water, climate, and soil conditions as limiting factors in the regional economy, see Álvarez (1958, 1964) and Demyck (1973: 238–242 and passim). It is estimated (D.P.E.S., 1968: 52) that of the 108,000-hectare land surface of the municipio of Lagos, only 40,000 hectares are arable. (One hectare is equivalent to 2.47 acres.)

cloud-free skies, bright sunshine, and pleasant temperatures contrast with a dusty, parched, brown landscape. Particularly in the driest parts of the region (northern Lagos and the municipio of Ojuelos), by March or April all of the reserve water in earthen dams has evaporated or been drained off for cattle, home use, and some irrigation. In the north, many of the fields are reduced to inches of dust which blows around in frequent dust-storms. Cacti stand out as welcome greenery. It is difficult to spot the adobe houses at a distance, so easily do they blend into the landscape. But by August, one would never recognize the hills and fields as part of the same landscape. With even scant rainfall, grass and wildflowers sprout; depressions appear where they were unnoticed before, becoming small watering holes and washing areas; and with the changing sunlight and shadows cast by swiftly moving clouds, the landscape is bathed in hues of green, purple, and blue.

The economy of the municipio of Lagos de Moreno has evolved in part as an adaptation to the local configuration of these regional climatic constraints. Lagos and adjoining Ojuelos are the most arid municipios in Los Altos. More hectares per animal are required for grazing lands here than in the wetter and more fertile southern and eastern municipios of the region.[2] Thus, larger landholdings evolved in the early years of cattle-raising. These larger landholdings could also be more readily supported by the town of Lagos' location at a major rail and highway intersection, offering access to transportation to markets (see Figure 2). Thus there were more haciendas and larger landholdings in Lagos than in other municipios in Los Altos.[3] Partly as a result of this land tenure pattern, Lagos has more ejidos than any other municipio in the region.

Today the agricultural economy of the region is based upon the cultivation of maize and beans and on dairy farming. Larger landowners grow crops which can be used to feed their cattle and to market as fodder. In addition to commercially profitable chiles and winter wheat, they grow alfalfa, oats, and sorghum. The smallest landholders and most

---

[2]Demyck (1973: 236, 241) estimates that in the Los Altos region as a whole, 1 irrigated hectare can support 5–6 animals, whereas 1.5–2 hectares of rainfall-dependent farmland (*tierras de temporal*) or 6–10 hectares of grazing grasslands (*agostadero*) are required per animal.

[3]Gándara Mendoza suggests that elsewhere in the region large haciendas may have evolved from smaller land grants through assertion of user or occupier rights to unclaimed empty lands (Martínez Saldaña and Gándara Mendoza, 1977: 177). This may have been a contributing factor to the development of large haciendas in Lagos de Moreno, which was more sparsely settled than municipios closer to Guadalajara.

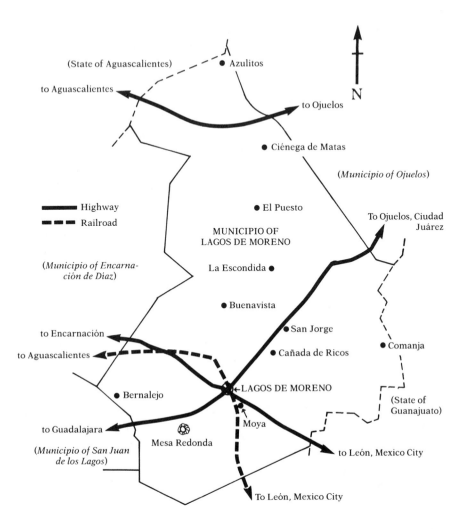

Figure 2. Municipio of Lagos de Moreno.

ejidatarios are generally subsistence farmers who feed their cattle dried cornstalks, retain most of the dried ears for family consumption, and sell anything that remains to purchase other household and farming supplies; generally they have few if any cows.[4]

While the Lagos economy is clearly agriculturally based, with even the largest industries agriculture-related or derivative, it is not strictly a

[4]The Departamento de Economia of the state of Jalisco (1973: 92) has estimated that 74% of the value of agricultural production in the municipio of Lagos de Moreno is locally consumed.

rural municipio. According to the 1970 census, 51 percent of the munici-pio's 65,950 residents lived in the municipio seat (the town of Lagos), while the rest lived in 325 smaller localities, 294 of which had fewer than 250 inhabitants. The town of Lagos had more than quadrupled its popu-lation since 1940, largely due to in-migration from the surrounding countryside. High unemployment and underemployment in rural com-munities (an estimated 32 percent of the municipio's population over the age of 12 were unemployed in 1971), inequitable land tenure patterns, a high rate of natural population increase, and a severe urban bias in the distribution of government investments and employment opportunities have all contributed to the rural exodus. This is reflected not only in the explosive growth of the town of Lagos but in high rates of out-migration from the countryside to Mexico City, Guadalajara, León, and other princi-pal cities within Mexico, as well as very heavy temporary wage-labor migration to the United States.[5]

Scholars' descriptions of the people of the region tend to coincide with the popular stereotype of the Alteño personality which is widespread in Mexico. The Alteño is said to be: hard-working, fiercely individualistic and independent, bellicose, a crafty trader; a traditionalist and political conservative, clinging to established custom (including deep religious devotion and obedience to the clergy) and resisting change; deeply at-tached to the land, committed to a system of private landholding, and proud of his *tierra* (the place he comes from). Alteños are considered to be closed, mistrustful of outsiders, and wary of forces which might introduce limitations on local and personal autonomy. They are also said to be the prototype of the traditional Mexican *charro* (roughly, "cow-boy"): able horsemen, avid rodeo fans, gamblers on cockfights, pistol-packing, hearty drinkers—in short, *machos*.[6] The women of Los Altos are reputed to be beautiful, fair, tall, and strong-willed—an important power within the family. A variety of historical factors (racial and cul-tural heritage, land tenure patterns and other aspects of economic orga-nization, regional political history) are customarily cited to explain the emergence and resilience of these traits.

Such characteristics as deep religiosity, sense of attachment to the land, political conservatism, and distrust of outsiders are hardly re-

[5]This pattern of out-migration is found in the Los Altos region as a whole. See Álvarez (1964: 106–107); Cornelius (1976, 1981); Demyck (1973); and Taylor (1933).

[6]For examples of such characterizations, see Berthe (1973); Demyck (1973: 227–234); D.P.E.S. (1968: 16); J. Meyer (1973a); Rivière d'Arc (1973a, 1973b, n.d.); Robe (1970: 30-31); Taylor (1933).

stricted only to Mexicans living in the Los Altos region.[7] Moreover, even if they were prevalent among Alteños at some point in the past, some traits (e.g., the charro comportment and appearance) are now seldom observed except at local fiestas. These changes have occurred in the wake of social changes brought by urbanization, class and occupational differentiation, and return migration from the United States. In fact, many of the traits included in the popularized conception of the Alteño are broadly characteristic of mestizo Mexico, which includes more than 90 percent of the country's total population.

While the distinctiveness of the Alteño personality as described by popular tradition and scholarship is highly debatable, some of the historical evidence cited to buttress such characterizations is nonetheless important. Racial heritage, land tenure patterns, and religiosity are key factors in the region's development. They were also important in the development of the agrarian reform movement.

The Early Settlement of Lagos de Moreno

The Spanish first entered Los Altos de Jalisco in about 1530–31. They found a small, widely dispersed Indian population, which was decimated in the second half of the sixteenth century by epidemics and battles. As a result, and because of the profound isolation of the region well into the present century, there has been relatively little Indian racial, economic, or cultural influence in Los Altos, as compared with other parts of Mexico.[8]

Scholars who have reviewed Church records believe that the Spanish settlers of Los Altos probably came from Castilla, Andalusía, and Extremadura (Taylor, 1933; J. Meyer, 1973a: 150). Popular tradition and some writers (e.g., D.P.E.S., 1968: 16) contend that the Spaniards who came to Los Altos were Sephardic Jews. But the evidence usually cited in support of this argument is weak, ranging from the tendency toward

[7]See Craig and Cornelius (1980: 340–378). Most authors writing on Los Altos imply that the mass media, expanding networks of political and economic dependency, and increasing ease of communications have tended to diminish the regional distinctiveness of these traits.

[8]See Berthe (1973: 138–139); Robe (1970: 30); Taylor (1933: 6–9). The Los Altos region is almost totally lacking in archeological zones and handcrafts associated with Indian Mexico. Indian mounds have been found in the municipios of Arandas and Teocaltiche, and there are reported to be small private collections of archeological artifacts in Lagos. Old men told me that Indian clay *monitos* ("dolls") had often been discovered in their youth in the adjoining municipio of Unión de San Antonio, but that these relics had been used for target practice by youngsters or had been taken away.

religious fanaticism among converts (from Judaism to Catholicism, in this case) to character traits (individualism, trading skills), and even the climatic and topographical similarity of Los Altos to the lands from which the Sephardim came.

Whatever the origin of the Spanish settlers, it is true that many present-day Alteños are (compared to Mexicans in the capital and in the southern states) taller, with fairer complexions and lighter eyes; they have few Indian features. These physical traits are very important elements in the Alteños' image of themselves and in the popular characterization of them. This is especially true for the landed families of the upper class, whose self-image as a well-bred local aristocracy is reinforced by reference to their predominantly European ancestry.

More significantly, the absence of an Indian population has had important economic consequences for Los Altos. With poor lands, mostly unsuitable to large-scale commercial agriculture, and without a ready supply of indigenous labor (nor of great mineral deposits requiring the importation of such labor), the Spanish settlers became small and medium-sized landholders—principally cattle ranchers. Cattle-raising was considered a higher-status occupation than farming, and it was well suited to the land in this region (Rivière d'Arc, 1973a: 39). This manner of land use gave rise to a settlement pattern consisting of small villages and even smaller economic-residential units (*ranchos*) interspersed with larger commercial centers. This pattern of settlement was well suited to the needs of the colonial administration to populate and protect that part of Nueva Galicia known today as Los Altos de Jalisco.[9]

By the mid-sixteenth century, the colonial administration had decided to build defensive outposts in Nueva Galicia to protect travelers, missionaries, and caravans carrying supplies to mining sites and raw ore from the mines to refining sites. Protection was needed against robbery, and from small roving bands of Indians. One such route to be defended was the Guadalajara-to-Mexico City road; another went from the mines of Zacatecas and Guanajuato to Mexico City, passing through what would later become the towns of Lagos de Moreno in Jalisco, and León, San Miguel de Allende, and Celaya in Guanajuato (Rivière d'Arc, 1973a: 34–37). Santa María de los Lagos—now called Lagos de Moreno—was founded on March 13, 1563, at the crossing of these two roadways. It was

[9]Nueva Galicia, one of the major politico-administrative districts of the Spanish Empire in the New World, included the area now covered by the Mexican states of Zacatecas, Jalisco, Nayarit, Colima, Aguascalientes, and parts of San Luis Potosi and Sinaloa.

established by decree of the Audiencia of Nueva Galicia to serve as a defense outpost.[10]

The Royal Crown and later the Audiencia began to grant land titles to Spanish settlers in the Los Altos region late in the sixteenth century (Berthe, 1973; Rivière d'Arc, 1973a), but title-holders did not immediately occupy the lands. In many cases, the lands were first worked by persons who acquired them from the original grantee through inheritance or purchase. This was particularly true in the case of the larger grants, although few of the original land-grants were large by the standards of the time. They often measured 1 or 2 *sitios de ganado mayor* (for cattle grazing; 1 sitio mayor is equivalent to 1756 hectares) and from 1 to 6 *caballerías de tierra* (for cultivation; 1 *caballería* is equivalent to 43–44 hectares).[11] These lands were usually worked by renters or sharecroppers as free laborers, or by a system of debt peonage administered by a manager or foreman. Even more common were grants associated with the establishment of towns, in which colonists were given a homesite, a garden, and 2 caballerías of crop and grazing land. In the specific case of Lagos, the original decree authorizing settlement of the town allowed each settler to have 1 *sitio de ganado menor* (approximately 780–800 hectares) and 1 caballería de tierra.

Up through the early nineteenth century, some Alteño families were able to acquire additional land on which they established haciendas, particularly in the municipios of Arandas, Unión de San Antonio, and Lagos de Moreno.[12] However, vast haciendas of the scale or productive capacity familiar in northern Mexico, or in Puebla, Morelos or Yucatán have never been characteristic of the region. Most of the original land-grants were subsequently subdivided many times by inheritance or debt

[10]The most detailed published local histories of Lagos de Moreno are de Alba (1957), anonymous (1972), and Vega Kegel (n.d.). Scattered historical essays were occasionally printed in the following local newspapers: *Ecos de Lagos, El Defensor del Pueblo, Labor,* and *Notas y Letras.*

[11]For comparisons of colonial and contemporary land-surface measurements, see Bazant (1975: 6) and Taylor (1933: 25-30).

[12]For histories of the development of land tenure and economic patterns in colonial and early nineteenth-century Los Altos see Chevalier (1952); Jones (1974, n.d.); Martínez Saldaña and Gándara Mendoza (1976: 50–63, 175–181); and Taylor (1933: 25–30). Bazant (1975) provides a very detailed history of 5 haciendas in the adjoining state of San Luis Potosí that were similar in some ways to the haciendas which developed in Lagos. González y González' (1974) history of the village of San José de Gracia in the state of Michoacán can be usefully compared to that of Lagos de Moreno, although San Jose de Gracia's developmental pattern is more like that of the southernmost portion of the Los Altos region.

repayment. As a result, most private landholdings in the Los Altos region as a whole are now relatively small. Except for isolated haciendas in other municipios, Lagos de Moreno was the only Alteño municipio with enough large landholdings by the 1920s and 1930s to warrant a sizable agrarian reform movement. Elsewhere in the region, the pattern of small landholdings reinforced political and religious conservatism, establishing a solid block of opposition to the federal government's land reform policies.

The written historical record is quite sketchy about local events from the founding of Lagos to the town's social-cultural zenith at the end of the nineteenth century. As the population slowly grew, many of the families—both wealthy and humble—whose descendants still live in Lagos began to establish their homes. Roads and bridges were improved, including the route connecting Guadalajara with Mexico City through San Juan de los Lagos and Santa María de los Lagos. Regular monthly *diligencias* (carriage runs) were established in 1794. Travelers on the carriage route brought income to many inns and rest stops in town, as well as news from the outside. Religious pilgrims to the shrine of the Virgin of San Juan de los Lagos (only 45 kilometers from Lagos) must have added to the normal flow of commercial travelers, as they still do. Moreover, as the carriage service became safer and more heavily used, especially in the nineteenth century, hacienda main houses and compounds (*cascos*) were built near the carriage route to take advantage of the ease of travel and the transport of supplies and crops along the road.

Lagos in the Nineteenth Century

It has been said with probable accuracy that political factionalism in Lagos, chiefly between "liberals" and "conservatives," dates from the struggle for independence from Spain (Azuela, 1942: 95).[13] Possibly because of this, relatively little was recorded about local events or senti-

---

[13]The independence movement opened political debates in Mexico between "centralists" and "federalists" and later between "liberals" and "conservatives" over the relative balance of power between federal and state authority, and the rights and privileges of special interest groups (especially the military, the Catholic Church, foreigners, and large landholders). These debates, with varying labels applied to advocates of each position, have continued into the contemporary period. For brief summaries of the issues, see Bazant (1977: 1–95) and Cline (1963: 39–56). "Liberal" is a term used today in Lagos to refer not so much to one's placement on a left-right ideological continuum, but to a position favoring reduced influence of the Catholic Church in social, economic, and political life.

ments during the independence movement, save for the heroic personal histories of Lagos' native sons and daughters Lic. Primo Verdad y Ramos, Doña Rita Pérez de Moreno, and Don Pedro Moreno, all of whom fought on the winning side. In a decree issued in 1829, the national congress authorized the change of the town's name from Santa María de los Lagos to Lagos de Moreno—in honor of Pedro Moreno.

With independence, the political stature of Lagos within the state of Jalisco became apparent, reflecting its relative size and cultural and economic development. Lagos, already the seat of a *departamento* of the state, received the title of *ciudad* (city) in 1824. In 1845 Lagos became the seat of the *cantón*[14] of Lagos de Moreno, second in size and importance in the state of Jalisco only to the cantón of Guadalajara. The cantón of Lagos included the municipios of Lagos de Moreno, Unión de San Antonio, San Diego Alejandría, Ojuelos, and San Juan de los Lagos. As a result of Lagos' political status as the seat of a major cantón with important commercial activities and major landholdings within its jurisdiction, and its location at a transportation crossroads, Laguenses had more access to political information (if they sought it) and more contact with government representatives than did the residents of most small towns in the region. There is, however, no evidence that this produced any significant material advantages for the municipio that would not have accrued from local economic resources. In fact, it may only have served to reinforce a negative attitude toward the government. As elsewhere, local authorities were appointed from Guadalajara and were generally not natives of Lagos. Their mission was to administer the laws and extract taxes.

Basic urban amenities can also be dated from the mid nineteenth century. Lagos had an uninterrupted tradition of local education dating back to the seventeenth century, for those with financial means or interest in serving the Church. (The children of the very wealthy, however, have always been sent away to school in Guadalajara, León, or Mexico City.) A public hospital, staffed as it is today by the Sisters of Charity, was built in 1851. These and other services rarely available in small Mexican towns of that era added to Lagos' importance as an urban center.

Members of the Rincón Gallardo family, which owned by far the largest haciendas in the region, were responsible for many of the early

[14]The *cantón* was a political-administrative unit of a state. After the Revolution of 1910, the cantones were abolished and replaced by the smaller administrative units of municipios, which had been sub-units of the cantones. Lagos retained its position as a municipio seat. It now is also the seat of state and federal legislative districts.

industrial and public-service establishments in Lagos. In about 1853, José María Rincón Gallardo built a local grain mill; about seven years later his Fábrica La Victoria, a textile mill which was later to figure prominently in the local organized labor movement, was opened. Soon afterward the family's Fundición La Victoria began operations, serving as a foundry for repairing textile machinery and forging bells, well pumps, school benches, and machine parts. Much later, in the first decade of the present century, rudimentary potable water and electricity were provided to the town by extending the lines serving the Fábrica La Victoria. These improvements are cited even today by members of the landed elite in Lagos as evidence of the genteel, urbane past—a time of local progress truncated by disruptive social change.

Locally written history conspicuously avoids discussion of local conflicts, including those periods when national and state political turmoil might have been reflected in local tensions. For this reason we know little of events in Lagos during the period of President Benito Juárez' liberal constitutional reforms (1855–76). The churches in Lagos lost much of their wealth as a result of a series of national Church-state confrontations (the Juárez Reform, the Revolution of 1910, and a rebellion of Catholic guerrillas in 1926–29). The strong local tradition of political and religious conservatism and faith in priestly guidance must have collided in heated debate with the winds of liberalism espoused, among others, by Father Agustín Rivera y Sanromán and the four Laguenses who signed the "Reform" Constitution of 1857. Small wonder, then, that this period gave rise to a favorite Lagos anecdote. It is said that President Juárez came through Lagos and stopped to visit on his way to Guadalajara in 1858. As he was leaving, he was asked what he had liked most about the town. His reply: "That they asked me for nothing." Referring to this anecdote, one of my informants explained that "Lagos has a certain seigniorial dignity. There is much provincial pride in her people. . . . So Lagos has never been helped [by the government]; it is neither helped nor hindered."[15]

---

[15]This attitude persisted well into the middle of the present century, reflected in a preference (particularly among the wealthy and small private landholders) for maintaining the greatest possible distance between themselves and the government, thereby foregoing any assistance that might be solicited from government agencies. *Labor*, a local newspaper, reported on October 6, 1946: "During the visit which General Cárdenas made not long ago as President of the Republic, neither commerce, nor the cattle raisers, nor the farmers went to speak with him, since no one wished to ask him for anything, just as they have not asked for anything from other Presidents when there has been an opportunity, nor of the Governors, nor of any other authority. They like to be well removed from

The Aristocracy's Golden Years: Lagos at the Turn of the Century

To members of the local elite who love it, Lagos de Moreno is known as the "Athens of Jalisco." The intended image of architectural beauty, refinement of the arts, intellectual debate, and genteel living is most accurately applied to the period which coincides roughly with the dictatorship of President Porfirio Díaz (1875–1910). It was a status achieved through gradual transformation, and lost in a slow decline over the first 40 or 50 years of this century. During the Porfiriato, as most of the large haciendas reached their maximum size and the local aristocracy attained its cultural zenith, the town's traditional August fiesta, instituted in 1872 to commemorate Lagos' patron saint, became the social highlight of the year. Aside from numerous religious celebrations and processions, the fiesta brought extensive visiting between haciendas, country picnics, horse races, bull and cock fights, elegant dinners and balls, literary and musical contests, and poetry recitals.

Local culture flourished. Education and intellectual accomplishments were highly prized. Poets (Francisco González León, José Becerra), composers and musicians (Apolonio Moreno, Antonio Gómez Anda), fablists (José Rosas Moreno), orators (Agustín Rivera y Sanromán), and other cultural figures rose from the upper class and a small local middle class of administrators, teachers, and professionals. Lagos had a local printing company and newspaper (*El Diablo Cojuelo*) as early as 1850, and in subsequent years several periodicals were published intermittently in the town. The most enduring among them—a literary magazine, *Notas y Letras*, and a sometimes progressive newspaper, *El Defensor del Pueblo*— were published sporadically by the López Arce family after 1888. Newspaper accounts of this period document the importance accorded locally to erudition and education, as demonstrated not only at public celebrations but in private gatherings of Laguenses as well.

Generally, the landed aristocracy of Lagos spent some time on the land—often the summer months. The haciendas had large, comfortably furnished main houses, and many had their own chapels and stores (*tiendas de raya*). All had stables, granaries, servants' and laborers' quarters.[16] Most of these families maintained large, elaborate houses in the

---

everything, even though they well know how much Lagos needs to ask for. All of this is regarded with pride, boastfully, as their very own and nearly unique coat of arms."

[16]In addition, there were 11 rural representatives of municipal authority and the police (*comisarios* and *tenientes de policía*) based in *cuarteles rurales*. Of these, all but 3

town of Lagos and, except for business, shopping, or vacation trips out-side the region, they were not absentee landlords. Haciendas were man-aged by foremen and administrators under the supervision of the owner, who received at least weekly reports in Lagos.

The expansion of urban services and other amenities in Lagos con-tinued. By the turn of the century these included a telegraph office, regular railroad passenger service, and a mule-drawn streetcar.[17] A sys-tem of street lighting was in operation by 1906. By 1907, 100 homes had potable water. Both services were criticized for their deficiencies: the lights were turned off on moonlit nights and often failed at other times; the water system was blamed for periodic typhoid epidemics (Gómez Flores, 1973). In 1909 a telephone line was installed, connecting the center of town with the railroad station.

In 1907 the ornate Rosas Moreno Theater was inaugurated. Regular Sunday concerts, open to all social classes, were also held in the munici-pal park and in the main square. There, three concentric rows of benches helped to separate the strollers, and protectors of order sta-tioned at the corners of the plaza assured that the upper class could occupy the inner ring undisturbed by lower-status intruders.[18] The poorest were allowed to occupy the "bleacher" seats on the steps of the main church, as they still do today.

As the Porfiriato drew to a close, Lagos de Moreno was a prominent and prosperous town, exceptional within the region and the state. The amenities described above insured a life of reasonable comfort and stim-ulation for the local upper class and the small middle class of merchants, artisans, and professionals serving their needs and those of travelers. While economically and socially very significant, these groups still con-stituted a small proportion of the population in the town and in the municipio, and living standards among the majority of Laguenses re-mained very low. In the first decade of the present century, *El Defensor del Pueblo* published scattered articles (both original and reprinted from other sources) in which the upper class was subtly and sometimes

---

were located on the largest haciendas, according to the municipal government records (*Libros de Actas*) for 1901. This may have contributed to the ease with which hacienda administrators could punish petty theft, crime, and insubordination among agricultural workers during Porfirio Diaz' regime.

[17]The first train came through Lagos de Moreno on December 15–16, 1882 (*Ecos de Lagos*, December 15, 1942), but regular passenger service did not begin until 1884-85.

[18]Informants recalled that the middle row of benches was removed when the main square was renovated during the late 1940s. No one could recall with certainty when the formal class segregation system was discontinued.

The decaying chapel and main house (*casco*) of the Hacienda Tlalixcoyán, in 1976. The casco is of moderate size compared with those of other large landholdings in the municipio of Lagos, although the domed chapel is larger and architecturally more elaborate than most. The household servants' quarters, granary, and threshing area were located behind the main house.

openly warned that social changes were overdue. The articles called for higher wages to factory and field laborers, for respect and improved treatment of employees, for abolition of the hacienda stores—in short, for labor relationships which would result not only in financial benefit to the employer but also a decent livelihood for the worker.

On the haciendas, the best-paid hands were the cattle herders. Field labor was provided by sharecroppers, *peones acasillados*, and day laborers. The sharecroppers usually received half of the harvest, minus costs of seeds and animal forage (if they had their own plow animals) or rental of a plowing team. The peones acasillados were laborers with closer ties—sometimes involving hereditary debt peonage—to the hacienda owner than the sharecroppers or day laborers. They resided in housing provided by the *hacendado*. On haciendas which had irrigated land, the major crops were winter wheat, chile peppers, corn, and beans. The more valuable, irrigated crops were planted by the peones acasillados and day laborers. These were the hacienda owner's crops, for his own use or sale and to pay laborers' rations. The planting, cultivation, and harvest of these crops took priority over sharecropped fields.

Sharecroppers depended on rainfall, and their planting and harvesting could be completed only after their work in the owner's own fields (cf. Brading, 1978: 205–206). Sharecroppers who were fortunate sometimes planted small plots of chiles (which was a very profitable crop) and occasionally had a team of mules which they drove, supplementing their income in the winter season by selling wood, charcoal, or lime crudely manufactured in the fields, or by acting as small tradesmen. Although informants differ on this point, it seems that sharecroppers (who might own their own home and a minuscule agricultural plot) were free to choose where they worked. Peones acasillados generally had to secure permission to change employers.

Survivors of the agrarian reform movement report that field laborers worked from dawn to dusk on the haciendas, eating their meals in the fields. Any of their own chores—such as tending animals—had to be done before or after the hacendado's work. Children as young as 5 or 6 began fieldwork as planters, dropping seeds into the furrows behind the plows. By the age of 12, most joined adult male laborers in the field, guiding plow teams. Some haciendas had schools, although they served primarily for instruction in the catechism, and then only when children could be spared from fieldwork, looking after younger siblings, and housework.

The wage system was *"real y ración"*—wages and a ration of corn and beans. Wages ranged from 12 to 20 cents a day, plus a liter of corn.[19] Debts were subtracted from wage payments; and supplies such as salt, chile, lime (used in making tortillas), and lard could be purchased from the hacienda's store. On at least one hacienda, Ciénega de Mata, laborers were paid in bars of soap redeemable in the hacienda's store.[20]

In the town of Lagos de Moreno, the major source of employment, apart from domestic service, was the Fábrica La Victoria. But the factory was periodically closed due to national recessions, mismanagement,

[19]There are no summary data available on the changes in agricultural or urban wages in the municipio during the Porfiriato. However, the national average minimum wage of 23.5 centavos per day in 1908 (Simpson, 1937: 37–38) was higher than wages reportedly paid in Lagos as late as 1930.

[20]According to local informants, on haciendas with their own stores it was often common to pay agricultural workers in tokens redeemable at the store. Simpson (1937: 38) explains that this practice was widespread throughout Mexico at the turn of the century.

The Fábrica La Victoria and the mule-drawn trolley which ran from the main plaza of Lagos de Moreno to the railroad station. (Reproduced from a photograph in the local literary magazine, *Notas y Letras*, August 6, 1904.)

mechanical problems, and the owner's long residence abroad. Around the turn of the century, the plant closed again, and the town lost numerous residents who went elsewhere in search of work (*Notas y Letras*, August 6, 1904). In 1903–04 Gustavo A. Madero (brother of Francisco I. Madero, who was to launch the Revolutionary movement against Porfirio Díaz) and Juan B. Rincón Gallardo provided new capital and inspiration to set the factory into operation again. Laborers returned, and the enterprise of La Victoria y Anexos, which included the factory, the foundry, some urban properties, and a small ranch, temporarily flourished. But by November 1907 the enterprise was once again in difficulty, and La Victoria y Anexos went up for sale at an asking price of one million pesos (*El Defensor del Pueblo*, November 24, 1907). Thereafter, it operated intermittently under different owners and managers until sometime in the mid 1920s, when it was closed permanently.[21]

As early as 1907, *El Defensor del Pueblo* began publishing articles

---

[21]The last owner of the building which housed the factory—who never operated it as a textile mill—says that the factory closed in 1923. Reports by early members of the labor movement suggest, however, that the factory was still operating in 1925.

bemoaning the municipio's high levels of emigration to the United States. These articles argued that laborers would continue to resort to migration as long as landowners did not raise wages or plant and irrigate more land, and as long as they continued to dismiss sharecroppers just as the harvest was about to begin. They also blamed local authorities, whose obstructionism and evasiveness reportedly did nothing to resolve the few complaints filed by agricultural laborers against their employers.

Enduring the Revolution

The Revolution of 1910–17 was the indirect progenitor of change in Lagos de Moreno. The state of Jalisco actually played a relatively minor role in the Revolution. Walton (1977: 35) attributes this to three factors: the distance of Guadalajara from the geopolitical center of the Revolution; the "relatively less pernicious" role of large landholdings and of foreign participation in the economy; and a political culture predisposed to theory rather than revolution.[22]

Locally, the Revolution did not take the form of a great social upheaval, nor a popular revolt against the tyranny of Porfirio Díaz and his brutal rural police, nor a popular outcry for agrarian reform and social justice. Early in my research, inquiries about local consequences and participation in the Revolution were met with the question, "Which revolution?—Madero's? Villa and Carranza's? Or the Cristeros'?" Respondents inevitably made a distinction between the political revolution which deposed Porfirio Díaz and brought Francisco I. Madero to power as the first President of the Revolution, and the conflict among military leaders and their support groups which beset the country from 1912 to 1920.

When Francisco Madero began his political movement against Porfirio Díaz, his principal objectives were the extension of suffrage and a change of leadership in national government ("Effective suffrage, no reelection"). There is little evidence to indicate that there was much support for the Maderistas in Lagos in this early, nonviolent phase of the

[22]Ronald Waterbury (1975) has pointed out that the Revolution in the state of Oaxaca contrasts sharply with the same period in the state of Morelos and in the north of the Republic. He argues that geographic isolation, a local tradition of conservatism, and a large indigenous population all combined to minimize the state's participation in the political and military phases of the Revolution, and also delayed implementation of the Revolution's reforms. His argument, with the exception of the part referring to an Indian population, also applies to Lagos de Moreno.

Revolution. The novelist Mariano Azuela, a Laguense and early Maderista, has written that before Díaz was overthrown, as far as the "more correct" citizens of Lagos were concerned, being a Maderista "was the same as being a perverse criminal, alienated and at least abnormal. . . . We formed a local anti-Porfirian nucleus, comprised of workers who knew how to read, small merchants, farmers angered by the government injustices, youthful dreamers and enthusiasts" (Azuela, 1974: 110–112). The sometimes liberal paper, *El Defensor del Pueblo* (June 26, 1910) supported the reelection of Porfirio Díaz, arguing that the process of democratization in the Republic should proceed gradually from local elections, moving upward to higher offices in order to prepare the citizenry for the responsible exercise of self-government.

Once Díaz had been removed from the presidency, Laguenses adapted to changed circumstances. Although Porfirio Díaz surely had his defenders, descendants of landed families who lived through that period in Lagos' history claim that they were all glad to see him removed from office, for he had grown old and had governed too long. Always political pragmatists, the town fathers soon welcomed the Revolution. Azuela writes (1974: 111–112) that when word reached Lagos that Díaz had sailed into exile, "even the worst of Madero's enemies rushed to portray themselves as his most ardent supporters, . . . the most merciless enemies of the Revolution, proudly displaying the badge of Maderista soldiers. . . . Rich men with foresight suddenly appeared as supporters of the new cause and devotees of the winning leader, with [troops] recruited from among their own servants."[23] In the local annals, the ravages of a flood in June 1911 figure far more prominently than the change of national government. Relief efforts by Maderista troops (over 3000 were left homeless by the floods), and Gustavo A. Madero's involvement with Lagos through the Fábrica La Victoria, may have insured local acquiescence in the change.[24]

In the years that followed the assassination of Francisco Madero in

---

[23]Azuela's novels portray the corruption of the Revolution, the local conservatism, and the festering destructiveness of the conflict. In *Andrés Pérez, maderista* (1945), he portrays the men who found it politically and personally profitable to support Madero. Azuela describes his reaction to the local response to the Revolution in his autobiography (1974: 106–153). Another Laguense, José Pérez Moreno, has also fictionally portrayed Lagos during the Revolution in his novel *El tercer canto de gallo* (1957).

[24]Rural respondents claim no political knowledge of nor participation in this stage of the Revolution. As one man said, "We were like this," placing his hands over his eyes, "with our eyes covered."

February 1913, Lagos de Moreno, along with the rest of the Republic, suffered the greatest losses and hardships of the revolutionary period. Reactionary and revolutionary military leaders and their armies fought to gain control of national and local governments. One informant described these years in Lagos as follows: "The Revolution came—a horrible thing. Hunger came with the Revolution. Then later came the plague, all the people scavenging, covered with ticks. The rich had left, and there were almost no priests. The hacienda peones kept alive by robbing."

The relative calm of the Madero period was broken in the state of Jalisco by the "northern revolutionaries," most notably Francisco ("Pancho") Villa's troops.[25] As one observer recalls: "Jalisco suffered greatly from Villismo. The rest it enjoyed in the Maderista revolutionary period which was, in a military sense, scarcely perceptible here [in Jalisco], ended when Huerta took power; only then were genuine uprisings registered in our territory" (Zuno, 1964: 93). The fact that it was Villa's troops, and not Emiliano Zapata's peasant armies, which invaded the region was a significant factor in the gradual evolution of the agrarian reform movement and its opposition. Villa's men robbed, and sometimes redistributed harvested crops and animals among the poor peasants. In one resident's words, "The Villistas were the most terrible, because they were the ones who were most devoted to pillage and burning." Villa's troops occupied houses and commandeered cattle, horses, and forage for animals. They also killed at least one local hacienda owner, Celso Serrano Hermosillo, and another prominent citizen, Jesús Gómez Portugal. No informant could recall any efforts during this period to organize peasant communities, land invasions, or other efforts toward agrarian reforms.

Despite the poverty of its urban and rural poor, Lagos was basically unmoved by the call to military revolt. Laguenses did not leave in substantial numbers to join any of the revolutionary armies,[26] nor did they join forces to attempt local changes in keeping with the ideals being fought for elsewhere. Of the period of the armed conflict, Laguenses now invariably say, "Some [armed groups] would leave and others would

[25]The "northern revolutionaries" included the armies of Pancho Villa, Alvaro Obregón, Venustiano Carranza, and Pascual Orozco. Of these, Villa and Obregón had the greatest impact on Jalisco (Paez Brotchie, 1940; Zuno, 1964).

[26]Cf. Rivière d'Arc (1973a: 49), who claims that Jalisciences joined the revolutionary armies "in large numbers." The experiences of one native son who did join the Villistas were fictionalized by Azuela in Los de abajo (1971), first published in El Paso, Texas, in 1915.

arrive. They were all alike. One did what they demanded. We didn't take sides." So although the Revolution had profound effects on the municipio, they were primarily demographic and economic, not political or social. During the periods of greatest political uncertainty and civil strife, families of means abandoned rural areas and provincial towns. Prominent landowning families from Lagos went mainly to Mexico City, where they clustered together in a few neighborhoods (Colonia Juárez and Santa María la Ribera). Haciendas and town houses were left in the care of trusted employees, who were not always able to defend the properties against the roving bands of revolutionaries. Agricultural laborers continued to work the fields for their own sustenance and, in periods of relative calm, for the owners as well. The years 1914 to 1917 were the worst in terms of hunger, disease, and economic chaos.

When possible during the conflict, fathers and sons of landholding families returned to Lagos to inspect their properties. Most of the men of landowning families had returned by 1917. But because of the destruction wrought by guerrilla bands, politico-economic uncertainties, and currency and population fluctuations, the local upper class suffered severe financial setbacks. Another casualty of the Revolution was Lagos' illustrious tradition of education and the arts. In view of the economic situation, even the landholding and middle-class families could not afford to educate their sons as their fathers had been—a financial constraint which extended into a second generation in some families. Women and children often remained in Mexico City, Guadalajara, and León into the 1920s, even after peace was finally restored to the countryside. Men spent these years trying to rebuild their capital and the local economy.

Yet another important consequence of the Revolution in Los Altos was depopulation of the countryside and smaller towns. Old-timers say that in the worst months the town of Lagos was "abandoned," but that probably refers to the wealthy families. Most residents with financial means moved to safer, larger localities—usually León, Guadalajara or Mexico City. And some moved to the United States, including among them many individuals of scant financial resources who were attracted north of the border by employment opportunities which did not exist in Mexican cities at the time.

Local historians contend that many wealthy families never returned after the Revolution. More likely, the Revolution produced a reversal in emigration trends. In previous generations, it was the rare son or daughter who for education, profession, or marriage moved permanently away from Lagos. With the Revolution, fewer members of the younger generation stayed on in the town. Data presented in the next chapter, however, demonstrate that the largest landholdings were neither permanently abandoned nor broken up as a result of the Revolution. As late as 1930, most of them remained, in legal title at least, in the hands of the same families if not the same individuals who owned them in 1900.

In time, the Revolution led to social change in Lagos, but it came via a circuitous and considerably delayed route. It took two decades before Laguenses who had been exposed to experience and ideas outside of Lagos, and politicians harboring personal ambitions or ideological convictions, were able to work together to effect significant change in the municipio of Lagos de Moreno.

3

Agrarian Reform:
The First Steps

Relatively little changed in Lagos de Moreno after the Revolution and before 1930. There were, of course, economic and population dislocations resulting from the Revolution of 1910–20 and the Cristero rebellion. Occasionally a burst of reformist zeal in the state capital produced a municipio president who would attempt to implement certain limited reforms. Some aspects of town and municipio life changed, but the essential structure of social, economic, and political relations which obtained at the turn of the century was still intact in 1930.

When asked why there had been no major changes in the wake of the Revolution, one Laguense explained, "A radical change? Well, you know, those things are very slow [in coming]. Those things, those social changes, are produced only in time, when people become convinced of the merits of something." Or, one might add, when the issue is forced. Until the 1930s, there were not enough men in Lagos with the right political connections to force the issues of political or agrarian reform. Moreover, not until the mid-1930s was there consistent backing and encouragement for such reforms from the state and federal governments.

This and the following chapter provide a detailed analysis of the development and fruition of the agrarian reform movement in the municipio of Lagos de Moreno. Attention is focused on the group of reformists and their leaders based in the municipio seat. These men, whose political activism initially was directed toward the implementation of new federal labor laws, eventually became the core of a growing group whose attention shifted gradually to rural organization and agrarian reform. It is this urban-based core of activists, led by skilled craftsmen and white-collar workers, which distinguishes the agrarian reform movement in Lagos de Moreno from previously studied local land-reform movements in Mexico.

The rising and falling fortunes of these labor reformists and, later, the agraristas, demonstrate how intimately the success or failure of local reform efforts is related to support and protection—or the lack of it— from local, state, and national authorities. Local economic conditions alone would have justified the reform movement. However, these local conditions were not sufficient to galvanize and strengthen a group of reformists in the face of intense and well organized local opposition to the reform. The reform group began to grow stronger and larger as potential participants were mobilized not only by their own work experiences and economic necessity but also by the support of important political patrons outside of the municipio.

Lagos Between Revolution and Reform

Population

After a precipitous loss of population in the town and municipio of Lagos de Moreno following the Revolution, the population of both began to grow slowly (see Table l). But there was also a high rate of out-migration, and the distribution of the population within the municipio also changed. From 1900 to 1930, the municipio as a whole retained its predominantly rural character: nearly two-thirds of the inhabitants lived outside of the municipio seat. Rural population losses are apparent, however, when figures are disaggregated to specific localities. There were three basic types of rural localities in the municipio: communities which grew up around the main compound of an hacienda, communities of sharecroppers and day laborers who worked on nearby landholdings, and communities of small property-holders. According to the decennial census figures, between 1900 and 1921 nearly 90% of these small communities lost population, while the rest remained stable or grew slightly; in the following decade (1921–30), only 36% of them suffered a net loss of population. But during the decade of agrarian reform (1930–40) over one-half lost inhabitants.

Pre-1930 population fluctuations reflect the impact of civil disorders associated with the Revolution and the Cristero rebellion, during which times it was more dangerous to reside in rural localities than in urban centers. During these periods, many families moved to Lagos de Moreno, to other larger towns in the region of Los Altos, or to Guadalajara, León, or Mexico City. But other factors also contributed significantly to popula-

Table 1
Population of Lagos de Moreno (Town and Municipio), 1900–1970

	1900	1921	1930	1940	1970
Inhabitants in Lagos (town)	15,999	10,012	12,054	12,490	33,782
Inhabitants in municipio	53,205	33,385	35,933	37,097	65,950

Source: Dirección General de Estadística, *Censo General de Población: Estado de Jalisco,* various editions.

tion changes during these decades. First, some of the large haciendas were subdivided through inheritance into smaller ranches, with each owner moving some of the agricultural workers and their families to new population centers. Even more important were the capital losses suffered during the Revolution by large landholders, particularly from 1914 to 1917. Although the land was not lost, many of the haciendas were only minimally farmed, and many laborers and their families had to move elsewhere. In addition, the hacendados employed only a fixed (sometimes declining) number of cattle herders, sharecroppers, household servants, and field hands, and the natural increase in population could not continue to be supported by a fixed number of breadwinners. Finally, some communities lost population between 1930 and 1940 when ejidatarios were granted land to establish a separate ejido "urban" area. For example, new localities were formed by ejidatarios from the haciendas of El Maguey, La Punta, San Nicolás, and Tlalixcoyán.

Some of the men whose departures are reflected in village and ranch census figures stayed in the municipio of Lagos or moved to other Mexican towns and cities. Many, however, went to the United States, sometimes with their families and sometimes as groups of young men. After construction of the railroads through Los Altos in the 1880s, recruiters for the railroad companies often came to Mexico seeking track-repair crews and strikebreakers. Some men were recruited to work cotton, sugar beet, and potato harvests. The accounts of these early emigrants who returned to their home communities encouraged others to migrate to the United States. The invasion of the region by revolutionary armies in 1914, and the Cristero rebellion in the 1920s, served to increase the outflow (Taylor, 1933: 12–13, 35–41). The result was a pattern of regional economic dependence on wages brought or sent back by seasonal workers in the United States—a pattern which persists today. Until 1929 it was relatively easy to enter the United States and find employment in agriculture or on the railroads. During the Depression, however, the United

States carried out a program of "repatriation" in which more than 400,000 Mexicans were expelled from the country. Many of the early agraristas in Lagos de Moreno, and nearly all of the movement's survivors who were interviewed for this study, had been to the U.S. and returned to their homes by 1930.[1]

Life-style

In 1930 there were still vast differences in the standard of living between urban and rural areas in the municipio, and between social classes. The large landholders continued to live in the center of town, with access to urban services and communication with other urban areas. The town was also populated by domestic servants, skilled craftsmen, shopkeepers, and a few professionals (attorneys, doctors, teachers, etc.). In town, the separation between upper and lower classes was enforced by custom in every facet of life, from concerts in the park to where people sat during Mass. One person, whose mother inherited a small part of an hacienda, described the rural living conditions as follows: "They lived in shacks where the wind blew between the cracks day and night, with straw roofs that burned easily. One saw a situation of dire poverty that broke one's heart—that is, for anyone who had some humane feelings, . . . but that was the custom."

While the landholders who visited large cities dressed in the latest fashions, rural dwellers continued to dress in their traditional clothing, described by one informant: "In those days the peón acasillado wore white pants with a blue belt, a white shirt with long sleeves, sandals, and a ranch-style [wide-brim] hat. Those who led pack animals [muleteers] wore a sort of leather apron to protect their clothing." Features of this manner of dress—the traditional style among rural, agricultural workers in Mexico—can still be seen in photographs taken during the 1930s.

On some of the haciendas, it was the custom for the foreman or manager to pay the employees on Saturday at the hacienda. Many other landholders preferred to have the workers come into town on Saturdays, where they sat patiently along the sidewalks in front of the employer's house waiting to be paid. When in town, it was the custom for campesinos to step down from the sidewalk, ceding passage to members of the upper class. On at least one hacienda, Ciénega de Mata, if the landholder

---

[1]See the section on "Los Norteños" at the end of this chapter, and Chapter 6, for further information on the agraristas' experiences in the U.S.

dropped anything, the peón never handed it back directly, but placed it first on the inverted brim of his own hat.[2]

The larger haciendas were self-contained communities, with a store, a chapel in which a visiting (or resident) priest said Mass, and a place of employment. Some of the haciendas had schools, used mainly to teach the catechism. The municipio was divided into small political-administrative districts (*delegaciones*), so that rural residents did not have to travel far to register births, deaths, and marriages—or to be arrested.

This "self-sufficiency" of the hacienda—and the idealized image of a paternal employer-employee relationship which it entails—was often cited by prosperous landholding families in Lagos as an argument against the land reform. Former hacendados and their descendants whose families' lands were expropriated for the ejidos consistently maintained in interviews that the campesinos had no *need* to petition for the land. "They had everything"—medical care, a little milk, some meat, their ration of maize and beans. The following statement, by a man in his late sixties whose family lost parts of their landholdings in the reform, was typical:

> Really it was unjustified, because the people were well off. . . . At the time that agrarismo began here, the rural people ate meat, meat such as any person could eat. They drank milk, ate bread; they had whatever they wanted. And they had their stores of maize and beans, and they lived happily. . . . On the hardest jobs, like the cattle herders, where they have to go where there are thorny trees, well, they all dressed in leather [chaps], something which today would be impossible, right? . . . Everything was extremely cheap.

Moreover, the landed elite contended, rural people must be firmly supervised or they won't work, for they are by nature lazy and incapable of leading orderly lives. They cannot manage their own money, nor make optimal use of the land. The ejidatarios, they argued, were simply lazy people who took advantage of the legal means to acquire easily what they were unwilling to work to attain. The expropriated haciendas rightfully belonged through inheritance to people whose class heritage prepared them to properly manage the land.

---

[2]These practices were repeatedly described in my interviews with agrarista leaders. The image of the servile peón—stepping into the street, and paid at a time convenient to his employer—symbolized most vividly for them the terms of the old relationship between patrón and peón. Such scenes were invariably described with anger and resentment.

This landholders' image of the campesino class must have influenced their early expectations about the ejido petitioners' chances of actually obtaining the land they sought. It clearly influenced their opinions on the rights of the petitioners to the land.

Wages and Working Conditions

Efforts to secure changes in working conditions and wages in the municipio of Lagos came first from urban laborers, specifically employees of the textile factory, La Victoria. The wage issue was first raised between December 1917 and July 1918. The death of the factory owner, Juan B. Rincón Gallardo, apparently precipitated the crisis. The management closed the factory for a period, contending that it was losing thousands of pesos monthly because of high wages and taxes, the low quality of the cotton fiber available, and the disrepair of machinery. Over 300 workers were suspended from their jobs. By May 5, 1918, *El Defensor del Pueblo* reported that "the majority of the workers of the factory have had to emigrate from Lagos because of the condition of extreme poverty in which they find themselves." In the same article, the newspaper claimed that the local government was not making a serious effort to promote settlement of the factory dispute because the workers had opposed the incumbents in the last election. This is the first written record of tension between labor and the local government. Subsequent developments in the effort to organize urban labor in Lagos are detailed later in this chapter.

By all reports, rural working conditions changed little after the Revolution. For example:

> The working day, the same; the peoples' wages, the same; benefits, none. The work hours were the same as had been customary in earlier times. They made them work from 6 to 6. But before the workers left to work in the fields at 6 a.m., they had to feed all of the animals. That meant they had to get up at 4 in the morning.

In the nearby municipio of Arandas, wages rose higher and faster in the municipio seat than in the outlying, rural areas. Furthermore, during the Depression years of 1930 and 1931, wages dropped to their level of 15 years earlier. By the time of the agrarian reform, rural workers in the Los Altos region were receiving essentially the same wage they had been paid at the turn of the century, despite inflation (Taylor, 1933: 24–25). *El Defensor del Pueblo* reported on December 30, 1928, that Ramón B. Rivera, the municipio president of Lagos de Moreno, called for a fivefold increase in salaries, from 20 centavos per day plus a ration of maize, to 1 peso per day. He urged campesinos to denounce their employers if the treatment they received was unfair and if they were not paid by Saturday afternoons. Six years later, however, *El Jaliscience* (November 4, 1934) reported that at the hacienda Ciénega de Mata (in Lagos de Moreno), fieldworkers were still being paid the equivalent of 9 centavos per day in a ration of soap and salt, and that all of their purchases had to be made at the hacienda's store. Interview reports of the wages paid immediately prior to the redistribution of land ranged from 15 to 30 centavos per day, plus a ration of maize (usually 4 liters per day).[3]

As one participant in the movement explained, these low wages motivated some of the men who participated in the agrarian reform: "They had many children, and they couldn't support themselves on the low wage they earned. . . . [The hacendados] would not hire all of their sons. So the family income did not stretch far enough. There was hunger." Evidence presented in Chapter 6 demonstrates that the low wages, particularly compared with what the agraristas had earned elsewhere, were a major factor contributing to their decision to emigrate and/or to participate in the agrarian reform movement.

Land Tenure Pattern

The Lagos economy of 1930 was dominated by livestock-raising—beef and dairy cattle, and sheep. Cattle-raising required extensive grazing acreage. As one Laguense from a landed family explained: "It was obsolete to have many houses [in town]—that was a widow's business. The important thing was to have lots of land, lots of cattle, many servants to order around. That was what was considered a well-to-do hacendado."

Urban and rural real estate listed in the local property tax registries for 1900 and 1930[4] confirm the patterns described by this informant. In general, individuals who had extensive rural landholdings were not

---

[3]These wages compare unfavorably with wages being paid elsewhere in Mexico. Simpson (1937: 302–303, 712) cites a study by Ramón Fernández y Fernández which found that between 1920 and 1933 average nominal wages in Mexico fluctuated between a low of 68 centavos per day to a high of 1.03 pesos per day. Whetten (1948: 261), citing a later version of the same study, shows that the average daily wage in Jalisco was lower than the national average: 68, 68, and 74 centavos in 1925, 1929, and 1935 respectively, compared with national averages of 90, 93, and 94 centavos in the same years. In Lagos, there were no reports of wages to compare with the national average, nor even equal to the state average daily wage, during the years cited here.

[4]See Appendix C for an explanation of the contents of the registries. There are disadvantages to relying on tax records as the principal source of information on the distribution of land and wealth in the municipio. The assessed values are underestimated, since

among the largest owners of urban real estate. Municipal tax records suggest a class structure in which the wealthiest families owned large rural landholdings, a small middle class invested its wealth in multiple urban properties, and a very small proportion of the lower class owned rural plots or urban dwellings of inconsequential tax value.

The landholding system in the municipio of Lagos was varied. Within its boundaries there were a few extremely large haciendas, some of substantial proportions, many of moderate size, and a great many very small properties.[5] From 1900 to 1930, the number of registered properties increased, but their distribution by size remained essentially unchanged. In 1930, 60% of the landowners in Lagos owned less than 1% of the land, and their property-holdings were all less than 1 hectare in size. By contrast, 1.2% of the landowners, each of whom owned more than 500 hectares, owned 74.5% of the land in the municipio. (Nationally, 2.8% of the landholdings censused in 1930 measured over 500 hectares and represented 88.6% of the land surface.) The Lorenz curves shown in Figure 3 demonstrate that not only was the land in Lagos inequitably distributed to an extreme degree, but that the distribution was only

---

the declared acreage and land value were used as the basis for computing taxes. However, the initial registration in 1900 was a means of legalizing possession of land which might have changed hands over the years without having ownership properly recorded. There was, therefore, at least an initial incentive for property-owners to accurately declare the extent of their holdings. Another disadvantage of this data source is the time lag in correcting the landholder's name in the tax records. Some properties listed as part of an estate in 1900 had not been changed on the records by 1930. Property sales and subdivisions by inheritance which might have occurred prior to 1930, resulting in de facto separate holdings, are not reflected in the data used here if they were not recorded by December 31, 1930.

Despite these shortcomings, one of the strongest arguments for using these records is the fact that planning engineers from the state and federal agencies (Local Agrarian Commission, National Agrarian Commission, and Agrarian Department) often relied on official reports from the local tax registry to determine whether the size of an hacienda, or the total number of hectares owned by an individual, made them legally subject to expropriation (as seen, for example, in expedientes ejidales for Lagos de Moreno and Cañada de Ricos, in ASRA). Divisions of large landholdings, whether through inheritance or sale, that were recorded after the publication of an ejido petition which might affect them were not considered legally valid. In general, presidential decrees granting ejido petitions disregarded de facto owners, listing as the affected landholders and haciendas those individuals and units on legal record at the time the petition was filed.

[5] In this study, 500 hectares is used as the dividing line between small-to-medium properties and large landholdings. Simpson (1937: 203) recommends 1,000 hectares, or a value of 30,000 pesos in 1930, as the most useful cutting-points for national analyses. However, given the pattern of land distribution in Lagos, and the number of very small properties, 500 hectares is a more appropriate measure of a large landholding in the local context.

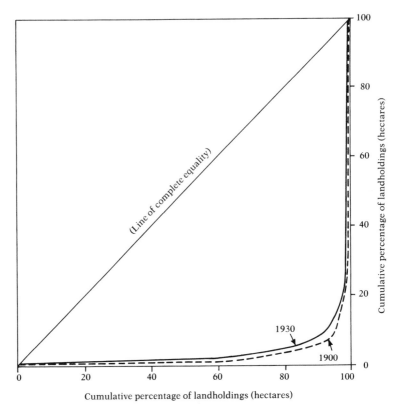

Cumulative percentage of landholdings (hectares)

Figure 3. Inequality of land distribution in the municipio of Lagos de Moreno, 1900 and 1930. (Data compiled from municipio property tax records.) The graph presents two smoothed Lorenz curves, one for the year 1900, the other for 1930. The degree of inequality in land distribution is indicated by the distance of the curves from the diagonal, representing the line of complete equality (i.e., the further the distance from the diagonal, the greater the degree of inequality). The raw data are reported in Appendix B, Table 1.

slightly more equitable in 1930 than it had been in 1900, a decade before the Revolution (cf. Simpson, 1937: 201–208, 640–653). Even the size of the local landholding aristocracy did not increase significantly between 1900 and 1930, although the size and number of their properties did change slightly, and the assessed tax value of the largest landholdings generally doubled between 1900 and 1930.[6]

---

[6]According to data compiled from the local tax registry (see Appendix B, Tables 4 and 5), 64 individuals in the municipio owned more than 500 hectares each in 1900. This land was in the form of 106 discrete properties, with a total area of 190,144 hectares and a total

Compared with haciendas of the same size in other states (e.g., Veracruz, Puebla, Morelos), landholdings in Lagos de Moreno had a lower commercial agriculture potential, and consequently a lower value. Only a small fraction of each of the largest haciendas in Lagos consisted of arable lands. For example, according to the *Manifestaciones Prediales de 1900*, Ciénega de Mata, with a total area of 31,277 hectares, had only 156 hectares of irrigated and 351 hectares of rainfall-dependent farming land. Similarly, El Tecuán, with 4,921 hectares, registered a total of 804 arable hectares, of which only 64 were irrigated. The land quality and value must be considered in any comparison between haciendas in Lagos and those elsewhere in Mexico. Because of the poor soil quality, low average annual rainfall, limited access to irrigation facilities, and little associated capital investment, haciendas in Lagos were generally much less elaborate operations than the largest and most commercially profitable properties in other parts of the Republic.[7]

Finally, I analyzed tax records to determine whether the largest landholdings had remained intact between 1900 and 1930 or whether they had been subdivided through sale or inheritance. Table 2 lists the haciendas or ranches in Lagos de Moreno which were registered as including 500 or more hectares in a single property unit in either 1900 or 1930. Some of these properties were subdivided during the 30-year period, and almost all doubled in value. Clearly, however, despite local belief to the contrary, the large landholdings were not abandoned by their owners after the Revolution. In general, until 1930 the large estates remained within the same families, even when they were broken up into separate units. The pre-Revolutionary land-tenure system in Lagos had survived two decades of civil strife. In the late 1920s, however, this highly unequal distribution of land and wealth came increasingly under challenge, as

---

tax-assessed value of 2,111,068 pesos. By 1930, there were 68 individuals who owned more than 500 hectares. However, because a few individuals owned many (10–47) pieces of property whose total surface added up to 500 hectares, the number of discrete properties trebled, to 322. Simultaneously, there was a slight decline in the total land area involved, to 184,401 hectares, although the value of the land increased considerably, to 4,209,060 pesos.

In the tax registries, irrigated land had up to four times the value of rainfall-dependent property of the same size. In general, properties closer to Lagos town had a higher per-hectare value. Proximity to Lagos implied easier access to the milk market, lower transportation costs to the railroad line for cattle and marketed crops, and proximity to the small rivers and springs of the municipio and to a higher water table.

[7]Compare, for example, Fowler (1970: 13–16); Friedrich (1970: 43); and Ronfeldt (1973: 10).

Table 2

Landholdings of 500 or More Hectares in Lagos de Moreno, 1900 and 1930

Name of Property	Size in Hectares		Tax-Assessed Value		Ownership Status, 1900–1930[a]
	1900	1930	1900	1930	
Los Ángeles	—[b]	601	—	20,000	X
Bajío del Purgatorio	—	690	—	—	X
Bellavista	571	702	4,100	9,500	B
Betulia	1,894	1,894	26,000	52,000	F/6
Betulia	—	750	—	32,000	X
*Las Cajas	1,936	2,151	38,000	85,000	B
El Cajón	556	556	8,000	16,000	B
*La Cantera (de Moreno)	727	727	9,827	19,600	A
Las Cardonas	513	513	2,412	4,820	E
La Ceja de Bolitas	770	770	9,213	18,400	A/4
*Ciénega de Mata	31,277	29,801	175,000	238,775	B
*Cieneguilla (de González, de Serrano)	1,579	1,758	32,000	68,000	E
*Rancho el Circo (now La Paz)	550	610	7,000	15,200	C/2
*Las Cruces	2,693	2,693	12,000	98,000	E
*Estancia Grande (formerly El Centro and Coecillo)		6,922		175,000	A/5
El Centro	4,415	(above)	50,000	(above)	
Coecillo	5,295	2,788	62,000	47,000	B
*La Estanzuela	1,070	1,070	10,792	21,500	A
*La Galera	818	818	22,000	44,000	A
Granadillas	570	—	18,000	—	X
Jaramillo el Alto (de Arriba)	4,294	4,294	46,000	92,000	A
Jaramillo el Bajo (de Abajo)	872	—	14,600	—	X
Labor de Hermosillo	646	—	13,800	—	X
*Labor Lagunita y la Cuchilla (same as Labor de Hermosillo?)	—	660	—	23,000	X
*Labor San Agustín y Portugalejo	984	1,580[c]	40,000	123,048[c]	D/2
*Laborcita de González	1,412	—	23,000	—	X

Name					
Ladera	813	—	11,800	—	X
*Ledesma (Ledesma, Alamitos, y La Troje)	3,424	4,723	51,000	200,000	E
Llano del Crespo	1,883	1,882c	17,000	34,000c	D/2
*Lo de Avalos	3,553c	3,553	44,000c	88,063	B
Lobos y Soledad	669	393	3,500	3,327	E
*Los Magueyes (San Juan de los Magueyes)	3,174	3,174	38,000	76,000	E
*La Merced	4,378	4,378	45,000	90,000	A
*Moya, Castelhondo y Anexos	1,285	1,542c	40,000	89,200c	D/2
*Nazas de Velázquez	770	661	15,400	21,210	E
Noche Buena	—	743c	—	13,080c	X
La Ordeña	607	607c	6,800	13,600c	E
*La Palma (La Palma Grande)	529	599	7,000	14,000	C/3
El Pedernal (El Pedregal)	620	689	3,000	6,700	A
*El Portezuelo	1,369	1,540	19,130	38,200	A
El Portezuelo de Briseño	652	789	6,930	15,800	E
*Providencia	—	524	—	18,400	X
*El Puesto	7,450	7,872	70,000	140,000	B
*La Punta	24,319	21,275	232,000	396,249	C/2
Rancho Nuevo	681	844	7,701	19,785	A
*Los Ranchos	1,634	1,634	20,000	40,000	B
Salto de Zuritas	784	784	10,000	20,000	B
*San Bernardo y Anexos	5,605	4,551	65,000	87,150	C/4
*San Cristóbal (San Cristóbal, La Troje y Anexos) (see La Troje)	3,246	12,143	28,500	125,000	C/2
San Fandilas	513	513	10,000	20,000	A
*San Francisco y Rancho Seco	2,396	2,396	47,000	94,000	B
San Isidro	619	—	4,700	—	X
San Isidro y Anexos	556	1,010	8,000	15,000	X
*San Isidro de Abajo		556	10,000	10,000	A
San Joaquín	924	1,677c	14,000	35,500c	D/3
San José del Potrero	1,284	1,251c	15,600	39,100c	D/5
*San Juan sin Agua	899	333	11,000	7,333	B
San Marcos	1,284	—	11,000	—	X

Name of Property	Size in Hectares		Tax-Assessed Value		Ownership Status, 1900–1930[a]
	1900	1930	1900	1930	
*San Nicolás	4,975	4,975	52,500	105,000	B
San Nicolás	899	899	10,275	20,500	B
*San Pedro (Nazas de Serrano)	655	620	19,800	26,920	B
*San Rafael	1,284	1,284c	21,000	42,000c	D/5
*Santa Cruz	2,653	2,604c	38,000	74,110c	D/6
*Santa Emilia	539	840	15,000	38,000	B
Santa Rosa	—	—	6,300	—	X
*Santa Rosa	499	517	—	7,500	X
Santiago	1,284	—	13,000	—	X
*Sauceda y Anexos	3,934	—	26,900	—	D/5
Sauceda		501		5,220	
El Roble		760		8,217	
Noche Buena		1,700c		17,680c	
Palomas		745c		17,630c	
*El Sauz	1,637	1,770c	18,000	37,832c	F
El Sauz de Calvillo	1,498	1,448	11,900	23,800	B
Sepúlveda, San Antonio, Chipinque, y Anexos	941	491	28,000	34,000	C/2
*El Tecuán	4,921	4,500	90,000	150,000	E
*Tlalixcoyán	1,284	1,284	24,600	49,200	A
*La Troje	668	693	28,000	57,000	E
*La Troje (see San Cristóbal above)	15,847	6,049c	140,000	167,000c	D/6
El Zapote	506	490	8,300	16,100	A

Source: Manifestaciones Prediales de 1900 and *Catastro Antiguo, 1900–1947*, Delegación de Hacienda del Estado de Jalisco, Lagos de Moreno, Jalisco.

[a]Property ownership based on the name and number of title-holders listed in the state tax registries, as cited above. The code which follows is based on paternal family name (e.g., Celso *Serrano* Flores to Oscar and Genaro *Serrano* Estrada). Transfers of ownership to other families (codes E and F below) may be overestimated, because a code based on father's family name would not include transfers of title to a daughter's husband or a wife's relatives. Ownership status is coded as follows, with co-owners in 1930 indicated by numeral:

A—Same owner in 1900 and 1930.

B—Title transferred by 1930 to a single individual, member of the same family as the owner in 1900.

C—Owned within the same family in 1900 and 1930. Property title shared by 1930.

D—Owned within the same family in 1900 and 1930. Property sub-divided into separate units by 1930.

E—Owned by 1930 by a single owner with a different family name than the owner in 1900.

F—Property subdivided into separate units by 1930 among several owners with family names which differ from the 1900 owner's name.

X—Data on property not available for 1900 or 1930.

[b]Data not available.

[c]Multiple property units belonging to the same or different owners. The total number of hectares and the total tax-assessed value of these separate units have been recorded in the table. For example:

1. Lo de Avalos in 1900 was owned by a single individual, but title is listed for 2 separate parts of the ranch measuring 2,671 and 882 hectares, valued respectively at 29,000 and 15,000 pesos.

2. Sauceda y Anexos was divided by 1930 into 6 units owned by 5 heirs. Of these, Noche Buena was divided into 2 units, owned by 2 heirs; the units, measuring 902 and 798 hectares, were assessed at 8,840 pesos apiece.

*Parts of these properties were later expropriated for the formation of one or more ejidos.

pressures for land reform began to mount at both the national and local levels.

Mexico in the Wake of Revolution

Constitutional Changes

The Constitution which emerged from the Revolution of 1910–17 created new options for would-be social reformers. It provided a sweeping re-definition of the legal rights of workers and campesinos, and imposed new restrictions on the Catholic Church.

Article 27 of the 1917 Constitution declared that ownership of all land and subsoil resources is vested in the nation, which alone has the author-ity to transfer ownership (or more accurately, usufruct). Article 27 did not legislate outright expropriation of all landholdings, nor the collectiv-ization of expropriated lands, but it did leave open the possibility for both actions. It declared null and void the alienation of communal lands which had occurred since 1856 under the Juárez and Díaz regimes. It provided the government with the authority to break up large landhold-ings through forced sales which would result in small and medium-sized private farms. State and federal governments were empowered to pass laws specifying how the large estates would be divided. For the first several years, this provision of the 1917 Constitution was implemented only in states such as Morelos, where the campesinos (because of their participation in the Revolution) were already organized.

Article 123 prescribed rights for workers which were more advanced than those prevailing in most industrialized countries at the time: the right to organize labor unions, to strike, to share in profits, to work an eight-hour day, and to receive a minimum wage. The same article pro-vided for the establishment of Boards of Conciliation and Arbitration with legal jurisdiction to settle disputes between labor and management. The article included a variety of other provisions, but those just men-tioned had the greatest impact nationally—and on the workers of Lagos de Moreno. In 1918, the Confederación Regional Obrera Mexicana (CROM) was established by Luis Morones and other radical labor leaders whose antecedents were in the Spanish anarcho-syndicalist movement and the House of the Workers of the World. The CROM became a national umbrella organization for unionized workers and campesinos, although numerous independent labor unions were established throughout the country during the 1920s.

Finally, there were articles limiting the power of the Church. The

Catholic Church had generally sided with the Díaz regime and had opposed Madero. Revolutionary leaders tended to be anticlerical because of this history of opposition, as well as philosophical beliefs many of them had adopted through association with the Liberal Party and the Flores Magón brothers.[8] Articles 3, 27, and 130 were especially important in this regard. Church wealth—buildings, convents, monasteries, art-works, and land—were to be nationalized. Priests of foreign nationalities were prohibited from serving in Mexico; Mexican priests were denied the right to vote or to participate in politics in any way. Religious services were prohibited outside the walls of the churches. Education—texts, curriculum, instructors—was to be controlled by the government. Primary education had to be secular. From the beginning, the Church and lay organizations opposed these restrictions on the Church. However, because the "anticlerical provisions" of the Constitution were only intermittently enforced, the Church and conservative Catholics did not organize militantly against the government until provoked by President Calles in 1926.

In Lagos de Moreno, these Constitutional provisions raised the specter of fundamental challenges to core values of the upper class. They made possible (but did not insure) land reform and campesino political activism, labor reform and the establishment of labor unions, and restraint of the temporal power of the Catholic Church and its priests. For workers and campesinos, the Constitutional changes were significant for two reasons. First, because they reflected the demands of organized interest groups active elsewhere in the Republic, they implied the possibility of affiliating with well-connected organizations which might provide practical political guidance and protection. Second, by providing legal legitimacy to the claims of workers and peasants, the Constitution facilitated the task of local political mobilization. Thereafter, campesinos could petition the state for the recognition of legal rights; provided the state was responsive, they no longer needed to organize *against* it. The risks of campesino political activism had not been eliminated, but they were reduced. The collective organization of campesinos was a necessary precondition for land reform in areas such as Lagos de Moreno, because the Constitution did not automatically mandate land reform. A complex peti-

[8]For detailed analyses of the Mexican Liberal Party and its most prominent organizers, the Flores Magón brothers, see Bartra (ed.), 1977; Córdova, 1975a, 1975b; Gómez-Quiñones, 1974; Hernández, 1975; and Quirk, 1953.

tioning procedure had to be pursued by any group of campesinos who wished to secure ejido lands.[9]

Political Change in the 1920s

The 1920s was a decade of political ferment in Mexico, as regional and local political leaders sought to consolidate, broaden, and assert their authority vis-à-vis the new federal government. Simultaneously, the federal government was engaged in efforts to consolidate its own authority. A frequently changing cast of state governors tried either to vigorously enforce or to suppress enforcement of the agrarian, labor, and anticlerical provisions of the Constitution. Regional military leaders engaged in assorted revolts against national or state governments. Local leaders of various ideological persuasions tried to organize followings in defense of their goals. Fluid, generally personalistic political parties emerged at election time to fight pitched electoral battles, dissolving in the off years.

Some land redistribution was achieved during this period, but it was selective and often confined to particular regions. Mass-based peasant leagues began to form in some states, especially Veracruz, Puebla, Tamaulipas, and Michoacán. Most of them were organized by politicians who regarded the leagues as personal political vehicles.[10] The most important of these nationally—and subsequently to the agraristas in Lagos—were the leagues in Veracruz (organized by Governor Adalberto Tejeda in 1923 under the auspices of the Partido Nacional Agrarista [PNA], with Ursulo Galván as a principal leader), and in Michoacán (organized in 1922 with the help of the CROM, with Primo Tapia and Francisco Múgica as principal leaders). By 1926 the CROM claimed 1,500 campesino members (Huizer, 1968–69: 117). In the same year, the PNA and the Veracruz league met to establish the first national peasant union, the Liga Nacional Campesina Ursulo Galván.[11] Even earlier, campesino organizations had proven useful to the federal government, which was able in 1923–24

[9]The petitioning procedure and the obstacles which might be encountered at each stage of the process are described in detail in Appendix A, with case materials from the ejidos in Lagos de Moreno.

[10]Huizer and Stavenhagen, 1974: 385. For studies of these movements, see Brading (ed.), 1980; Falcón, 1975; [Fowler] Salamini 1976, 1978; Gómez-Jara, 1970; González Navarro, 1968; and Huizer, 1968-69.

[11]The Liga's declaration of principles called for adoption of Articles 27 and 123 of the 1917 Constitution as rights of peasants; perfection of the ejido as a form of land tenure; socialization of the land and other means of production; attention to the international nature of peasant problems; and solidarity with all proletarians (Huizer, 1968-69: 122).

to employ organized labor and agrarian reinforcements to quell the de la Huerta rebellion. This was the first time that armed agrarista troops fought in support of the federal army.

On December 1, 1924, General Plutarco Elías Calles took the presidential oath of office succeeding General Obregón. Calles occupied the presidency until November 30, 1928. During those four years in office, however, he succeeded in establishing his domination of national politics and public policy—a control which extended into 1935. Calles used the official party and the Congress to impose a series of puppet presidents (Emilio Portes Gil, Pascual Ortiz Rubio, and Abelardo Rodríguez) from 1929 to 1934. Although his public statements became much more conservative in later years, during his own presidency Calles advocated vigorous enforcement of many of the more radical and controversial articles of the Constitution.

Partly as a result of the existence of Article 123, partly fostered by the reciprocal influence of state and national organizing efforts, this was a period of relative liberalization for labor. Luis Morones, leader of the CROM, served as Minister of Labor, Commerce, and Industry. State and national labor organizations experimented with a variety of tactics and ideologies. Socialist agrarian and labor movements flourished in Yucatán, Veracruz, and Michoacán. For a time (until it was declared illegal in 1929), the Communist Party operated openly, concentrating its efforts in mines, textile mills, and the largest urban areas (Schmitt, 1965: 7–14). Several newspapers of a liberal-to-radical bent had at least limited circulation between 1910 and 1930, including *El Machete*, the Communist Party publication; *Sagitario*, published by Librado Rivera, a Flores Magón follower in Tamaulipas; and *Espártaco*, the organ of the Unión de Mecánicos Mexicanos (the railroad workers' union). Issues of all of these periodicals circulated among the reform leaders in Lagos de Moreno.

Despite the enlarged tolerance for "radical" political activities on the national level, it was still dangerous in many places to be a radical, or even an aspiring reformer, especially in rural areas and small towns distant from the largest cities where persons seeking change could find support. Labor and agrarian radicalism was also dangerous in the most pro-clerical states, where the opposition was quick to link the implementation of labor and agrarian laws to government enforcement of restrictions on the Church. In Lagos it became quite common to consider all restraints on the Church as atheistic, and it was not far from such a belief to the notion that all reformers were communists. Usually, reformers gained followers only when state and local authorities endorsed their efforts, particularly when they guaranteed protection. They were endangered when government protection was withheld and when authorities acted in concert with opponents of reform.

As the relations between leaders of the CROM and the federal government became closer, national labor leaders and their organization became less radical. In effect, they facilitated state control over organized labor. Intense factionalism was to develop within the Mexican labor movement in the early 1930s because of the co-opted leadership of the CROM.

While neither Calles nor the presidents he sponsored during the 1929–34 period vigorously encouraged community petitions for agrarian reform, more land was redistributed than ever before (Simpson, 1937: 96–97; Whetten, 1948: 124–127). Calles himself distributed about three million hectares. But in 1929 Calles spent eight months in Europe and witnessed the agricultural production problems faced by small landholdings in France (Weyl and Weyl, 1939: 80–83). After his return to Mexico in June 1930, Calles declared that the agrarian reform in Mexico had been a failure. He recommended that state governors set deadlines beyond which petitions for land reform would not be considered. The redistribution of land dropped markedly in the next three years, as Calles shifted his support to promoting small private landholdings which could maintain higher levels of production. Two of the state governors who refused to fall in behind this policy of agrarian retrenchment and who continued to grant land reform petitions were Tejeda of Veracruz and Cárdenas of Michoacán.

Lagos de Moreno in the 1920s

The first open rumblings for labor and agrarian reform in Lagos were heard in 1924. They coincided, significantly, with José Guadalupe Zuno's tenure as governor of Jalisco (from March 1, 1923, until his resignation on March 23, 1926).[12] In Lagos, the upper class regards the Zuno family

[12]Zuno was a young man, in his late twenties or early thirties while Governor. He had long been a part of a group of intellectuals (poets, novelists, muralists, political cartoonists) based in Guadalajara which favored the enforcement of revolutionary doctrines. Zuno described this group and its activities in *Reminiscencias de una vida* (1972). Zuno resigned as governor in the face of charges of corruption lodged against his administration in the Federal Legislature. He was found guilty by that body, and sentenced to the suspension of his political rights for six years. Moreno Ochoa (1959) claims that Zuno was charged with supporting the De la Huerta rebellion against the federal government, a charge which he claims all Jalisciences recognized as a pretext to remove Zuno from

as the scourge of Jalisco and blames "the old man" (José Guadalupe senior) for all manner of vile atrocities and crimes.[13] They regard his administration as socialist, corrupt, and anticlerical. Agraristas who were in Lagos in the 1920s said that Zuno encouraged and supported their labor and agrarian organizing activities. Reform leader José Romero Gómez recalled:

> There was a terrible struggle, before the Cristero revolution. The Knights of Columbus tried to break up the revolutionary group in Lagos. . . . The struggle between the two went so far that the state governor, that is, [José] Guadalupe Zuno, sent the Anaya brothers— Obregonista military officers, one a General and the other a Colonel—to Lagos to see if they could control the situation and give us support. . . . The revolutionary group stuck by the Anaya brothers; and the Knights of Columbus with the local group of petit bourgeois were led by the elite of the bourgeoisie, the hacendados.

The upper-class and the agrarista images of Governor Zuno are not necessarily contradictory. It is clear that he promoted agrarian reform more than any other governor of Jalisco before the presidency of Lázaro Cárdenas (1934–40).[14] During his tenure in office, Zuno gave provisional state approval, pending final presidential approval (which frequently was not granted), to approximately 107 agrarian communities, benefiting 22,157 individuals with 113,636 hectares (see Table 2 in Appendix B). In the municipio of Lagos, six of the seven earliest community petitions for land redistribution were filed during the Zuno administration.[15]

---

office. The real reason, he contends, is that Zuno was a supporter of former President Alvaro Obregón, as were all of his cabinet members, and that President Plutarco Elías Calles was afraid that in the event of a conflict between himself and General Obregón, Calles could not count on Zuno's loyalty. Even today, state governors are occasionally removed from office by the Federal Legislature at the behest of the President, usually for committing grave errors of political judgment.

[13]Zuno's daughter, María Esther Zuno de Echeverría, is the wife of Mexico's recent President Luis Echeverría Alvarez. During Echeverría's presidency, Zuno's sons held a variety of official posts in Jalisco and managed to regain much of the power which the family had periodically held and lost in the state. It is difficult to know how much "the old man" was reviled for his progeny and how much for his own policies and ideas.

[14]See Moreno Ochoa (1959) and Zuno (1964: 123–124). Admittedly, there was a rapid turnover of state executives, and the variable length of service makes it difficult to compare accomplishments. Zuno served longer by two months than any other governor of Jalisco until Everardo Topete, whose four-year administration began on March 1, 1935. One governor, Clemente Sepulveda, served only two months in 1926; the terms of others ranged from six months to two years (Paez Brotchie, 1940).

[15]Mexico's Agrarian Reform Law defines the procedures which must be followed before ejido lands can be granted in response to a community's petition for land reform.

The Lagos petitions were filed at the urging of Susano Castañeda, municipio president of Lagos in 1925 and member of the municipio government council *(ayuntamiento)* in 1926. Castañeda, and a successor, Clodoaldo Gómez, were the only two municipio presidents who urged local agrarian or labor reform in Lagos until 1935. As José Romero described them: "They were the two municipio presidents that they sent to us from Guadalajara who had more or less revolutionary ideas, but not committed because . . . they weren't going to struggle, they were going to make money. . . . They took advantage of the strength of the [labor] organization to maintain their [political] position." In fact, the reformists developed mutually beneficial relationships with these "more or less revolutionary" municipio presidents.[16]

Organizing Urban Laborers and Campesinos

Following common practice, Castañeda arrived in Lagos as a political nominee of the state government. Quoting Romero again: "He called all of us, of the revolutionary group in Lagos, and we made an agreement to keep struggling and to help him with his administration. Because of that, Lagos took an upswing. We sprouted wings!"

The "revolutionary group" to which Romero referred consisted of a small band of urban laborers who were concerned primarily with labor and political issues. Castañeda shared this concern, but he was also interested in encouraging community petitions for ejidos. The few Laguenses who had discreetly held radical or reformist ideas began to come forward and to join Castañeda. This was the beginning of a coalition between laborers and agraristas, held together primarily by leaders committed (for political advantage or for ideological reasons) to reform of urban *and* rural working conditions. This coalition held together in varying degrees of formality for 13 years, leaving a distinctive imprint on the agrarian reform movement in Lagos de Moreno.

José Romero was among the first to emerge publicly as a member of

---

The bureaucratic process is complicated and potentially quite protracted. It involves several review stages, many government employees, and countless individuals representing the interests of the petitioning community and the potentially affected landowners. The sheer number of people, agencies, and steps involved provides abundant opportunity for delay and subversion (see Appendix A for examples).

[16]An article in *El Defensor del Pueblo* (December 2, 1928) lamented the manner in which the state government imposed its candidates for municipio president. The newspaper charged that recent municipio presidents had come as "veritable political bosses to impose their will and ridicule Lagos society." Susano Castañeda, Clodoaldo Gómez, and Miguel Rábago Soto were cited as recent examples.

the "revolutionary group." His political life history and ideas are recounted in detail in Chapter 5. A short, stocky man of assertive de-
meanor, Romero was raised in Lagos and worked as a carpenter and
cabinet-maker. He had some formal education and enjoyed reading a
wide variety of political publications, creating, as he said, his own amal-
gam of ideas and hopes for reform. By his own account he had read the
newspaper of the anarcho-syndicalist Flores Magón brothers, *Regeneración*,[17] as well as novelists such as Emile Zola. He began to take an
interest in local and state politics, working in political campaigns and
serving on the regional labor arbitration board. Most important, he began to discuss his ideas with a few other men in Lagos, and with occasional politicians and outsiders temporarily posted to the town.[18]

In the mid-1920s, most of the other Laguenses who entertained
thoughts of agrarian or labor reform were laborers and skilled craftsmen.[19] Most of them were or had been employed at the textile mill. Those
not employed at the factory had developed other trade skills. Nieves
Ortiz was a leader among them, an uneducated shoemaker reportedly in
his sixties by 1930 and very "revolutionary," according to all who knew
him. Several of the first agraristas traced their earliest contact with the

---

[17]*Regeneración* was a newspaper published intermittently between 1900 and 1918,
mainly in the United States, by Enrique and Ricardo Flores Magón. Influenced by the
Spanish anarcho-syndicalists, they helped to establish the Mexican Liberal Party.
"*Magonismo*" opposed the re-election of Porfirio Díaz as early as 1903, and advocated
many of the most radical social reforms later partially incorporated into the Constitution.
For analysis and reproduction of articles from *Regeneración*, see Bartra (1977).

[18]Romero had become interested in radical ideas by 1924. The earliest documentation
of this interest is a letter to him from Pedro Moreno Mitre, apparently a laborer from
Lagos then residing in Mexico City, dated June 24, 1924. Moreno wrote that since October
of the previous year he had met Romero's request to send him "liberal press and other
propaganda," and berated Romero for not keeping him informed about what was happening in Lagos. He went on to encourage Romero to become involved in the upcoming
elections to insure that someone *genuinely* interested in the welfare of the people was
elected (AJRG).

[19]As noted in Chapter 2, a few local intellectuals such as Mariano Azuela had been
critical of the abuses of the Revolution and the corrupting effect of political and economic
power. Prior to the Revolution, Gabriel López Arce, publisher at the time of the local
newspaper, *El Defensor del Pueblo* ("The Public Defender"), had espoused a variety of
unpopular causes such as wage increases, improvement in the treatment of urban workers and agricultural laborers, and laborer self-help groups. For this and other offenses,
the newspaper became known as "El Ofensor del Pueblo" ("The Public Offender"). As far
as one can determine, however, none of the local "liberals" went so far as to advocate
unionization of labor for collective bargaining or wage increases, much less the redistribution of property through land reform.

reform movement to "Nievitos" Ortiz. Ortiz later became presiding officer of one of the first unions in Lagos, the Unión de Obreros Libertarios. One informant described Ortiz this way:

> He was a revolutionary as if he were 18 or 20 years old, with a tremendous spirit for struggle. As if he had been educated in the time of the struggle. He was wholeheartedly anticlerical. He personally would go to Buenavista, Cuarenta, wherever it was necessary, and would look after the [community] organizations that were aborning, as old as he was.

Fabián Espinoza was a master mechanic at the factory. As one agrarista described him, "He took a interest in agrarianism from the heart only, because he was already old. He liked the movement and began to distribute propaganda." Maximino Espinoza, Agustín Espinoza, Aniceto Martínez, and a man known as "Chupiros" also worked at the factory. Francisco Navia senior had been employed at La Victoria, but by that time had four looms of his own for making blankets. There were others, but these men were the more vocal members with the most sustained involvement in the reform movement. Of all the men who participated in this early organizational phase, only José Romero and Francisco Navia junior were alive in 1975.

Aniceto Martínez in particular later played an important role in the local movement's development. He was only intermittently employed at the factory; during those periods when the factory closed down, Martínez would return to being a "*maricatero.*" As José Romero recalled, "He had a little donkey which he would load with his boxes of merchandise. He'd even sell *novenas*—those little books they used to sell in those days to pray to saints. . . . They were a big sale item in the ranchos. . . . That's how he wandered all over the municipio of Lagos." Along with the novenas, Martínez sold thread, needles, spices, and other merchandise, in exchange for maize, beans, or money. This second vocation as itinerant rural merchant was later to prove an important vehicle for recruitment into the reform movement, distribution of propaganda, and gathering intelligence on rural community developments.

In 1924, the only labor union in Lagos was the Sindicato de Obreros Católicos (Catholic Workers' Union). It was little more than a self-help group, a means of satisfying the constitutional requirement that factories must have unions (cf. J. Meyer, 1976: 21–23). By various accounts it had been formed either by Acción Católica—a Catholic lay organization—or by a local priest, Father José Alba. It was primarily a mutual-aid

society, apparently modeled on the workers' societies organized by Catholic priests in Guadalajara before the Revolution (see Calvert, 1973: 224; Zuno, 1964: 30) and on Catholic labor unions organized as a means of evading constitutional limitations on religiously affiliated political parties (see Bazant, 1977: 167). In the case of the organizations in Guadalajara: "The intent of these activities was not to promote a violent revolution; instead, it was reduced to a sort of education of the workers, so that united they might help each other more effectively in their home needs, and to get them accustomed to saving and parliamentary procedures" (Zuno, 1964: 30). After the Revolution, some of these societies in Guadalajara joined with other unions and student groups to become the precursors of national labor organizations. But there was no such radicalizing effect in Lagos.

The reformist laborers at the Victoria factory eventually grew impatient with the Catholic union's reluctance to demand wage increases for the factory's workers. They formed another union which they called the Unión de Obreros Libertarios (UOL), the Organization of Libertarian Workers. Although he didn't join the UOL, José Romero was soon drawn into its activities.

In May 1924, the UOL registered its newspaper, *La Palabra*, of which one remaining issue (for September 7, 1924) has been preserved in a private local press archive. That issue announced a meeting of the union's members, described Plutarco Calles' pro-worker philosophy, offered a short account of the vile treatment of workers on haciendas before the Revolution, and concluded with an article explaining why workers should be organized. The latter article read in part:

> Beyond the well-known reason that "unity builds strength," the laborer, the worker, will only be able to demand his rights with complete success when he has the undeniable strength of unity. But the laborer who knows his rights, the worker who retains intact his faculties as a man and as a citizen, must never recoil nor be afraid of the cardboard gun of the members of the bourgeoisie; instead he should become braver and more determined to join with his *compañeros* and form the laborer's organization, the basis and beginning of his social and economic betterment.

La Palabra also argued that workers in general, *both* in the fields and in the town, should always be united. This foreshadowed the subsequent involvement of the labor unionists in organizing agrarian communities.

The style of these articles suggests that either there were, within the UOL, laborers with some education and preparation capable of producing a newspaper, or—more likely—that outside organizers were involved with the local movement. Many of the early agraristas credit Susano Castañeda with formation of the UOL. However, there is no evidence that Castañeda was in Lagos in 1924 in any official capacity. Romero's assertion that dissident factory workers formed the UOL seems more plausible, with the caveat that organizers from the national labor union (CROM) or its state affiliate were probably at least apprised if not involved as promoters. The credit accorded to Castañeda for forming the Unión may reflect his influence in legitimating its relations with institutions external to Lagos, and in expanding its sphere of activities.[20] Whatever its origins, the UOL served a dual purpose as an advocate for workers' rights and as a political support group for Castañeda and Zuno.

At about the same time, the Victoria textile mill closed permanently. The closing of the factory (sometime between late 1923 and 1925) was probably due to a combination of factors: several changes in ownership, financial mismanagement of this and other businesses of the same owners, aging equipment, scarcity of raw materials, the predominance of other cities as textile centers, and the labor ferment in the textile industry nationally. Its closing created a severe employment problem for the laborers, many of whom moved away from Lagos.[21] Recruiters came to Lagos from other textile mills in search of experienced workers. Some found employment in nearby León, Guanajuato; others moved farther, to Puebla, San Luis Potosí, and Aguascalientes, other major textile centers.

Among those who left was Aniceto Martínez, who found work at a mill in El Salto de Juanacatlán, near Guadalajara. There he joined the labor union in the mill, becoming its secretary and principal mediator between the workers and management. Roughly from the mid-1920s until 1930–31, Martínez reportedly traveled in Veracruz, Michoacán, and Jalisco, and possibly in other states as well. As José Romero observed, "Since he was restless by nature, it wasn't hard for him to cover lots of ground." He established contacts with politicians in these states, and also with worker and agrarian movements and their leaders. In subsequent years Martínez helped to keep Laguenses informed of reform movements elsewhere, and his contacts were instrumental in developing outside support and protection for the movement in Lagos.

Before concluding this account of the Unión de Obreros Libertarios, it is important to stress its political function and the connection which it established between the labor and agrarian reform movements in Lagos as early as January 1925. Romero reported that with Castañeda, the Unión members formed "a political group, genuinely political." Another

[20]A letter from the UOL dated January 17, 1925, asked that the Unión be formally registered, a request being made "at the urging of Susano Castañeda." It described the organization's motto as "land and worker emancipation," and its members as "concerned about proletarian emancipation." It bears some 60 names, and the Unión's president is listed as Nieves A. Ortiz. (Expediente ejidal, Lagos de Moreno, Comisión Local Agraria, Guadalajara, Jalisco.)

[21]Estimates of the number of employees at the factory at its closing range from 300 to 500, based on estimates of about 175 looms and three shifts of workers.

agrarista described Castañeda's objectives as follows: "What he was trying to do was to organize the people in town as well as those in the fields.
Those were his ideals." The pivotal roles of both Castañeda and the UOL
in the local agrarian reform movement are demonstrated by the first
petition for land for the agrarian community of Lagos de Moreno (expediente ejidal, ASRA), which reads as follows:

> In the city of Lagos de Moreno, state of Jalisco, on January 17,
> 1925, with the undersigned gathered in the meeting room of the
> Unión de Obreros Libertarios at the urging of Compañero Susano
> Castañeda, an agreement was reached to form an agrarian commu-
> nity in this city.
>
> Accordingly, in keeping with the relevant Article of the applica-
> ble law, it was agreed to direct a respectful petition to the State
> Executive, asking for authorization to form the agrarian group we
> propose, with the objective of granting ejidos to the signers, since
> we are all workers of the field and currently we are harshly op-
> pressed by the large landowners [latifundistas] of this region, who
> until now have not known how to appreciate our labor for its real
> worth—which, together with the evil eyes with which they look
> upon us since we are members of this Unión which has concerned
> itself with proletarian emancipation, is what has made us resolve to
> respectfully ask the State Executive, as we hereby do, to authorize
> us to form in this city an agrarian group to bear as its motto "LAND
> AND WORKER EMANCIPATION."

One of the numerous signatures on the petition is that of Nieves Ortiz,
who, as president of the UOL, signed for those who did not know how to
write.

Nieves Ortiz and Francisco Navia also organized the agrarian community of Buenavista, which was granted land provisionally by Governor
Zuno in 1925 and finally authorized by President Calles in 1927. The
other agrarian communities which filed petitions during these early
years were Cañada de Ricos, Ciénega de Mata, La Escondida, and Moya.
Four of these are among the ejidos closest to the town of Lagos, and that
proximity was undoubtedly influential in facilitating travel, mobilization, and communications among organizers and interested campesinos,
and in affording some degree of protection to petitioners by sympathetic
authorities in Lagos.

The cooperation between urban labor and campesinos in the municipio of Lagos continued through the Sindicato de Oficios Varios (SOV),
successor to the UOL. At times this coalition worked to the disadvantage

of agrarian reformers. One of the accusations lodged against petitioners for land, to invalidate or discredit their petitions, was the charge that they were not campesinos at all, but urban laborers without any ties to the land. On its surface, there was merit to this charge; but it ignored the fact that while urban laborers and other "outsiders" may have provided encouragement, the majority of those who signed petitions and most of the first recipients of land in the ejidos were indeed campesinos.

The Cristero Rebellion Intervenes

When asked what defused the agrarian reform movement of the 1920s, Lagos' agraristas invariably pointed to the Cristero rebellion—"*se atravesó la cristiada.*" Between 1926 and 1929, Laguenses became enmeshed in a complex set of conflicts which originated outside their communities but had severe local repercussions. Nationally, the Cristero rebellion was a critical confrontation between the revolutionary government, with its policies for social transformation and political centralization, and the Catholic Church and its devoted followers, representing the country's principal traditional authority structure and the set of conservative customs and values attached to it.[22]

The Cristero rebellion was brought about by President Calles' determination to enforce constitutional restraints on the Church, and the Church's campaign against these laws and Calles' enforcement mechanisms. Since 1917 the national Church hierarchy had barely tolerated the constitutional restrictions. As plans for their enforcement advanced, the Archbishop in January and February 1926 reaffirmed the Church's opposition to the constitutional articles and its intention to undertake a campaign against them. Calles countered by signing a decree on July 31, 1926, specifying the terms for national enforcement of the constitutional provisions, including penalties for violation.

---

[22]This is a highly controversial period in Mexican history, about which it is nearly impossible to have a dispassionate discussion—especially with persons who lived through the rebellion in intensely Catholic regions such as Los Altos de Jalisco. Among the principal scholarly studies of the national religious movement and the international politics of the conflict are J. Meyer (1971, 1973–74, 1976), D. Bailey (1974), Olivera de Bonfil (1966, 1976), and Quirk (1973). Scores of polemical treatises and politicized histories have also been published on this period. See, for example, Larín (1968), Moreno Ochoa (1959), Paez Brotchie (1940), and Zuno (1964). Novels about the core region of the rebellion dramatically portray the personal consequences of the movement and the traditional religious values which nourished it. See especially de Anda (1974), Rulfo (1973a, 1973b), and Yáñez (1975).

The Church Episcopal Committee and leaders of lay organizations objected strenuously to the "Calles law," and particularly to the provision that priests had to register with the federal government. The Church refused to submit to what it regarded as government usurpation of its authority over its own ministers. It was announced that after July 31 all religious services requiring officiation by priests, except the administration of sacraments, would be indefinitely suspended. Lay leaders called for a nationwide economic boycott. There were demonstrations and skirmishes between the government and Church supporters during the second half of 1926, but neither the boycott nor suspension of religious services forced a change in federal policies. Finally, lay Catholics organized a popular army, and in January 1927 the armed rebellion began. It lasted, with setbacks and advances on both sides, until 1929. Religious rites were not officially reinstated by the Church until June 21, 1929.

Thousands of faithful Catholics in the central region of the country, believing that they were being deprived of their rights to open religious observance by an unjust government, joined together in small guerrilla bands to fight against the federal government. Their battle cries were *"Viva Cristo Rey!"* ("Long live Christ the King!") and *"Viva la Virgen de Guadalupe!"* ("Long live the Virgin of Guadalupe!"). For thousands, the Cristero rebellion was a religious war against an unbelieving (some thought atheistic) government.

The heartland of the Cristero movement was in the center of the Republic, in the states of Michoacán, Colima, Jalisco, Querétaro, Zacatecas, Nayarit, Aguascalientes, and Guanajuato. Important lay and Church leadership of the movement, and substantial financial support for it, were based in Jalisco. The largest contingent of participants in the fighting came from the Los Altos region of Jalisco. There, the traditional Catholic conservatism of the region's residents, the large number of priests, nuns, and members of lay organizations,[23] and the Alteños' tradi-

---

[23]Jean Meyer (1973a: 161) writes that as late as 1950, one-third of the region's population belonged to lay Church organizations. This is an indication not only of the religious devotion of the region's people, but also of the high incidence of organized groups which were in frequent contact with priests. That organization and contact would facilitate mobilizing Alteños on issues affecting the Church and Catholicism. In 1975 and 1976, conservative Catholics of the region—mobilized by local priests as well as itinerant lay organizers—once again rebelled against federal government authority, though in a nonviolent manner. Protesting a newly published edition of the government's series of basic primary school textbooks (which failed to mention the Church at all, but did include references to Fidel Castro as well as material on sex education and Darwin's theory of

tional resentment of federal government constraints on local autonomy combined to produce substantial support for the rebellion. During the years of the fighting, Los Altos and the mountainous areas in adjoining states became havens for guerrilla groups. Many who did not leave to fight provided protection, food, and shelter to the rebels.

The rebellion and its hard core of supporters in Jalisco put a severe strain on the state government and on its relationship with the federal government. The state government was under pressure to quash the armed rebellion, despite extensive support within the state for the Cristero rebels. From July 1926 to July 1929, Jalisco had three governors who held office long enough to bear mentioning. Margarito Ramírez served the longest, from April 1927 to August 1929. As governor, Ramírez devoted more of his political resources and energies to labor and agrarian reform than had most of his predecessors, except for Zuno. He approved 36 petitions (denying 28 others), benefiting 3,995 campesinos with 21,158 hectares (see Table 2 in Appendix B).

The Cristero stronghold in Los Altos was to the west and south of the municipio of Lagos de Moreno, but Lagos was also involved in the conflict. After the first major battle in the vicinity, the federal army brought the bodies of the dead into town and displayed them in front of the main church to discourage local support for the rebels. Bands of rebels and of federal troops garrisoned in Lagos alternately descended on the haciendas and rural communities, extracting whatever tribute they could.

While this was a tense and unsettled period in Lagos, the municipio escaped the heavy casualties and material damages suffered by neighboring municipios. Most Laguenses cite as the principal hardships of the period the population reconcentrations attempted by the federal government, and the extreme poverty resulting from the civil disorder. On three different occasions, the federal government attempted to isolate the Cristero rebels by relocating the rural population which was allegedly providing protection and support to them. From October to December 1927, and again from January to May in 1928 and 1929, residents of rural communities were ordered to move to urban areas of their choice (see Taylor, 1933: 38). One of the towns designated as a resettlement site was Lagos de Moreno. The sudden influx of rural people strained local resources, producing food shortages and health problems.

---

evolution), large numbers of Alteños withdrew their children from the public schools, engaged in heated debates with municipal officials, and in some places even burned the textbooks.

Wealthier landowning families, particularly women and children, once again withdrew to the safety of larger cities. Again the population of Los Altos declined, not only due to combat casualties but also because many of the families which left the region's rural areas did not return after the rebellion ended, or left some family members behind in cities outside the region. One of the leading agraristas, a young man at the time, describes the period as follows:

> Life was very hard, because really, the rich people gave nothing. But the poor people . . . one could see that they were barely surviving. It was extreme poverty—not to have the means or the place to go to earn a living. Those who were in society [working for rich people] could count on their small ration and what was given to them, but there were no jobs for other people. . . . The resettled people suffered hunger, misery, poverty, all that. . . . They would eat one meal a day, whatever they could.

Bitter Enemies: "El Clero" and "El Capital"

The Cristero rebellion seriously impeded the agrarian reform movement in Lagos de Moreno. In part this occurred because government attention and resources were directed to other, more pressing tasks. However, agraristas in Lagos firmly believe that the Cristiada was, at least in part, an attempt to frighten would-be reformers, to delay or prevent the redistribution of land. In their view, the Cristero movement represented a conspiracy between the rich ("*el capital*") and the clergy ("*el clero*"), whom they regarded as their bitterest enemies. The following comment was typical:

> To me, the priests and the rich people have always been allied. So when the Cristero revolution came, there were priests who led uprisings. And there were rich people who sent their pennies to support the war of the Cristeros, surely thinking that the situation would change for them if the Cristeros won.

The Cristiada may not have begun as a movement against the agraristas.[24] However, within a short time, the agraristas and the Cristeros did

---

[24]Jean Meyer, whose detailed study of the Cristero rebellion is based on numerous interviews with former leaders and rank-and-file participants in the movement as well as archival materials, rejects the charge that the movement represented a deliberate assault on the agrarian reform, or a form of collusion between wealthy landowners and the Church. He cites Catholic congresses held in Guadalajara and several other cities during the 1903–09 period in which large landowners were harshly criticized by the clergy for exploiting their workers (J. Meyer, 1976: 9). However, there is considerable evidence that

become enemies. The region was plagued by their conflict in the 1920s and well into the 1930s.[25] There were several reasons for the conflict. First, the government's anticlerical policy and later its military action against the Cristeros provoked hostility among conservative Catholics in Los Altos and resulted in opposition to the government and to all those associated with it. As recipients or seekers of government largesse through land redistribution, agraristas were regarded as government supporters. As one informant explained, the Cristeros were opposed to the agraristas "because the agraristas belonged to the government, and the Cristeros did not belong to the government but were instead in rebellion against it."

The Cristeros were correct in believing that there was cooperation between some agraristas and some public officials. Agraristas often believed or were told that to enhance their chances of receiving land they had to support the government.[26] Governor Margarito Ramírez used agraristas to supplement federal troops in the defense of Guadalajara against the Cristeros in 1929. Also in 1929, a military district was created in Los Altos de Jalisco, and General Saturnino Cedillo was charged with its defense. Cedillo brought his 10,000-member veteran agrarista army from the adjoining state of San Luis Potosí, supplemented by an equal number of federal soldiers. They advanced into Los Altos against the Cristero rebels in three columns, originating in Lagos de Moreno.[27]

A second, closely related reason for the conflict between Cristeros and agraristas is that many of the leading supporters of agrarian and labor reform were also anticlerical, or at least favored imposing constitutional limitations on the power of the priests and the Catholic Church. This was certainly true of nationally prominent figures such as President Calles, Governor Adalberto Tejeda of Veracruz, Governors Lázaro Cárdenas and Francisco Múgica of Michoacán, the leaders of the national peasant league (Liga Nacional Campesina Ursulo Galván) and labor organization (Luis Morones of the CROM), and state agrarian leaders such as Primo

---

during the 1920s the Church opposed the government's land reform program (see Huizer, 1968–69: 118; Huizer and Stavenhagen, 1974: 384; Weyl and Weyl, 1939: 4, 78; and Meyer himself, 1973b: 226).

[25]Demyck (1973: 229); Díaz and Rodríguez (1979); Fábregas (1975: 44); Rivière d'Arc (n.d.: 4–5); and Taylor (1933: 30-32).

[26]See, for example, J. Meyer (1973–74, vol. 1: 161 and passim); Rivière d'Arc (n.d.: 4–5). Agraristas were also used to reinforce federal government troops against unsuccessful rebellions in 1923 (Bazant, 1977: 166) and 1929 (Weyl and Weyl, 1939: 90).

[27]D. Bailey (1974: 249–253); J. Meyer (1973–74: vol. 1: 298–309); and Paez Brotchie (1940: 161–173).

Tapia in Michoacán.[28] Similar ideas were espoused by labor and agrarian activists in Jalisco, and especially by Governor José Guadalupe Zuno.[29] Finally, the interviews with agraristas in Lagos revealed that they, too, were anticlerical. Such was true of some of the principal leaders of the reform movement in the 1920s (Romero, Nieves Ortiz, and Aniceto Martínez), as well as the men who became agraristas in the 1930s (see Chapter 6). Clearly, then, Cristeros could easily associate opposition to the Church and clergy with support for agrarian reform.

Andrés Fábregas (1975:44) offers yet another explanation for the tension between agraristas and Cristeros. He argues that the Cristiada can be interpreted as a war of local interests against the state, in which the Cristeros represented local unity and religion standing against the social change and economic development promoted by the government (cf. J. Meyer, 1973b: 146–170). Thus the Cristeros had at least three reasons why they regarded the agraristas as allies of their opponents or as a threat to basic values of conservative Catholics. And the agraristas had their own reasons for despising the Cristeros.

During the Cristiada and well into the 1930s, the Catholic Church was aligned against the agrarian reform: if not an official Church policy, priests in Los Altos nevertheless preached openly against land redistribution.[30] In sermons, they denounced agrarianism as robbery and therefore a sin.[31] Conservative Catholics believed that agrarianism was communism and an idea inspired by outside agitators. One educated Laguense who helped the agraristas denied vehemently that the Cristiada was a plot against the agrarian reform. But, he explained,

[28]See Bazant (1977: 167–168); Cornelius (1973: 419 and passim); Fowler (1970); [Fowler] Salamini (1978); Friedrich (1970); and Weyl and Weyl (1939: 79).

[29]Zuno (1964: 24) lists J. Merced Cedano and A. M. Rivera among the early revolutionaries in Guadalajara and Jalisco who had the valor to stand up and make a special contribution to the anticlerical movement. Cedano also organized the Liga de Comunidades Agrarias de Jalisco (the state peasant league) and was, according to Zuno, an early and enthusiastic agrarista in the state. Rivera was mentioned frequently in interviews with José Romero, as the organizer of a Liga de Comunidades Agrarias in Ocotlán, a participant in the state league, and a good friend to the agraristas in Lagos.

[30]At the national level, the Church's opposition diminished when Cárdenas began to make peace with the Catholic Church late in 1935 (see D. Bailey, 1974: 297; Cornelius, 1973: 427, 448).

[31]Jean Meyer (1973b: 226) acknowledges that such sermons were delivered, particularly in the 1920s. Opposition to agrarian reform by priests in various parts of Mexico has been described by Simpson (1937: 429), Friedrich (1970: 27, 48) and Weyl and Weyl (1939: 78).

The priests opposed agrarianism, and since they had their religious principles deeply rooted within themselves, they felt that asking for land was robbery. That is why the Cristero always refused to accept land, because he considered it robbing the patrón.

Agraristas took the opposition of the local clergy personally: priests described agrarian reform as a sin and further threatened to excommunicate the agraristas and to deny confession and other rites of the Church to them and their families. Such threats were reported unanimously by all of the agraristas in Lagos. Many added that, particularly in chapels on the haciendas, the priests would inquire during confession about sins against the hacendado (such as taking maize or beans) and would later tell the hacendado which workers were cheating. Whether or not such things actually happened, the agraristas of Lagos believed that they did. The priests may have believed that land reform was sinful. It is also conceivable that priests, knowing that their tenure depended in part on the local oligarchy, and knowing that much of the financial support of the Church came from those same families, may have been inclined to preach more fervently on themes affecting elite interests. Taylor (1933: 37), who studied a southern municipio in Los Altos, found that there were "more or less formal alliances of government and agraristas, of Church and conservative landowners."[32] The alliance need not have been formal, but in this region it appears that the Church and the oligarchy found common cause in opposing the government and its agraristas.

The priests' opposition to the agrarian reform affected group objectives as well as personal interests of the agraristas. The threats of excommunication and the charges that land redistribution was sinful convinced many campesinos to completely avoid any association with agrarian reform. Agraristas report that the Cristeros would hang aspiring ejidatarios and leave small sacks of dirt suspended from their necks with notes reading, "You want land, here it is" ("*Quieres tierra, aqui la tienes*"). Three informants whose life histories are reported in Chapter 6 also told of being held, hunted, or attacked by Cristeros for their agrarian sympathies. Others mentioned friends or neighbors who had similar experiences. Thus opposition from faithful Catholics delayed reform in its early stages by reinforcing community resistance, by reducing the

[32]Luis González y González (1974: 184–190) traces the evolution of a similar Church-landowner alliance and the philosophy behind it in a community he studied in Michoacán.

number of petitioners for land, and by forcing the daring few to go underground and to proceed secretively—and slowly.

In communities such as Buenavista and Moya, which had solicited lands in 1924–25, technical surveys and temporary land grants were obstructed by opposition from within the communities. Official records (expedientes ejidales, ASRA) for the ejidos in the municipio of Lagos de Moreno offer numerous examples of community opposition to land reform and resultant delays in the land grant process. Several examples illustrate this problem. The first census to determine the number of men eligible to receive ejido lands in La Escondida was delayed when residents refused to be censused. Government engineer Roberto Plasencia Ortiz reported to the Local Agrarian Commission in Guadalajara on June 21, 1929, that "The residents of La Escondida are absolutely unwilling on the question of the ejido and tell me categorically that they have not authorized any petition for an ejido nor have any intention of supporting it, given that they live from wage labor and would have no tools to become independent of the landholdings [on which they work] and cultivate the ejido." In Ciénega de Mata, after the agrarian census was completed, 31 community residents filed charges which raised questions about the authenticity of the community's petition for an ejido. They charged that their names had been forged on the petition and "that we have never asked for lands from this hacienda because we have all the necessities of life, and we don't need them [the lands], since we all sharecrop on the same property and we freely keep our animals."

Finally, community opposition could be detrimental to the ejidos even after the land had been granted. On June 30, 1927, engineer Roberto Vázquez filed a report in which he noted that when he attempted to implement the presidential decree granting an ejido to the community of Matanzas in the municipio of Ojuelos, the residents had been afraid to accept the land "because with this [accepting the land] they would find themselves more attacked by the hacendados, who never let up molesting them, and more so now that in this vicinity there are some fanatics in rebellion [Cristeros] who help out the capitalists."

Many individuals and communities did not join the agrarian reform movement until the mid-1930s because of the dangers of activism in the 1920s. And many of the original petitioners from the 1920s were frightened off or forced to leave because they were boycotted and could find no work. Agrarian Reform Ministry records show that the potentially affected landowners frequently argued against the legitimacy of a community's petition for land on the grounds that the persons whose names appeared on the original petition or in the agrarian census no longer resided in the community. Often they were said to have moved away or to be working in the United States.[33] In many cases the members of the committee of petitioners (comité ejecutivo) monitoring the community's petition for land in the 1930s are not the same as those listed for the same committee in the 1920s. This was true, for example, in Ciénega de Mata, Moya, and Lagos de Moreno. This change of personnel can be attributed to a variety of causes (death, forgery of names of early petitioners, moving, political infighting); but fear—whether of moral consequences or of physical danger—was surely the most common cause.

The available documentary evidence from ejido records confirms only that the agraristas perceived the Cristeros as their enemies. It neither sustains nor undermines the presumption of a direct link between the priests and the large landowners. Liberal and radical newspapers, some of which circulated in Lagos during those years, also report confrontations between Cristeros and agraristas. For example, El Machete (the Communist Party organ, with a pro-agrarista and anticlerical bias) reports extensively on such clashes, such as the one described in the June 9, 1928, issue in which 18 agraristas were killed by Cristeros in La Blanquita, Zacatecas. Such accounts would have reinforced agrarista perceptions of a conflict between themselves and the Cristeros.

While the formal national peace agreement between the federal government and Church leaders was signed in 1929, the Los Altos region continued to suffer sporadic outbreaks and attacks by groups labeled "Cristeros" well into the 1930s.[34] Some of these groups were Cristero factions whose leaders had refused to sign the peace accords or had rebelled again, in response to what they regarded as government violations of the terms of the treaty (J. Meyer, 1973a: 159 and passim). Some were simply bandit groups who used the conflict as an excuse to loot and rob. Others were guardias blancas, the so-called "white guards" hired by the large landowners to protect their interests. There was an armed Cristero uprising of some magnitude in 1935–36 which was of particular importance in the town of Lagos de Moreno because of the climactic battle which occurred atop a nearby hill, the Mesa Redonda, in which armed agrarista platoons from the municipio participated.

As late as 1934, the Cristero movement and Church opposition to reform continued to be an issue with considerable inflammatory potential

---

[33]Expedientes ejidales for Matanzas, Moya, and Paso de Cuarenta (ASRA).

[34]As can be seen, for example, in numerous issues of El Jaliscience during 1932.

in national agrarian circles. At the State Agrarian Convention in Guadalajara, the delegate from Guanajuato spoke of

> today's campesino, the current agrarista, the one who yesterday, with his weapons in his hands and drenching the soil of Mexico with his blood, defended the revolutionary institutions killing Cristeros who wanted to snatch from him the piece of land which provides the bread for his children. (*El Informador*, November 28, 1934.)

The government's Cristero opponents found other targets besides the agraristas. Many informants mentioned that Cristeros persecuted public-school teachers when the rural schools were first introduced.[35] Some agraristas served as protective escorts to the teachers on journeys between their communities and Lagos. Many also recalled that local priests warned parents against enrolling their children in the government schools, threatening them again with excommunication. Such opposition was due to the allegedly socialist content of the public-school curriculum (see Raby, 1973: 149–165).

The reported opposition to rural-school teachers may have occurred in the few federal or state rural schools which were established in Lagos in the 1920s, but it is more likely that the agraristas' personal experiences of Cristero opposition to teachers and schools occurred primarily in the 1930s. Most of the federal rural schools were not established in the municipio until after the ejidos were granted in the mid-1930s. By that time there were more teachers, and the federal government, especially under President Cárdenas, urged them to assist and to encourage ejido petitions whenever possible.[36] During this time, teachers were persecuted in other parts of Los Altos (Weyl and Weyl, 1939: 6–7). It was also primarily during the 1930s that campesinos were advised not to send their children to the public schools.

It was this later period of Cristero activity in the 1930s—in which

[35]A teacher was killed in Las Cajas, and others were beaten and frightened away from their jobs in La Escondida and Tecuán.

[36]However, local agraristas could recall only one community, Ciénega de Mata, in which the teacher had provided important support for the ejido petitioners. The teacher, Sra. Virginia Escobar, was still alive in 1976 and living in the same community. She and the agraristas provide conflicting testimony on the importance of her contributions to the ejido in Ciénega de Mata. They agree only that she provided encouragement, financial support, and some assistance with the paperwork. Raby (1973: 125–146) reports numerous instances, in other parts of Mexico, in which rural teachers assisted ejido petitioners during the 1930s.

religious rebels, bandits, and white guards attacked the government and its agrarista supporters—which strengthened the agraristas' image of the Cristero movement as a reactionary response to land reform. This is not to underestimate the inhibiting effect of the Cristiada during the 1920s. However, by the 1930s there were more men interested in agrarian reform, and with national government support, it promised to become a reality. As a result, local opposition became more strident and turned to tactics more violent than priestly persuasion and moral intimidation.

Nor were Catholic militants and priests the only local opposition to the agrarian reform movement. Before the outbreak of the Cristero rebellion, local landholders ("el capital") had begun to join forces and plan strategies to block the reform petitions. The Cristiada provided a respite during which landowners had time to seek allies, to refine their tactics, and to file objections with the courts. José Romero described the opposing forces as the battle lines were drawn toward the end of the Cristiada:

> The struggle was with the clergy, the government, and the municipal presidents. Each one was an enemy of the movement for its own reasons. First, the municipal presidents, because they were not of a revolutionary ideology, and they came from the middle classes, or were imposed by the governors or their friends, especially the representatives [in the Legislature]. Then, the [military] garrison commanders in the towns . . . would put themselves in opposition to the campesinos, whom they called bandits, cattle-rustlers—there was no lack of epithets—and accuse them of the most outrageous crimes imaginable. . . . The commander of a garrison would arrive, with a certain number of soldiers. If he was from the cavalry, the rich people would immediately go to place themselves at his service, providing him with forage for the army's animals. This was an advantage to the people in charge of that garrison, because they could save [pocket] all of the costs of the forage for the animals.[37]

Other Enemies: The Military and Local Authorities

Many agraristas agree that the military zone commanders were formidable adversaries of the early reform movement, as important (in their own way) as the landowners and the priests. The military's opposi-

---

[37]Similar stories of profiteering by local army officers were told by other informants as well. See also Gruening (1928: 328–329); Weyl and Weyl (1939: 4).

tion stemmed not necessarily from any political or ideological opposition to reform, but from its corruptibility; only the rich had the resources to buy armed protection. In addition, during the period of federal government retrenchment on land reform in the early 1930s, the army may have taken advantage of the federal policy shift to discourage the local agraristas.

The Lagos agraristas report that, whether on orders from superiors or because of a profitable relationship established with the local landowners, the federal troops did not support the local agrarian reform movement until 1935, when the Cárdenas administration formed armed volunteer brigades of agraristas. There is some evidence that military authorities encouraged—or failed to discourage—landowners from hiring white guards or forming *defensas sociales*—self-defense groups allegedly needed to protect landowners from pillaging by roving bands of rebels.[38] On May 26, 1929, *El Defensor del Pueblo* in Lagos reported that the Asociación de Charros Laguenses[39] had been formed in response to local interest and the fact that the commanders of the local garrison of federal troops were "providing guarantees" of protection. The agraristas could hardly ignore such displays of military-landowner cooperation.

During these years, when members of landowning families were not personally in local government, they maintained strong ties to local authorities. As a result, these authorities did not support the reformists, and often were accused of persecuting them.[40] As one agrarista explained:

> Even the authorities were anti-agrarista. They didn't want the agrarian movement—the municipal, and even the state authorities. . . . The authorities were exclusively in the hands of ha-

[38]For example, on January 9, 1932, *El Informador* (a Guadalajara newspaper) reported that military authorities had decided that under no circumstances would hacendados' self-defense groups be disarmed or deprived of license to bear arms. Less than a month later, on January 29, *El Informador* reported that "Yesterday the state Military Operations Headquarters received several petitions from farmers in the Los Altos region who were seeking authorization to arm some men to form defensas sociales. They are seeking to avoid becoming victims of some assailants who might possibly appear in the vicinity, trying to rob defenseless places."

[39]An upper-class equestrian social club. In Los Altos, these associations are often political groups of the landed gentry.

[40]Charges of collaboration between local authorities and Cristeros in persecuting the agraristas are also recorded in the expedientes ejidales (ASRA) of, for example, Buenavista and La Escondida.

cendados, so they were our worst enemies. And to my understanding, even the military authorities were [our enemies].

Support and Leadership

Despite the relative lack of progress on the pending petitions for land reform during the Cristiada, the small cadre of reformists in Lagos slowly expanded and strengthened their organization. They established relations with powerful political figures and peasant and labor organizations outside of the region, accepted into local leadership roles several outsiders who were later to make vital contributions to the local movement, and received encouragement from visiting proponents of radical ideologies.

During these years, Laguenses forged alliances with two important political figures, alliances which bore fruit in the following decade. One was with General Saturnino Cedillo, one of Mexico's strongest regional military and political leaders, based in the adjoining state of San Luis Potosí. The capital of San Luis Potosí is 150 kilometers from Lagos—50 kilometers closer than the Jalisco state capital in Guadalajara.[41] Cedillo had built up a formidable regional power base by providing arms to a personal army of between 10,000 and 15,000 agraristas in San Luis Potosí (Cornelius, 1973: 424; Falcón, 1975: 136). General Cedillo and his peasant army were called upon to aid federal troops in the struggle against the Cristeros. Leading his agraristas, he launched several attacks on the Cristeros, driving as far into Jalisco as Tepatitlán.[42] Coming from San Luis Potosí, the army had to pass through the municipio of Lagos de Moreno; so local reformists had an opportunity to talk with successful agraristas who had a powerful sponsor.

As one of the first recipients of land in the ejido of Moya explained:

> During the Cristero rebellion, many agraristas came from San Luis Potosí. They were brought here to fight against the Cristeros. . . . At the time, General Cedillo clearly headed [the agrar-

---

[41]Residents of the municipio had always maintained good commercial relations with San Luis Potosí, which was a more important commercial center than León and as accessible (or more so to residents of the eastern part of the municipio) as Guadalajara. Until the mid 1940s, when the highway between Lagos and Guadalajara was paved, to reach the state capital one either took the dirt road or traveled south by train to Irapuato, transferring there for Guadalajara—a journey of 11 hours.

[42]D. Bailey (1974: 249–253); J. Meyer (1973–74, vol. 1: 298–309); and Paez Brotchie (1940: 161–173).

istas] in San Luis. . . . He helped a lot, and that's when relations were established with the General and the people of San Luis.

None of the Laguenses could provide any specific details about their contacts with Cedillo during this period. They explained, however, that they later turned to him for protection and advice in the early 1930s, because they knew about his activities in San Luis Potosí and could find no comparable supporter in Jalisco.

In the late 1920s, the most powerful ally of reformist Laguenses in the state of Jalisco was Governor Margarito Ramírez (interim governor, April 1928 to August 1929.) By the 1930s, Ramírez was an important power broker in Jalisco.[43] He managed General Lázaro Cárdenas' presidential campaign in Jalisco in 1933–34. Romero described the first contact between Laguenses and Ramírez in May 1928, when the latter was serving as Governor:

> The district representative . . . sends me a letter in which he tells me, "I need you to bring together about 12 to 15 thousand men for Sunday night, because the Governor of the state is going to visit us." . . . So I mobilized myself, and at 7 o'clock in the evening, the Governor arrived in Lagos. I already had the whole railroad station full of people on horseback and on foot.[44]

At this time, Clodoaldo Gómez, a rare supporter of the agraristas, was municipio president in Lagos. Romero was asked to assist in mobilizing local residents to receive the Governor because of his involvement with the local labor movement and with the radical political group established earlier under the auspices of Susano Castañeda and supported by Gómez. This was the first of many exchanges—the most important of them in the 1930s—between Romero and the Lagos agraristas and Margarito Ramírez.

Ramírez also had early contacts in Guadalajara with Aniceto Mar-

[43]Ramírez gained political stature in the state under the patronage of General Alvaro Obregón, whose life Ramírez helped to save in 1920 (Dulles, 1961: 29–31). At various times, Ramírez served as federal deputy, senator, and governor of the territory of Quintana Roo under Presidents Alemán, Ruiz Cortínes, and López Mateos. Despite repeated efforts, I was unable to interview Ramírez, who was still alive but in delicate health in Guadalajara in 1976. He had secluded himself following the assassination of his son, a student union leader at the Universidad de Guadalajara.

[44]A copy of a letter from district representative Napoleón Orozco Romero dated May 12, 1928, in Romero's personal files corroborates this account. In his letter, Orozco instructed Romero about which groups should be represented in the reception committee, which he had promised would number 5,000 men.

tínez, who later returned to Lagos to play an important role in the reform movement. Martínez, it will be recalled, had been employed periodically at the Victoria textile mill and had worked with the early union organizers in the UOL. Romero described Martínez as

> a young man of ideals. . . . He wasn't a campesino; he was a laborer, of magnificent ideals, as though he had studied. . . . He had acquired his revolutionary ideas, I think, not by learning, just on his own. . . . He knew how to read and write, but he didn't have enough education to take charge of the situation. So when we got to know each other, we made common cause, and he served the organization as a propagandist wherever he went.

When the factory closed, in about 1923–24, Martínez returned briefly to work with his father, selling trinkets and spices in rural communities. Then he disappeared; his friends in Lagos did not hear from him for some time.

The sequence of Martínez' wanderings during his absence is uncertain. Because he was killed in 1932, we must rely on scanty documentary evidence and the recollections of his companions to describe his contributions to the reform movement.

His widow, Carmen Casillas Cornejo, met Aniceto Martínez when they were both working in the textile mill at El Salto de Juanacatlán, near Guadalajara. It was a large mill, employing some 1,600 to 1,700 workers by her estimate. Martínez was active in the local labor union, serving as Secretary-General of the district union and later on the Board of Conciliation and Arbitration.[45] His widow recalled that he was always defending the workers and that his opinions angered the management, although they respected him more than most of the union activists. In 1927, Martínez suggested that they leave the mill to organize agrarian communities: "We're going to go see if the campesinos want land."

During the 1920s, the mines and textile mills were the focal points of labor organizing outside of Mexico City, including the area surrounding Guadalajara. Given the size of the mill at Juanacatlán and its proximity to Guadalajara, Martínez could have had contacts through the labor unions with Governor Margarito Ramírez during his term of office. The nature of those contacts cannot be documented, but among Doña Carmen's

---

[45]These Boards (Juntas de Conciliación y Arbitraje) were established under the terms of Article 123 of the Constitution of 1917 to serve as arbiters handling complaints between workers and employers.

most treasured possessions was a letter of introduction for Aniceto on
personal letterhead of the Governor of Jalisco. It reads:

> Guadalajara
> November 14, 1927
>
> To Whom it May Concern:
>
> I hereby affirm that Sr. Aniceto Martínez is going to the munici-
> pios of Unión de San Antonio and Arandas of this federal entity
> [state] to organize the workers and campesinos of those areas.
>
> I beg the civilian as well as military authorities to take steps to
> provide all manner of protection to the aforementioned Sr. Mar-
> tínez.
>
> Interim Governor (sig.) M. Ramírez

Doña Carmen jointly credited Martínez and Governor Ramírez with
the inspiration for their quest, during which they suffered numerous
hardships:

> We traveled on foot . . . everywhere from Jiquilpan, Michoacán,
> until we reached Salvatierra [Guanajuato]. We covered the entire
> state of Michoacán, . . . pleading the issue of land. There were peo-
> ple who received us more or less well, and there were people who
> all but stoned us out of town. And we would sleep in the hills, even
> with the child [a toddler] like I showed you in the picture. . . . Our
> breakfast was a piece of cactus, and our dinner more cactus with-
> out so much as a grain of salt. . . . Imagine, isn't that suffering?
> Suffering and working with genuine goodwill for people.

Eventually, while the Cristero rebellion was still in progress, the Martínez family returned to Lagos de Moreno.

José Romero also stressed the importance of the relationships that
Martínez established with revolutionaries in Michoacán during his travels:

> In Michoacán [Lázaro Cárdenas] had already established a revolu-
> tionary movement which was reverberating throughout the whole
> country.[46] That's why Aniceto met with him and told him about the

[46]Lázaro Cárdenas was governor of Michoacán from 1928 to 1932. In 1929 he formed
the Confederación Revolucionaria Michoacana del Trabajo, incorporating workers,
campesinos, and students in an organization which pressed for land and labor reform. As
governor, he greatly expanded the redistribution of land in Michoacán, emphasizing
collective ejido organization, despite the federal government's policy of retrenchment on
land reform. His administration increased school construction and reorganized the curriculum to include the doctrine of the Revolution, support for labor unions and camp-

Doña Carmen Casillas, widow of Aniceto Martínez, photographed in 1976.

situation in Lagos. Then General Cárdenas told Aniceto, "Go to Lagos and begin to work on organizing the campesinos." That's when Aniceto came to me in my shop to talk about what was happening in Lagos. . . . We talked about all of the places he'd visited in Veracruz, in Mexico, in Michoacán. He carried a letter of introduction from the labor organization in Michoacán, the one that supported General Cárdenas in establishing the revolutionary movement in Michoacán. That's how all of us from the revolutionary movement in Jalisco and Michoacán got to know each other.

---

esino leagues, and increased community involvement in school governance. He took a temporary leave of absence from the governorship to return to active military duty during the Cristero rebellion, thus strengthening his credentials in the anticlerical political community. Throughout this period, Cárdenas' own views placed him in the moderate wing of the official party. However, because his administration included men whose views were more radical than his own, he acquired a reputation as a "radical" in agricultural, labor, education, and religious policy. On this period, see Falcón (1978: 339–347), González y González (1979: 221–233), and Weyl and Weyl (1939: 57-106).

Whether inspired primarily by Governor Cárdenas or Governor Ramírez, upon his return to Lagos Martínez rejoined the local reform movement. At the time, the reformists were still concerned primarily with urban labor issues. At the urging of Martínez and of Macedonio Ayala—who arrived at approximately the same time—the group began to turn their attention to encouraging more agrarian communities to petition for land and encouraging others to press for action on petitions already submitted. Martínez resumed his traveling-merchant role, selling trinkets in the rural communities and propagandizing for land reform. José Romero recalled:

> The first agrarian manifesto that we wrote to mobilize the campesinos we made up one evening when he came to my shop.... "How goes the movement?" he asked.... And I told him, "I'm organizing agrarian communities, and we are already in the Sindicato de Oficios Varios."[47] I began to talk with him, and he said, "Well, let's start a campaign [to convince] the campesinos." And so we set about writing what occurred to us ... against the large landholders, and that [the peasants] should learn from the communities that had already been liberated, as in Veracruz, Michoacán, Guanajuato.... That's how we made up the manifesto. And right away we were distributing it. Aniceto would distribute it inside the prayer books and song-sheets he carried; he'd go out to the ranchos to sell them. We didn't know where he was wandering. And then he'd come back saying "Look what I've got—a petition from such-and-such a place."

At approximately the same time (roughly between 1925 and 1927), the group received another infusion of leadership from two outsiders—Macedonio Ayala de la Fuente and Miguel Aguirre Salas. Both in their early twenties, they arrived as postal employees to work under Aguirre's half-brother, Enrique Rendón Salas. Aguirre was from the state of Mexico; little more is known of his origins.[48] He played a relatively minor role until the early 1940s, when he assumed leadership of the local campesino organization, a capacity in which he served until his death.

Macedonio Ayala's background was quite different from that of everyone else in the local movement. Born in Nadadores (now Nueva Rosita),

---

[47]The local labor union which succeeded the UOL.

[48]Aguirre's daughter, a schoolteacher in Lagos, recalled vaguely that her father had been a strong supporter of the Communist Party and that he used to say that he had been sent to Lagos by Vicente Lombardo Toledano, a Marxist (but not Communist Party member) labor union leader of the 1930s.

Portrait photograph of Macedonio Ayala, taken in about 1933.

Coahuila, he reportedly came from an important family of modest means. His widow, Doña Elvira Hernández, recalled that he had been educated at a commercial school in Saltillo and possibly in a military academy. He left home to travel, working briefly in a glass factory in Monterrey. Doña Elvira remembered his saying that he met a General Cedillo (there were four Cedillo brothers) in Monterrey, who told him about Lagos de Moreno and secured an appointment for him at the local post office.

From his photographs, Ayala would seem an unlikely candidate for agrarian leadership. Quite tall, he stood slightly stooped, his head inclined at an angle. He appears shy, a pensive man more than an agrarian activist. One companion described him as having "a jovial personality, a little serious. He was tall, moderately ruddy, robust, quite young." Ayala's widow said she despaired during a seven-year courtship and their brief marriage, for he was always giving away clothing, food, or money to someone in need. She complained that he was forever being called away to help with campesino family crises. Romero spoke of Ayala with the highest praise. "Ayala never had political ambitions, nor did he ever betray us. He devoted his entire self to the movement." Others who knew him agreed completely with this assessment.

When they arrived in Lagos, both Ayala and Aguirre held minor government positions as clerks in the post office, jobs which were critically important to the agrarian movement. Because the agraristas were poor—it was a hardship even to purchase the writing paper and stamps for a letter to a government agency—most of the transactions between petitioning communities and the government were handled by correspondence. Sometimes these communications involved compliance with deadlines or appointments between community representatives and government officials. One of the easiest ways for the opposition to obstruct the agraristas' efforts was to intercept letters or telegrams between the government and the agraristas. In this way, local landowners could discover the identity of petitioners, delay delivery of the communication until the deadline had passed, or simply be "tipped off" on current developments affecting their interests. It was clearly to the agraristas' advantage to have one of their men serve circumspectly as a postal clerk.

Thus it was a strategic as well as a leadership boon to the movement when a mutual friend introduced Ayala and Aguirre to José Romero and the rest of the "revolutionary group." With the most recent arrivals, Romero, Martínez, and Ayala constituted the top echelon of local agrarian leaders. Together they represented a broad range of political and working experience, and different personal and political styles. While they agreed on the ultimate objectives of land redistribution, improved wages and working conditions, and increased political participation for the working class, their diverse approaches to achieving these objectives complemented each other.

Romero was an urban-based political activist-ideologue. His contribution was to build and lead organizations, and to keep in touch with like-minded organizations and their representatives from outside of Lagos. On the other hand, Ayala and Martínez had some experience with the process and philosophy of agrarian reform elsewhere. Most accounts describe Martínez as an activist, ideologically radical, who was moved by the conditions of human deprivation and suffering he encountered in his travels through the countryside. In personality and motivation, Ayala is described as having a combination of the qualities attributed to Romero and Martínez: moved by individual suffering, well-educated, well-read, reserved, and politically skillful.

Romero's generalized goals of social and political reform were focused by Ayala and Martínez, who urged that the group concentrate its attention on agrarian issues. Such a recommendation must have been based not only on abstract ideals and compassion, but also on experience and information about agrarian reform elsewhere in the Republic, as well as a strategic assessment as to where a group interested in "the social struggle" ("*la lucha social*") might find its manpower and strength in an agricultural region.

One final actor in the Lagos reform movement was introduced during the years of the Cristiada—Lt. Col. Roberto Calvo Ramírez, who served with the 35th Regiment in Lagos. Those who remembered him described him as a communist "to the marrow of his bones."[49] At the time that he was stationed in Lagos, the reformists were meeting regularly. To inspire them, Calvo Ramírez had the regimental band play "The Internationale" after each meeting.

According to one youthful participant in the reformists' meetings, Calvo Ramírez attempted to supply more than musical inspiration. "He really did have communist inclinations.... He'd say, No, look, this is better yet, and he was encouraging us to go in the direction of communism." Was anyone among the reformists interested in moving in that direction? "Well, without forming a cell [sic] or anything, we did talk with him. But without destroying our union organization, or our agrarian goals. Quite the contrary, it reinforced us."

Romero claimed that Calvo Ramírez did inspire a local Communist Party organization, which Romero led. He described it as a small group, of fewer than 30 (probably fewer than 10), which also took an interest in the international programs of the Party. "All of the Communists contributed what we could to free the Reds who were held prisoners by the Whites in Russia, and in other parts of Europe where there were Red prisoners."

Romero recalled that the local Communist Party was formed some time around 1926, prior to the campesino organizations. A small item

[49]*El Machete*, the Communist Party newspaper, reported in its issue of December 4–11, 1924, that an agrarian Communist, Roberto Calvo Ramírez, president of the Partido Agrarista Oaxaqueño and member of the Communist Party of Mexico, had become a member of the Chamber of Deputies of the state of Oaxaca on December 1 of that year.

appearing in *El Machete* on August 26, 1927, reports that the "Local Comunista de Las Jiménez, Ocotlán, y Lagos de Moreno" was among the new groups joining the regional organizing committee during a convention of El Bloque Obrero y Campesino (the Worker and Peasant Bloc) in Jalisco. This item (which makes no mention of the size of the membership) and Romero's claims represent the only evidence (other than discernible influences on rhetoric) of an infusion of Communist Party information and ideas into the reform movement in Lagos.[50]

The question of communist ideas or Communist Party involvement in land reform is an extremely delicate issue in Lagos de Moreno. Even today, many new ideas with no relationship to Marxism-Leninism are regarded suspiciously, as potentially "communist." The charge of communist inspiration or involvement is used by former hacendados and their families, as well as by less affluent conservatives, to discount the legitimacy of the demands of the local agraristas. For that reason it is important to note that while Romero espoused communist ideals (see Chapter 5), none of the other agraristas interviewed claimed any particular information, exposure, or inclination toward communism or the Communist Party. A few of the agraristas recognized Romero's sympathies. For example:

> José Romero Gómez . . . *did* boast of being a Communist; he did claim his Marxist-Leninist doctrines. . . . [He acquired his ideas] I think from his readings, because he did read Marx.

> The only one who guided us was Romero, who did know more about socialism and communism. . . . But he never told us to do this or that. Our political life was entirely Mexican.

The agraristas did not acknowledge, nor do their historical accounts reflect, any communist influence on the ideas or rhetoric of the rank-and-file members. In this region, the widespread presumption of communist influence on the agrarian movement probably derives from the label "agrarian *communities*," the mental association of ejidos with Soviet collectives, the anticlerical views of the agraristas (linked to the presumed atheism of communists), and Romero's rhetoric. Explaining why they were labeled communists, the agraristas said:

---

[50]Romero recalled reading *El Machete*, the Communist Party newspaper, and *Sagitario*. *Sagitario* was published between 1922 and 1927 in Tampico, Veracruz. It was founded by Librado Rivera, an old Flores Magón supporter. I have found no references to any Communist Party affiliation for either Rivera or *Sagitario*. (*Regeneración*, tercera etapa, nos. 56–57 [1961], 67–68 [1962], and 88 [1965].)

They associated the communities with communism. . . . They said that we were communists, but they had only vaguely heard of communism.

They think that everybody who doesn't believe in God is a communist.

The truth is that I don't know what communism might be. But if what I believe and want, that the worker be able to improve himself, that he be paid what his work is worth, if that is communism, then I'm a communist.

Because it is a controversial issue locally, and because the question of communist influence as an external impetus to organization might be critical in explaining the evolution of the movement, this issue was carefully explored in the interviews. In my judgment, Romero was the only local agrarista who accurately understood what was involved in Marxism-Leninism, and the only one who was inclined to embrace its ideals.[51]

The War Horse: El Sindicato de Oficios Varios

As noted above, the early collaboration between urban labor and agrarian reformers in Lagos continued under the auspices of the Sindicato de Oficios Varios (SOV). One interviewee aptly described the SOV as the reform group's "war horse" ("*nuestro caballito de batalla*"). It was to play a central role in the struggle which culminated in land redistribution in the 1930s.

The SOV's precursor, the Unión de Obreros Libertarios, dissolved some time after the textile mill closed. Of the core group of union members, the men who remained in Lagos continued to meet off and on during the Cristiada. Their meetings were generally secret except when local officials such as Clodoaldo Gómez and Roberto Calvo Ramírez provided the protection which permitted more open gatherings. Eventually, at some point during the Cristiada, they formed the SOV.

The original members of the SOV included José Romero Gómez, Francisco Navia, Fabián Espinoza, Agustín Espinoza, Elías Prado, Francisco ("Quico") Prado, and a few others. They were all laborers or skilled

---

[51]Macedonio Ayala and Aniceto Martínez are excluded from this judgment. There is insufficient information about their political affiliations to make any assessment of their relationship to communism or the Communist Party. However, José Vallarta, a non-local influence on the Lagos reform movement (see Chapter 4), apparently did share Romero's communist sympathies. In an undated letter (AJRG), he tells Romero that *Callismo* (support for General Calles) must serve "as the banner of our Leninism."

craftsmen, and what they formed was a labor union. Most of them were self-employed or worked in small shops. Romero recalled that since there were not enough workers in each trade to form separate trade unions, "nor were all workers [in a trade] of a mind to unite to form a guild," they formed a "varied trades" union. The group included barbers, cobblers, butchers, carpenters, blanket-weavers, small merchants, and mechanics. As explained by Francisco Navia, the only other survivor of the founding group, the membership was so small that "a Secretary-General[52] was named—Romero Gómez; and a Secretary of External Affairs, one of Internal Affairs, one of Labor; we all managed to be named Secretaries. So the union was formed, and we sent away to register ourselves in Guadalajara."

While it lasted, most of the members of the SOV, and of the specific trade unions which spun off from it in the late 1930s, continued to be self-employed or employees in very small shops. There were no large, factory unions in Lagos de Moreno until the Nestlé factory union was formed in the late 1940s.

The objective of the original members of the SOV was to "organize the labor movement in Lagos." The two survivors described their understanding of that goal as follows:

> *Navia:* We thought that, organized, we would have protection, that we might enjoy other privileges. *Organizations can always achieve other benefits.*
>
> *Romero:* The movement was entirely a union movement, but it supported the political movement. *Our thinking was to take over the power: power in the hands of the workers.* And that's the path we followed with the movement, until it was achieved. . . . And we would participate in every political activity—for elections of governor, of president, of local government.

The laborers who joined the SOV in the years that followed described its purpose as seeking minimum wages or higher assured fees for craftsmen, or protection ("*garantías*") for workers.

The SOV became, then, a dual-purpose organization. One objective was economic strength in numbers: organized, its members stood a better chance of being able to secure higher wages or craftsmen's fees. Second, and more significant, was the goal of political strength through organization. Before there was a strong official, national political party (the Partido Nacional Revolucionario, PNR), a permanent local interest

[52]The highest-ranking official in Mexican labor unions.

group like the SOV could be politically useful both to its members and to aspiring politicians. If such a group were active in elections, its chances of securing appointive or elective office—or better yet, support or favors—for its members would be enhanced.

Either objective—wage improvement or political bargaining—could be better served through alliances, so the SOV became affiliated with the Unión de Mecánicos Mexicanos, the federal railroad workers' union.[53] It is not clear why this particular affiliation was chosen. In Lagos, *El Defensor del Pueblo* of May 4, 1930, eschewed publication ("for lack of space") of a detailed account of the May Day celebrations for that year, but did briefly report that festivities in which red and black flags (the colors of the national labor organization, CROM) were displayed were held in the Rosas Moreno Theatre. The celebration was organized by the Unión de Mecánicos Mexicanos, employees of the federal treasury stationed in Lagos, and employees of the local government. So by 1930, the labor organizations in Lagos had become bold enough to participate in public ceremonies.

Neither Navia nor Romero mentioned agrarian reform as one reason for establishing the SOV, although its predecessor, the Unión de Obreros Libertarios, had become involved in organizing agrarian communities. The SOV's subsequent involvement in agrarian problems seems to have been the result of local leadership commitment and initiative, combined with encouragement from outside leaders and political organizations.

Local landholders were correct in charging that the SOV reformists were not even tillers of the soil. As Navia explains, "That's why the rich people, the hacendados, would say: 'But these men aren't even campesinos.' And really, we weren't even campesinos." But it was not long before their ranks were augmented by genuine campesinos.

Los Norteños

The decision to move into agrarian activism can be attributed to ideology and leadership, but timing and the availability of manpower were also important factors. With the 1929 stock-market crash and the Depression, unemployment rose in the United States. As in the past, Americans turned against the foreigners in their midst, blaming them for high

[53]The Unión de Mecánicos Mexicanos was based 83 kilometers north of Lagos in the city of Aguascalientes. I was not able to establish any connection between the railroad union (one of the first to be organized in Mexico) and the initiation of the union movement in Lagos de Moreno. According to a local employee of the railroads, the first railroad union representative based in Lagos, one José Aguiñaga López, arrived in 1932.

unemployment. In order to open up jobs for U.S. citizens, Mexicans who could not produce documents to prove that they were legally in the U.S. were deported. There were also more informal, local efforts by social workers and government authorities to encourage Mexicans to leave "voluntarily," with their transportation back to Mexico subsidized by U.S. government agencies. It has been estimated that nearly half a million Mexicans were either deported or "voluntarily" repatriated during the period from 1929 to 1935 (see Hoffman, 1974).

Until that time, it had been relatively easy for Mexicans to enter the United States.[54] They crossed the border in search of work or adventure, to escape political persecution or private vendettas, or to find a new way of life. Alteños began to emigrate—usually as unmarried men, in groups of friends or relatives—as early as the mid-1880s. The *norteños*[55] were often recruited by the railroads, who sent agents to Mexico to seek cheap labor. They worked on track-repair crews from Oregon to Texas, from California to Kansas, and sometimes in roundhouses as strikebreakers. They also worked harvesting the potato, sugar beet, and cotton crops in Idaho, California, Texas, and the Midwest. At first, migrant workers simply crossed the border; later, small bridge-crossing fees were required; and still later, visa fees were instituted. In general, however, it was an open border, and jobs in the U.S. were relatively easy to obtain. All of this changed, however, with the Depression, the repatriation, and the establishment of the U.S. Border Patrol in 1929. The normal two-way flow across the border was severely disrupted.

The Mexican government became concerned about the treatment of its nationals in the U.S. and about the huge influx of unemployed Mexicans returning home. Newspapers during these years carried accounts of the harsh treatment received by many repatriatees, and announcements by Mexican authorities urging their citizens to return home. Partially in an attempt to cope with the returning Mexicans, ejido lands were offered to them, particularly in the northern states.

Laguenses returning from the U.S. provided the manpower for the agrarian reform efforts of the SOV, filing new community petitions for

[54]Particularly useful studies of migration to the U.S. during the period when the first agraristas were involved in the flow include Cardoso (1980), Gamio (1930), García y Griego (1973), Hoffman (1974), Reisler (1976), and Taylor (1933).

[55]In Los Altos, people who have worked in the U.S. call each other "norteños," referring to their sojourn in the north. The term is used particularly by men who were in the U.S. prior to the official migrant-labor program (the Bracero Program, 1942-64).

ejido lands and renewing earlier petitions.[56] Most had returned by Christmas 1930—some a few years earlier. Most were young (usually under 30) and had growing families. The majority had worked on the railroad track gangs and had additional experience in migrant agricultural labor or sharecropping.[57]

All of the surviving norteños agreed that while in the United States they had seen "another life" and "they did not come back to live the [typical] life of the region." Having earned higher wages and experienced a different kind of employer-employee relationship, and having heard about the advantages of unions,[58] they had little desire to return to the old pattern of sharecropping or debt-peonage. Moreover, through Mexicans from other parts of the country whom they had met and worked with in the U.S., they had heard about land redistribution in other parts of Mexico. Finally, their exposure in the U.S. to other religious beliefs and authorities made the migrants less susceptible to threats by the priests who were opposing the agrarian reform. Romero described what followed:

> The campesinos began to organize, not the ones on the haciendas, nor on the ranchos; no—how were those people going to organize if they were afraid of the owner's shadow, and of the white guards? So, I took advantage [of the opportunity], and the campesinos who had been to the U.S. and who were returning joined me ... all of them. They weren't going to return to the haciendas to earn the 15 centavos that was paid then. They had seen another life, had learned about other wages, so they returned to their homes, ... but already with the idea of not returning to the hacienda to work for the patrón. ... Many who returned [from the U.S.] set up their

[56]For example, representatives of the ejido of Paso de Cuarenta on May 6, 1931, urged prompt resolution of a conflict over the land grant to that community, because many men had returned from the U.S. and were hoping to dedicate themselves to agriculture. In another case, Francisco Munguia Torres, the Procurador de Pueblos for Jalisco and Colima, reported to the National Agrarian Commission on August 8, 1932, that an ejido was urgently needed for Lagos de Moreno. He referred to the local problem of unemployment among men recently forced to return to Mexico from the U.S. He appended a list of the names of 32 men who had returned from the U.S. and who had the resources and interest to work ejido land. (Expedientes ejidales, ASRA.)

[57]The U.S. experiences of the surviving agraristas and the impact of those experiences upon them are described in greater detail in Chapter 6.

[58]Only three out of all the agraristas interviewed had belonged to unions in the United States, but others had witnessed the benefits which accrued to the skilled Anglo workers who belonged to these organizations.

little stores, became merchants, but they didn't return to the hacienda. When I started the movement, well, right away they joined it. And then they went to work on their relatives and their companions.

There is one final reason why the norteños were disproportionately represented among the first agraristas. Few of those who went to the U.S. and returned were *peones acasillados* (agricultural workers who lived in hacienda housing and were dependent on the hacienda for employment, goods, and services, often resulting from an inherited pattern of debt peonage). It would have been difficult for peones acasillados to migrate without taking their entire families, and they could not have left them behind as hacienda dependents. As a result, most of the migrants had been sharecroppers, mule drivers, or seasonal laborers on the haciendas. When they returned, they followed the same patterns of employment or turned to small-scale commerce. Consequently, at a time when peones acasillados were not eligible to petition for or receive ejido lands, the norteños represented a significant proportion of the population of campesinos in Lagos who were *both* eligible and willing to join the agrarian reform movement.

4

Agrarian Reform:
Fruition

One of the most important features of the agrarian reform movement in Lagos de Moreno was the essentially political, legal, and nonviolent strategy adopted by the agraristas. Their objective was to persuade the state and federal governments to enforce existing laws. The Laguenses were not involved in a confrontation with the federal system in which they were trying to *change* national laws. The basic strategy was to establish alliances with organizations and politicians who could contribute to the strength and success of the drive for land and labor reform in Lagos. Simultaneously, the agraristas persevered with the legal procedures for securing land, as specified in the Agrarian Reform Code. This chapter traces the implementation of this strategy by the Lagos reform movement during the period from 1931 to 1940.

The Agraristas Organize

Members of the Sindicato de Oficios Varios (SOV) continued to meet periodically during the Cristiada in the late 1920s. At the end of the decade, the core labor group was enlarged by the returned migrants from the United States and their relatives. Until the lands were finally granted in the mid-1930s, the group changed meeting places often, to maintain secrecy. The meetings were held generally every month. Romero and Ayala generally advised on the status of paperwork and wrote letters for the community representatives to sign. Correspondence was critical to the success of the local effort, since petitioners could not afford the expense of travel to lobby for their cause.[1] In addition, petitioners were told, as one participant explained, "how they should organize and be ready, particularly against the white guards."

The leaders of the SOV (and later of the Liga Regional de Comunidades Agrarias) served as intermediaries between community petitioners and the state and federal agencies (the Local Agrarian Commission, the National Agrarian Commission, or the Agrarian Department) which handled petitions for land reform.[2] While this was their primary task, the group and its leaders had another, equally important mission: to persuade other campesinos to join the movement.

The enlargement of the group was essential: a minimum of 20 persons had to sign each community petition for land reform. The same number had to be judged eligible to receive land when the community census was taken, and at least 11 had to accept the land when the lands were granted. It was possible to falsely represent the number of agraristas (though it became progressively more difficult at each stage of the petitioning process) by forging signatures or thumbprints, by listing nonresidents of a community, by having some individuals apply in a variety of communities, or by having laborers and craftsmen (not campesinos) apply. At each stage of the bureaucratic process, however, the petitioning group had to contend with the landowners whose properties were threatened by the community's petition. Landowners carefully reviewed the names of petitioners and people listed in the community censuses, and were quick to file lists of "disqualified" persons. So it clearly behooved each interested community group to engage, as one organizer explained, in

> a task of consciousness-raising [*una labor de concientización*], because the campesinos didn't want to accept [land]. They were, really, afraid of their *patrones*: that they would evict them from the little houses they lived in, that they would take away their jobs. They [also] didn't want to accept land because they were very submissive religiously—they said that they would be condemned. . . . The priests took care of that.

[1] The assistance provided to the petitioners by the reform group leaders also accounts for the remarkable uniformity in wording of agrarian community petitions and correspondence originating in Lagos, both in the 1920s, when petitioners gathered together under Susano Castañeda's protective urging, and later under the leadership of the SOV and the Liga Regional de Comunidades Agrarias, a regional peasant union established in Lagos de Moreno.

[2] This function is now performed by regional representatives of the Confederación Nacional Campesina (CNC) and the federal Agrarian Reform Ministry.

One of the most important contributions of non-agricultural laborers to the agrarian reform movement in Lagos was their participation in the task of convincing frightened campesinos to join the drive for land redistribution. In view of the continued opposition of the clergy, military and local government authorities, and large landholders, the agraristas faced a monumental "consciousness-raising task." First, in a very devout Catholic region, they had to convince campesinos that, despite priests' warnings, it was not a sin to ask for ejido lands. Then they had to convince them to confront the risks involved in petitioning for land. Reluctant campesinos could easily see that agraristas faced privation, unemployment, ostracism, and possibly even death. Local authorities and assailants would descend unexpectedly on the homes of known agraristas,[3] so secrecy was necessary to avoid reprisals against their families. The risks were increased because, while the opposition was armed, the local police forbade agraristas to carry weapons. It was literally true, as one participant said, that "one gambled with one's life." Many were attacked and some were killed, among them Aniceto Martínez, Macedonio Ayala, Jesús Márquez, a leader of the aspiring ejido community in Potrerillo, and the father of the ejido leader in El Tecuán.

Because of the obvious hazards, recruitment was conducted with the utmost caution. Although agraristas began by approaching trusted, close relatives whom they regarded as persuadable, even this strategy was risky. Within families there was much disagreement over agrarismo. Wives dissuaded some men from joining the reformists. The fathers of all but two of the agraristas interviewed for this study opposed their sons on the issue of land reform.[4]

When seeking new converts, the agraristas would travel to haciendas, "but of course we didn't just give ourselves away. We sought ways to get in touch with one or two people only, people we already knew. . . . We'd meet in the fields or out in the hills wherever we could." Once a campesino was convinced that land redistribution was a good idea, "then we'd identify ourselves, we made friends, we had more contact. . . . We'd in-

---

[3]Documented examples include an assault by local police on the home of the leader of the community of Buenavista and an attack on the agraristas in La Escondida in which alleged Cristeros pillaged, assaulted, and then branded the agraristas by cutting off the tips of their ears. These episodes were reported in numerous interviews (see, for example, Víctor Reyes in Chapter 6). Documents in the ejido records of the Agrarian Reform Ministry for Buenavista and Lagos de Moreno corroborate the agraristas' accounts.

[4]The agraristas attributed opposition of the women and the older generation to their closer ties to the Church, fear of reprisals from landowners, traditional loyalty to the patrón, and a generalized fear of change.

vite them to the meeting hall to talk and there we'd tell them, 'You ask for the land, we'll make out the petition for you.' And many would agree. . . . They would go back to their homes and keep it secret."

The Liga Regional Campesina Magdaleno Cedillo

The SOV initially drew most of its members from the communities and haciendas closer to the town of Lagos. One young man who joined the movement in the early 1930s estimated that there was a group of 150 to 200 agraristas when he joined. Based on interviews and documents in the Agrarian Reform Ministry, my own estimate is that the core of dedicated community leaders numbered about 30. The Liga Regional Campesina Magdaleno Cedillo derived its strength from this group. The Liga was a regional peasant union organized and based in Lagos de Moreno; 21 communities in Los Altos were represented initially.[5] It was named after the brother of the protector and advisor of the Lagos group, General Saturnino Cedillo. The Liga was established sometime before December 1931;[6] by then the group interested in land reform had grown sufficiently to support its own organization, separate from the SOV.

After the Liga was founded, the SOV and the Liga drifted apart. Surviving labor activists disclaimed any involvement in the agrarian reform movement after the initial petitions. While they continued to favor land reform, members of the SOV turned their attention to political and labor issues. Men involved in both groups, particularly Ayala, Romero, Navia, and Captain José Vallarta, continued to share the objectives of social justice and political power for the working classes. From interviews with the first agraristas, it is apparent that these ideals were only vaguely (and belatedly) shared by the campesino members of the Liga (see Chapter 6).

As a formal organization, the Liga Regional gave legitimacy to its officers in their exchanges with official agencies on behalf of petitioning communities. It enhanced their bargaining power with state and federal politicians. It facilitated contacts with other campesino unions in Jalisco

[5]As listed on the Liga letterhead (AJRG, ASRA), they were: Lagos de Moreno, Buenavista, Paso de Cuarenta, La Escondida, Bernalejo, San Jorge, Loma de Veloces, Las Cruces, La Trinidad, Moya, Cañada de Ricos, San Nicolás, Matanzas, Ojuelos, Letras, Chinampas, El Testerazo, Unión de San Antonio, La Noria, Las Palmas, and Encarnación de Díaz.

[6]Informants were unable to recall when the Liga was formally organized. However, a letter to Romero from Roberto Calvo Ramírez dated December 23, 1931, appears to have been written in response to a letter announcing the establishment of the Liga. Calvo Ramírez wrote to congratulate Romero on the formation of the Liga and to offer advice on the management of the group (AJRG).

and elsewhere in Mexico, enabling Liga representatives to attend conferences of other agrarista organizations. The Laguenses became more informed, and stronger, as they became affiliated with other organizations. However, it is doubtful that locally the Liga represented much of an organizational change from the informal agrarista network that existed prior to its establishment. The Liga's stationery carried a list of officers,[7] but many of those named could not recall serving in any official capacity, or remembered only holding a title without any real responsibilities. Such disclaimers suggest that the Liga was, in most respects, an organization on paper only. However, it did give the group a formal name, bringing with it protection and affiliation with an external political network and a set of protective patrons.

The Liga's mottoes, bravely emblazoned on its letterhead by 1936, were:

Campesino: the land belongs to him who tills it.

Defend it: freedom is won with blood and defended with a rifle.

The campesino organization is your soul, to impose your will upon the hypocrites and traitors.

May it cost you: so that your representative, your servant, won't sell himself out of hunger.

These slogans echo the language used in personal correspondence exchanged among the Liga's leaders. With such rhetoric, one can imagine some of the speeches by Romero and Ayala at the group's meetings. None of the first agraristas and labor union members interviewed could remember much about the ideas that were discussed at these gatherings, except that the participants were all fighting for "land and liberty." One ejidatario recalled that "Mostly what we talked about was that it isn't the same to work for the owner as to work for our families. So let's work for ourselves."

Were these meetings significant political learning experiences? Clearly, they did strengthen individual resolve and commitment to the reform group. They also reinforced the agraristas' commitment to the justice and feasibility of the idea of land redistribution. But the sessions did not, apparently, include discussions about systems of political ideas, nor about political ideologies more complex than "land and liberty." Important—and lasting—political lessons were imparted about the po-

---

[7]Officers changed from 1932 to 1938, but José Romero Gómez was always listed as Secretary-General, and Macedonio Ayala, until his death, as Secretary of Organization.

litical power of the wealthy in Mexico, about patron-client politics, and the way the Mexican bureaucracy could be greased. But they were primarily service meetings and "pep talks," not indoctrination sessions.

Just when the group of agraristas had expanded sufficiently to contemplate establishing their own organization, Captain José A. Vallarta came to Lagos.[8] Vallarta was a military officer whose visit was prompted by his impending marriage into a local campesino family that was actively seeking land reform benefits. Romero remembered their first meeting this way:

> They told Vallarta about the organization that had been formed. He became interested in talking with me. He arrived, introduced himself. . . . "Are you a revolutionary?" He opened up right away. "I have come because of this: I know that you are the one who is organizing the communities. I've come because I am a friend of the campesino leagues in such-and-such localities." I didn't trust him, because he was from the army—maybe he was a spy. Until at last he proved that he was friendly with all of the organizations. . . . He was protected by [General Saturnino] Cedillo, the Governor of Zacatecas, all of the revolutionaries of Zacatecas, Pánfilo Natera in San Luis, the brothers Cedillo. In Michoacán he had Don Dámaso Cárdenas, brother of the General [Lázaro Cárdenas].

Romero described Vallarta in superlatives, as genuinely committed to the struggle. "He'd go right into the workers' organizations, and the agrarian communities, in uniform and all. He didn't care; they'd harass him, punish him, and everything, but he was tenacious."[9]

Vallarta's contribution to the movement in Lagos was both symbolic and substantive. On the symbolic level, he designed the Liga's letterhead, complete with political artwork and slogans (see composite photo).[10] In

[8]Informants could not recall precisely when Vallarta arrived in Lagos. The earliest available personal correspondence between Romero and Vallarta is dated September 8, 1931. That letter indicates that since July of that year they had been discussing the possibility of naming Vallarta as formal representative of the "organizations" in Lagos. He later served as the "Representative-at-Large" for the Liga (AJRG).

[9]According to his letter to Romero dated September 8, 1931 (AJRG), Vallarta was serving with General Joaquín Amaro (who was Minister of War and the Navy) in Mexico City, where he continued to work during the next two years. There is no record of continued contact between Vallarta and the Lagos agraristas after Lázaro Cárdenas was elected President. Romero and other informants reported seeing him on occasion after he had been promoted to Major and then to General. Vallarta died in Mexico City in 1975.

[10]The insignia was quite similar to one used today by the Confederación Nacional Campesina. The letterhead included the mottoes cited earlier, as well as the organization's symbol (hammer, sickle, and rifle, embossed with the words "Peasants Unite"); a

LIGA REGIONAL CAMPESINA
"MAGDALENO CEDILLO"
DEL ESTADO DE JALISCO

(LIGA NACIONAL CAMPESINA "URSULO GALVAN")

CASA DEL CAMPESINO   LAGOS DE MORENO, JAL.

Liga Regional Campesina "Macedonio Ayala"
Adherida a la Confederación Campesina Mexicana

DOMICILIO SOCIAL,   LAGOS DE MORENO, JAL.
Aldama # 13,

Oficio núm. 599.-Hoja # 2.

Letterheads of the Liga Regional Campesina. They have been reproduced, from the top down, in the sequence of their use by the Liga. The second and third were designed by Captain José Vallarta, whose initials appear on the designs.

his correspondence with Romero and Ayala, Vallarta's rhetoric was forceful, and very radical. He seems to have been a keen political strategist, urging Romero and Ayala in his letters to adapt to the context; to use

---

red sun rising on a new day, symbolized by an independent campesino; and slogans calling for the "Socialization of Wealth" and "Land and Liberty."

the agrarian reform to build a cadre of followers for (unspecified) future plans; and to avoid direct confrontations with enemies, which could only weaken the movement.[11] Yet he also worried about the practicalities of campesino survival. On April 16, 1932, while working in Mexico City on "negotiations" for communities in the Lagos region, Vallarta wrote to Macedonio Ayala. He suggested that while grants of ejido land were pending, two campesinos might share the costs of planting and harvesting a single parcel in those communities which had been given final or provisional ejido grants. Agraristas from other communities did work parcels in the ejido of Buenavista (at a minimum) while their land grants were pending.

Vallarta's more important contribution to Lagos' agraristas, however, came from his network of contacts with important military officers and campesino organizations throughout the Republic. In correspondence cited earlier, he referred to contacts he had made in Mexico City with elected and appointed government officials from Jalisco as well as with General Cedillo. As he traveled around the country, Vallarta helped similar agrarista organizations elsewhere in Jalisco and in other states, and was able to keep each organization informed about the others.

Because of the predominance of medium-to-small landholdings elsewhere in Los Altos de Jalisco, there were relatively few agrarista organizations in the region. In part due to Vallarta's contacts, some scattered, smaller groups of agrarian communities—such as Ojuelos, Ocotlán, and Encarnación de Díaz, where Aniceto Martínez had concentrated his organizing efforts—became affiliates of the Liga in Lagos. It was also at Vallarta's urging that the local league was named after Magdaleno Cedillo, brother of General Saturnino Cedillo from San Luis Potosí.

As noted in Chapter 3, Lagos' agraristas had already sought support and advice from General Cedillo. Vallarta suggested that this protection might be increased if the organization were named after the General's brother. This relationship was advantageous, Romero explained, because

> At the time, our struggle wasn't only with the large landowners—for that would have been the least of our troubles. More than that, our struggle was against those who joined forces with the landowners [for example, the Chief of Military Operations in a region]. . . . To protect ourselves from assaults by the military and the government, we sought protection from the other organizations

[11]See, for example, the letter quoted in Chapter 5, note 17.

that existed in Guanajuato, San Luis Potosí, Zacatecas. . . . We weren't protected by the state of Jalisco . . . because there were too many interests that intervened, a lot of money that came between, . . . so for that reason, we turned mainly to General Cedillo.

By 1933, the relationship with Cedillo, reinforced by other ties, yielded invitations for Romero and Ayala to attend the conference in San Luis Potosí at which the Confederación Campesina Mexicana (CCM) was formed.

Shortly after its establishment, the Lagos Liga became an affiliate of the Liga Nacional Campesina Ursulo Galván.[12] In the four years that followed, roughly 1931–35, Romero and Ayala were able, through this affiliation and the intercession of José Vallarta, to attend conferences of other peasant leagues. When they did not attend, they were kept informed about policies formulated at those conferences and at national meetings of the Liga Nacional Campesina. Through correspondence and on trips to Mexico City and Guadalajara, they dealt with officers of the national league such as Manlio Fabio Altamirano, Adalberto Cortés, Antonio Echegaray, and Ursulo Galván. Laguenses also received propaganda mailings from the national organization.

The existence in Lagos de Moreno of the Liga Regional Campesina Magdaleno Cedillo—or more important, of an organized group of aspiring ejidatarios—became both an advantage and a disadvantage. Their contacts and affiliations raised their visibility and brought new patrons. Distinct political benefits accrued to the organization and its leaders, particularly when organized peasant groups became a key political base in the early stages of the 1933–34 presidential campaign. However, the increasing strength and visibility of the local peasant organization entailed costs paid by agrarista leaders, most dramatically by Aniceto Martínez and Macedonio Ayala.

[12]A similar affiliation was established with the CCM after it was formed in 1933. The Liga Nacional Campesina Ursulo Galván was established in 1926. It drew much of its strength and leadership from the state peasant league established in Veracruz in 1923. The Veracruz league flourished under Governor Adalberto Tejeda, a radical labor and agrarian reform leader who set important national precedents with the reform policies he implemented in his state. Like the movement in Lagos, the Veracruz league began with an urban and labor focus in its policies and personnel. One of its founders, Ursulo Galván, was a carpenter by trade who fled to the United States after the Revolution. He was also a Marxist and Communist Party member, but was purged from the Party in 1929 when he refused to follow Moscow's policy on rural reforms, preferring to support Mexican state and national policies as more suited to the Mexican context (see [Fowler] Salamini, 1978: 62–64; Schmitt, 1965: 15). The most detailed studies of the Liga Nacional and the peasant movement in Veracruz are [Fowler] Salamini (1978) and Falcón (1977).

The Price of Organization

During 1932, Aniceto Martínez, his wife and son had been living in Encarnación de Díaz, 42 kilometers north of Lagos town. They lived humbly, since while organizing agrarian communities he continued to make his living selling trinkets and spices in the countryside. By October of that year, Captain José Vallarta had already convinced Martínez and the agraristas in Lagos that the most promising candidate for their cause in the presidential elections upcoming in 1934 (for which the official party candidate would be chosen in December 1933) was General Lázaro Cárdenas. Early that October, Vallarta, at the time Representative-at-Large for the Liga Regional Campesina Magdaleno Cedillo, came to visit Martínez in the town of Encarnación. According to the agraristas, the landowners and military officers in Lagos had informed their counterparts in Encarnación that Martínez was an agitator, and as a consequence he was under close surveillance. He had previously been arrested in Encarnación on assorted pretexts, but he had always been able to secure his release. It was during one of Vallarta's visits that the local police, allegedly with the knowledge of the military authorities, ran Vallarta out of the state and arrested Martínez on October 15, 1932.

Martínez was held prisoner in Encarnación for three days. At dawn on October 18, with no forewarning, military guards removed him from jail supposedly to escort him to Lagos. The mounted guards led him afoot as far as Buenavista. Agraristas contended that the guards had orders not to bring him in alive, and so employed a ruse to make Martínez think that he could escape, and then shot him in the back. Later that day, the agraristas in Lagos were told that Martínez died while trying to escape. When they went to Buenavista to bring the body back to Lagos, the people in that community told them how Martínez had been killed.

Incensed by the killing, the agraristas demonstrated and wrote letters to the President of the Republic and to the Legislature protesting the crime. In addition, Vallarta wrote a circular to affiliated organizations outside of Lagos. A reply from the Liga Regional de Obreros y Campesinos del Municipio de Torreón (Chihuahua) is dated October 25, 1932, and addressed to Abelardo Rodríguez (President of the Republic), the Minister of the Interior, the Minister of War, and the national Attorney-General. The letter, probably reiterating the contents of Vallarta's circular, described the circumstances of Martínez' death. It also charged the local commander of the 35th Regiment with responsibility for Martínez' death by his relentless pursuit of agraristas, and requested his replacement, "because it has been clearly proven that he represents protection for the Cristeros, and a serious threat to the organized workers of the Republic" (AJRG).

Martínez' death brought a resurgence of contacts with outside organizations and authorities, and some attention to the plight of the agraristas in Lagos de Moreno. His death, and others, made the local activists much more cautious, but the attacks did not cripple the organization.

At about the same time Martínez was killed, Macedonio Ayala was fired from his job in the Lagos post office. Dismissed for being an agrarista, it would have been difficult for Ayala to find other white-collar employment in Lagos. Moreover, with so many communities' petitions being referred by the state government to the federal Comisión Nacional Agraria in Mexico City, Ayala could better serve the interests of Laguenses (and support himself) by seeking a job in the capital. With letters of introduction to congressional deputies from Veracruz and Michoacán—states with strong campesino organizations—Ayala left for Mexico City. By February 6, 1933, Ayala was corresponding with Romero as the official representative in Mexico City for the agrarian community of Paso de Cuarenta.[13] He gave his address at the time as Balderas 76, later the office of the Confederación Campesina Mexicana (CCM). Ayala had become a foot-soldier in the nascent national pro-Cárdenas campesino movement.

While in Mexico City, Ayala followed the progress of community petitions through the federal bureaucracy, keeping in constant communication with the Lagos agraristas about these developments. In one such letter, to José Romero, dated March 7, 1933, Ayala began by describing his discouragement:

> I don't really know what the fate of the workers will be; but I can tell you that it looks black and that only a "miracle" can save the Revolution right now. I don't wish to discourage you more than you rightfully are already, but I think that we should speak frankly with each other. Of course, we must not lose trust and faith in the ultimate triumph of our cause, although that triumph may be a long time in coming; and in these times of chaos and confusion, [we must] overcome everything, not fainting a single second, and be sacrificed if it is necessary.

[13]He was similarly described in a Guadalajara newspaper article announcing the final stages of government action creating the ejido of Paso de Cuarenta (*El Jaliscience*, May 20, 1933). Cuarenta is a community about 25 kilometers northeast of Lagos.

Then he explained his personal troubles:

> Moving on to something else, I shall begin by describing my
> personal situation, which could not be more strained. At the end of
> January I was laid off in Accounting, returning to the sad life of
> before. Sleeping in newspapers, eating sometimes twice a day and
> some days not at all. Many others have not been able to endure
> these experiences and some of them have deserted; and others,
> quite simply, have betrayed us.

Faced with these pressing personal circumstances, Ayala returned to
Lagos de Moreno, from which he subsequently made visits to Guadalajara to participate in the state agrarian congress, to Mexico City to moni-
tor community petitions, and to San Luis Potosí to attend the national
congress of peasant leagues at which the CCM was formed (see below).

The 1933-34 Presidential Campaign

The Agraristas Support Cárdenas

The Partido Nacional Revolucionario (PNR) had been established in
1929 by former President Calles, as a national political party embracing
all of the "revolutionary" organizations throughout Mexico. It was also a
convenient vehicle for achieving centralized control over the nomination
of candidates to public office at all levels. The PNR was to hold its nominating convention for the 1934 presidential election in Querétaro, in
December 1933. As one of the leading precandidates, General Lázaro
Cárdenas had been sounding out campesino and workers' organizations
throughout the country during 1932.[14] One of the splits within the Liga
Nacional Campesina Ursulo Galván which developed between 1930 and
1932 was precisely over the issue of whether to support Cárdenas or
Governor Adalberto Tejeda of Veracruz as the campesinos' presidential
candidate. Three different factions of the Liga Nacional emerged during
1932. The Cardenista wing, led by Graciano Sánchez and Enrique Flores
Magón, initiated an active campaign throughout the country to establish
state and regional peasant organizations, as steps toward a larger, more
structured national peasant union (Fowler, 1970: 323, 254–343; Brown,
1979; Falcón, 1978: 361), one which would help their candidate win the
nomination.

---

[14]By the early 1930s, approximately 200,000 campesinos (out of an estimated total
campesino population of 3.6 million) were nominally organized into state-level agrarian
leagues in various parts of the country (Portes Gil, quoted in J. Wilkie and E. Wilkie, 1969:
581).

To meet their objectives, the Cardenistas in the Liga Nacional hoped to take advantage of a series of state peasant congresses scheduled during 1933. The convention in Jalisco was to occur in March. Those attending included representatives of peasant leagues, independent ejido communities, and agrarian communities whose ejido grants were still pending. Participants were courted to insure a large turnout of men who would support the programs and reports which conference planners anticipated for the agenda.

The Liga Regional in Lagos, it will be recalled, was affiliated with the Liga Nacional Campesina Ursulo Galván. The Laguenses had friends in all three political factions of the Liga Nacional, but the Lagos group ultimately sided with the Cardenistas in the struggle for the presidency. They had been primed as Cárdenas supporters. They were already well acquainted with his accomplishments in labor organization and agrarian reform as Governor of Michoacán. Aniceto Martínez had early contacts with Cárdenas and his organizations in Michoacán, information which guided his participation in the Lagos group. Moreover, through the press and peasant congresses, Laguenses heard about other reform leaders from Michoacán such as Ernesto Soto Reyes, Luis Mora Tovar, Sansón Flores ("El Chino"), and Antonio Mayes Navarro (see [Fowler] Salamini, 1978: 110–111). Finally, Margarito Ramírez, José Vallarta, and others who were early Cárdenas supporters[15] urged the Laguenses to support their candidate and kept them informed about the campaign.

According to Romero, Severiano Casillas,[16] representing the state peasant league, came to Lagos to urge him to gather together as many community representatives as he could to attend the March 1933 conference.[17] Within a week of his visit, Casillas had sent Romero sufficient funds to bring three representatives from each Lagos agrarian community ("the best-prepared and brightest men"); 36 representatives from the municipio of Lagos attended the conference. It was probably at this

[15]José Romero, Francisco Navia, Aniceto Martínez' widow, and other agraristas all attested to Vallarta's support for General Cárdenas even before he was openly campaigning for the nomination. Vallarta was an employee in the Ministry of War and the Navy while Cárdenas was Minister of that agency, and later during Cárdenas' presidency. Margarito Ramírez was state campaign director in Jalisco for Cárdenas' presidential campaign in 1933-34.

[16]*El Jaliscience*, November 26–December 2, 1932, identifies Severiano Casillas and J. Guadalupe Santana as officials of the Liga de Comunidades Agrarias de Jalisco.

[17]Macedonio Ayala also wrote to Romero on March 7, 1933, from Mexico City, stressing the importance of attending an upcoming congress in Guadalajara. Presumably this is the same conference referred to here.

state agrarian congress in 1933 that Romero, Ayala, and the Lagos agraristas joined other participants in the meetings for the official photograph
reproduced here. Romero claims that because he led the largest local
delegation of representatives at the conference,

> I would have been [named] Secretary-General of the state orga-
> nization, but that wasn't to the Governor's political advantage, and
> he imposed one of his own people as president of the state league. I
> ended up as second secretary, . . . commissioned to resolve the land
> and water rights problems of all the communities in this and ad-
> joining states.

J. Guadalupe Santana was selected president of the Liga de Comunidades Agrarias de Jalisco. Romero served as the Jalisco Liga's Secretary for Lands and Waters from March 29, 1933 until March 1, 1936.[18]

To fulfill his responsibilities in the state league, Romero moved to
Guadalajara. There he continued to maintain close contact with the
agrarian movement in Lagos, but his attention turned primarily to a
broader set of political issues and to a larger number of communities.
Macedonio Ayala, who was then serving as the Lagos communities' representative in Mexico City, moved into the top local leadership position. A
variety of events coincided to enhance his leadership role: the assassination of Aniceto Martínez, the loss of his own job, and the development of
useful ties to officials in Guadalajara. By May of 1933 Lázaro Cárdenas, at
the time Minister of War, was the most serious contender for the presidential nomination of the PNR. He had built up a substantial constituency among labor and peasant organizations, within the junior military
ranks, and among key regional political leaders. He still had not, however, formally declared his candidacy, nor was he yet publicly supported
by General Calles, still the functional head of the official party. The lack
of an endorsement from Calles had restrained the more cautious of the
state governors and interest groups in the country, among them some key
politicians in Jalisco.[19]

---

[18]These dates are confirmed in a letter written by Guadalupe Santana, which also
praises Romero's loyal service to the state league (AJRG).

[19]Cf. Cornelius (1973: 426); Falcón (1975: 144–146). José Romero contended that Jalisco Governor Sebastián Allende was among those who refrained from joining the Cárdenas bandwagon until Calles gave tacit approval to Cárdenas' candidacy. (Falcón [1978:
378–379] confirms that Allende delayed his endorsement of Cárdenas.) This became a
source of tension between Allende and members of the state league who supported Cárdenas.

Participants in the state agrarian congress held in Guadalajara in 1933. Among those pictured (marked with arrows, left to right) are Víctor Reyes, José Romero, Graciano Sánchez, and Macedonio Ayala.

But between April and June 1933 the state political scenery changed rapidly.[20] On April 11, 1933, the Partido Agrarista de Jalisco became the first organized political group to publicly endorse a candidate (Cárdenas), despite Governor Allende's resistance to the endorsement. The Liga Regional Campesina Magdaleno Cedillo and the Unión Plutarco Elías Calles followed close behind. On May 1, the campesino leagues of several states issued a manifesto declaring that the organized agraristas had decided to participate in the upcoming election, and that they would be supporting Lázaro Cárdenas as their candidate (Dulles, 1961: 571). On May 16, Cárdenas resigned as Minister of War to devote full time to his campaign, which he formally opened that day. In the next few days, Jesús González Gallo, president of the Jalisco chapter of the PNR, joined Margarito Ramírez and Florencio Topete—who were already publicly supporting Cárdenas—in endorsing the General's candidacy; the Liga de Comunidades Agrarias de Jalisco declared its support for Cárdenas; and

[20]This sequence of events in Jalisco is based on accounts in *El Jaliscience* from May 11 through June 30, 1933, and on Falcón (1978).

Margarito Ramírez was named head of the state's pro-Cárdenas committee. José Vallarta, at the time in San Luis Potosí attending a national
peasant congress, wrote to Ramírez on June 4 urging that the members
of local Cárdenas campaign groups be "men of absolutely revolutionary
backgrounds" (AJRG). Three days later a pro-Cárdenas committee was
formed in Lagos de Moreno. Guadalupe Santana took the first of several
leaves of absence from the presidency of the Jalisco Liga to work full-
time in the Cárdenas campaign, and Romero became acting president in
Santana's absence.

    According to Romero, "the really rough part of the Cárdenas cam-
paign for us in Jalisco was that we had to fight against the Governor,
because the [state] government was not Cardenista; its loyalties were to
Calles." Romero remembered that once General Calles acquiesced in
Cárdenas' nomination as the PNR candidate, "the governors, instead of
persecuting the Cardenistas, began to give them protection."

The Confederación Campesina Mexicana

One of the most important tactics of the Cárdenas presidential campaign
was the establishment of a national peasant organization. The pro-Cárdenas faction of the Liga Nacional Campesina Ursulo Galván[21] called for
a national convention of the Liga to be held in San Luis Potosí from May
31 to June 2, 1933. They hoped that the conference would resolve the
conflicts within the Liga Nacional and that a unified national peasant
organization would emerge from the meetings. The agenda items, and
the resolutions approved at this congress, demonstrate that the meeting
was also designed to endorse policies which would extend and intensify
the agrarian reform program and increase protection for ejidatarios and
their organizations (El Jaliscience, May 31, 1933).

    By 1933 the agrarian reform program in Mexico was threatened with
extinction. Following Calles' criticism of the reform in 1930, the national
redistribution of land had declined appreciably. In May 1933, Calles
again spoke publicly of the failure of the national reform program, rec-
ommending that the distribution of land be halted. Calles' statement
reflected, in part, his long-standing concern with the modernization of
agriculture in Mexico.[22] He recommended that large landowners be

----

    [21]This faction was led by Enrique Flores Magón, R. Fuentes López, Adalberto Cortés,
and Graciano Sánchez.
    [22]Calles' later views on agrarian reform were consistent with his long-standing prefer-
ence for the small, privately owned plot as the basic form of land tenure in Mexico:

Representatives to the national campesino convention held in San Luis Potosí, May 31–June 2, 1933, at which the Confederación Campesina Mexicana (CCM) was established. Graciano Sánchez (center, front row) was elected president of the CCM. José Romero appears immediately behind and to the left of Sánchez.

forced to sell fractions of their holdings to promote the growth of small private farms for those campesinos in need of land and with resources to purchase it. His statement constituted endorsement of the "pre-emptive" land-title transfers occurring throughout the Republic—including Lagos de Moreno. Large landowners had been selling portions of their holdings to transfer the economic losses to others in case of land redistribution, and also to reduce the apparent size of their holdings (making them less likely to be expropriated). The agrarian activists were concerned that if Calles succeeded in nominating a like-minded candidate, the land reform program would be terminated.

Delegates representing campesino organizations in 23 states assembled in San Luis Potosí for the national peasant convention under the watchful eyes of Cárdenas' representatives and General Saturnino Cedillo. The official Jalisco delegates were Serapio Hurtado, José

"Calles had originally approved the expropriation of land from large haciendas and its redistribution into ejidos . . . [but] this was viewed as no more than an interim measure prior to creation of a class of small, middle-class proprietors with individually owned plots. . . . Calles' subsequent concern for increased agricultural productivity and efficient land use led him to oppose further land redistribution in any form on a large scale" (Cornelius, 1973: 418; see also Calvert, 1973: 256; Simpson, 1937: 441-442).

Romero Gómez, and José Vallarta, the latter representing the Liga de Comunidades Agrarias Plutarco Elías Calles of Ocotlán. Ayala attended, but not as an official delegate. All of the resolutions proposed by the Jalisco delegates were approved.[23] While the pro-Cárdenas groups engaged in a great deal of campaigning at the convention, there was no formal endorsement of any candidate. As had been hoped, the Confederación Campesina Mexicana (CCM)—predecessor of the Confederación Nacional Campesina (CNC), the current national peasant union— was formed at the congress.

The Cárdenas Upheaval

Finally, in December 1933, the PNR met in nominating convention and selected Lázaro Cárdenas as its presidential candidate. At the convention, the party acted on former President Calles' recommendation, made in May of that year, that the PNR develop a six-year plan to guide the new administration. The results, spawned from a series of compromises, were much more radical than Calles had anticipated (Osorio Marbán, 1970: 358–492). The six-year plan, which Cárdenas adopted as his campaign platform, was one of "cooperative socialism" (Bazant, 1977: 179). In addition to endorsing the principle of collective agricultural communities, it recommended the extension of eligibility to peones acasillados (resident hacienda workers). This endorsement of an expanded land-reform program followed an impassioned speech by Graciano Sánchez (see Osorio Marbán, 1970: 384–397), in which he charged that the failure of the land reform program was due to the way in which it had been implemented.

President Abelardo Rodríguez began implementing the new program in the last year of his administration. In January 1934 he created the Agrarian Department to handle petitions for land reform, thus separating this activity from the Agriculture Ministry. In March he signed the Agrarian Reform Law, which specified in detail the procedures for implementing Article 27 of the Constitution (see Appendix A).

The six-year plan also advocated strengthening labor unions into workers' cooperatives, and several policies by which the government would support the workers in collective bargaining with management.

---

[23]*El Jaliscience*, June 6, 1933. Romero appears in two official photographs of representatives attending the congress, one of which is reproduced here.

The platform, and Cárdenas' record as Governor of Michoacán, earned him the support of Lombardo Toledano and other leftist union leaders.[24] These leaders and their unions had begun to split from the CROM in 1932 in disputes with the conservative leadership, which had permitted government control of strikes.

Finally, the PNR convention endorsed an amendment to Article 3 of the Constitution, passed in October 1933, which provided for "modernization" of the public-school system in Mexico. The amendment required schools to teach "an exact and rational concept of the universe and social life." Opponents interpreted the change as the introduction of "sexual education," because the curriculum also included some health and biological education. Supporters of the amendment hoped that it would lead (as it did) to an emphasis in the schools on community cohesion, service, and collective effort—possibly also to a curriculum opposed to Catholic doctrine and closer to socialism or Marxism.[25] By 1934, the public school curriculum had been relabeled "socialist education," a change which did little to win support in conservative circles. This amendment, and Calles' anticlerical pronouncements in July of 1934 advocating complete Church withdrawal from the educational system, provoked a limited repetition of the Cristero uprising in Los Altos de Jalisco in 1934–36. Taken together, these changes in education and labor policy strengthened conservative opposition to the new government, and to those groups, such as the agraristas, who were regarded as agents of the government.

After his nomination, Lázaro Cárdenas took his political campaign to the people. Setting a precedent for all subsequent presidential candidates, he traveled over 16,000 miles by airplane, train, car, and horseback, to every state and countless rural villages. This was the first time that the votes of rural dwellers had been seriously courted. Cárdenas listened much more than he spoke; he declared that in the campaign he hoped to learn about the needs of the people. He received village petitions for land, schools, and services. As part of the campaign, supporters organized political groups—unions and agrarian leagues—at state and regional levels. Cárdenas' campaign not only brought him a landslide

[24]Vicente Lombardo Toledano was an intellectual, a law professor, who had joined the CROM in 1926. A radical leader, he had been influenced by communism, although without joining the Communist Party (see Kirk, 1942: 80–105; Krauze, 1976).

[25]For further analysis of the "socialist school" in Mexico during the Cárdenas period, see Raby (1973: 35–62) and Ruiz (1963: 45-64).

Campesinos in denim overalls line up in 1934 to cast their ballots at one of the election booths on the main plaza in Lagos de Moreno. Most of the agraristas voted for the first time in this national election, which brought Lázaro Cárdenas to power.

victory and earned him the support of mass organizations, but also established a nationwide network of labor and campesino groups which could be incorporated into national organizations. Moreover, his policy of going to the people did not end with his election in July 1934. He continued to travel until his inauguration on December 1, and spent roughly one-third of his term of office outside of the capital. An observer of his administration wrote:

> Cárdenas, by personally carrying the federal government to the people, brought to many for the first time the awareness of belonging to it, and the knowledge that they had a right to expect service from it, in exchange for loyalty and cooperation. (Kirk, 1942: 39.)

The Benefits and Costs of Political Activism

Beginning with the CCM convention in 1933 and the associated congresses, Laguenses participated in nationally important political assemblies. In January 1934, Ayala, Romero, Salvador Martínez, and Francisco Navia were all included in the Jalisco delegation to the national labor convention held in Mexico City. Participation in such meet-

Members of the Jalisco delegation to the national labor convention held in Mexico City in January 1934. Among those pictured (marked with arrows) are: front row, Macedonio Ayala; second row, Salvador Martínez (left) and José Romero (right); last row, Francisco Navia.

ings had significant political payoffs for the Lagos reform leaders individually and for the agrarian communities whose cause they were promoting.

Macedonio Ayala's personal fortunes began to improve. After losing his job in Mexico City, he joined Romero in Guadalajara. There, he gained favor with Governor Allende.[26] By June 4, 1933, he had been appointed Inspector of Ejidos for the state of Jalisco, reporting directly to the Governor. Ayala was becoming involved in influential political circles in Guadalajara.[27]

For seven years Ayala had courted Elvira Hernández, but they had not married because of his precarious employment situation. His job as state Inspector of Ejidos relieved some of the financial pressure, and they were married on October 7, 1933. For the next year or so they traveled back and forth between Guadalajara and Lagos. According to Doña

[26]Ayala's widow, José Romero, Francisco Navia, and Cipriano Barbosa all said that Ayala maintained a good relationship with Allende, despite the fact that the Governor was not generally helpful to agraristas.

[27]At some time during 1933 or 1934, Ayala was photographed in what appears to be Guadalajara's Parque Agua Azul with state and national political leaders, including Margarito Ramírez.

Elvira, they were lent a small house by the president of the state PNR (Jesús González Gallo). It was unfurnished, however, and without the means to buy things, they lived with boxes for tables and a shower made from a punctured tin can. Despite their relatively greater financial security, it was not yet personally profitable to be a spokesman for local peasant organizations in Mexico.

Doña Elvira recalled that during 1933 Ayala traveled a great deal as the "representative of the Governor, to install municipio presidents throughout the state," and that she occasionally accompanied him. In some towns there were large reception committees and great festivities in honor of Ayala and the events he was there to preside over. It is possible that Doña Elvira was in error about the purpose of these trips, for she freely admitted that Ayala did not discuss agrarian business with her.[28] If Ayala was still Inspector of Ejidos during these trips, their main purpose was probably to organize peasant support for the state and national elections.[29] By mid-1934 Ayala had reestablished his residence in Lagos, to preside over the final procedures for land redistribution.

Jalisco was scheduled to elect a new governor in 1934. Initially the agraristas in Lagos backed another candidate for the official party nomination,[30] but Everardo Topete was chosen, with the support of the incumbent governor, Allende. Topete began his campaign tour of the state, and as a municipio seat and one of the largest towns in the state, Lagos de Moreno was included on the itinerary. The hacendados and the *"grupo revolucionario"* (including the campesinos and labor union members) each gathered a large contingent of supporters to greet the candidate

[28]She did not approve of his political sentiments, for she felt that her husband's involvement in agrarianism and his financial generosity toward campesinos led only to public opprobrium, danger, and personal sacrifice, with little gratitude from those he served.

[29]It is difficult to reconstruct this period in Ayala's life; documentary evidence is negligible, and informants could remember little about his activities outside of Lagos. My own estimate is that he served only briefly as Inspector of Ejidos, either quitting or being terminated to participate in Cárdenas' presidential campaign. José Romero described the events of 1933–34 as the real proof of Ayala's commitment to the cause of the agraristas. He recalled that Ayala had just been married and appointed as Inspector of Ejidos when the Jalisco Liga declared its support for Cárdenas, against the Governor's wishes. Ayala, faced with a choice between his job or keeping faith with his companions, chose the latter course and was fired. Whether for this or other reasons, by November 1934 Ayala is listed in public documents as the representative of the ejidos near Lagos, but not as Inspector of Ejidos, under circumstances in which such an official title would have been mentioned.

[30]They supported Silvano Barba González, who instead became President Cárdenas' personal secretary, serving later in the Ministry of Labor, as Minister of the Interior, and as President of the PNR from 1936 to 1938. He did become Governor of Jalisco in 1938.

upon his arrival in Lagos.[31] This was a critical election in Jalisco; assorted interest groups throughout the state were jockeying to influence the candidates and the formulation of policies which would affect them during the Cárdenas administration. The hacendados and the revolutionary group in Lagos both had a great deal at stake, and their interests conflicted.

The gubernatorial campaign rally at the Lagos train station in 1934 was a critical turning point for Ayala. Romero was still in Guadalajara working in the state league; Ayala had become the leader of the local agraristas and the focal point of the landowners' opposition. The campesinos had become better organized and more assertive through their participation in the Cárdenas campaign—the first election in which most of them ever voted. In addition, their petitions for land reform were moving into the final stages of government review. At the railroad rally, Ayala led the contingent of *revolucionarios*, while Raul Romo organized the landowners and their supporters. There was jostling between the two groups for the prime position closest to the train. An argument broke out, and then some fist-fights, including an altercation between a landowner and one of the labor union members.[32] The landowners contend that Ayala encouraged his men to fight, while the agraristas argue that he was trying to calm them down. Since the agraristas had only sticks and knives to defend themselves, it is unlikely that they had been encouraged to escalate what could have been a fatal encounter. The arrival of the train broke up the confrontation; but in the weeks that followed, the local authorities watched the reformists ever more closely, frisking them and confiscating arms. Macedonio Ayala received numerous anonymous notes threatening his life if he did not leave town. The agraristas set up bodyguards to accompany Ayala and the government engineers who came to conduct final studies for the grants of land.

By October 1934, the agraristas were optimistic that the prospective local and national political changes would benefit them. Lázaro Cárdenas was to take the presidential oath of office on December 1. Everardo Topete, with whom Ayala had established good relations, stood as the

---

[31]Such symbolic gestures are essential in Mexican politics, for they offer opportunities to formally declare support for a candidate and to present interest-group petitions. Moreover, while presenting a large delegation at a campaign rally does not insure that a group's petitions will be answered, failure to marshal such a delegation can be detrimental when a group seeks to be heard in the future.

[32]According to one report, the fight broke out when one of the landowners tore down a banner which read "Down with the bourgeoisie, down with the clergy."

gubernatorial candidate for Jalisco. An announcement of the candidates for legislative office and for the local ayuntamiento, for elections scheduled in December, was expected shortly. The agraristas assumed that Ayala aspired to political office. As one of them explained:

> Ayala had friends—everywhere—and he was a political man, well-educated. . . . We'd all seek out Ayala because he had a very good way of dealing with rural people. And you know that a politician, and an educated man, aspires for more. . . . A man who understands many things has a right to something. . . . And like I say, he was a good friend of the Governor.

The final census was being conducted (again) for the ejido of Lagos de Moreno. Late in October, Ayala served as official witness of the procedures on behalf of the petitioners. At least two other censuses had been taken prior to 1934 to determine how many people in the community would be entitled to receive ejido lands. Since the quantity of land expropriated was determined by the number of eligible recipients, the census was a vital, closely observed, and hotly contested procedure. José María Nares Alvarez, the state Procurador de Pueblos, and government engineer Enrique Bancalari were in town to observe and conduct the census. The presence of the Procurador de Pueblos, who did not normally attend such procedures, attests to the delicacy of the situation in Lagos and to the importance it was accorded by state officials.

The personal safety of the agraristas was increasingly threatened as the Lagos ejido census neared completion. Ayala's safety was particularly compromised, because it was apparent to all that he was potentially a nominee for elective office. José Romero recalled that he intended to propose Ayala as a candidate for the federal or state legislature, and that Manuel Martínez Valadez, the federal deputy for the district, had agreed to nominate Ayala.[33] Doña Elvira remembered that on October 25 or 26 Ayala had received word by telegram that he was to be nominated as the candidate for municipio president of Lagos de Moreno.[34]

Because of the threats on his life, Ayala had a bodyguard of agraristas

[33]Martínez Valadez, a leading congressman supporting President Cárdenas in his final confrontation with former President Calles, was shot and killed in the federal Chamber of Deputies on September 11, 1935 (Paez Brotchie, 1940: 182).

[34]Other agraristas also recalled that Ayala had been selected to be the next municipio president. Two of them affirmed that he had received a telegram announcing his nomination. The same account is reported in a biography of Ayala published in the local newspaper, *Vértice*, November 4, 1973.

who accompanied him on his daily rounds. On the evening of October 26, the bodyguards had already withdrawn when Ayala and his wife, then two months pregnant with their first child, went out to the corner store. On the way back to their house they were assaulted by two men. Ayala was stabbed in the back and fatally wounded. The two unidentified as-

sailants also attacked Doña Elvira and then fled down the darkened street.[35]

Ayala survived only a few days. The agraristas were unable to secure the expert medical attention he required, "because really we were so poor, so strapped, that there weren't the means to provide adequate care." Ayala died on November 2, 1934, and was buried in a "first-class" gravesite provided by the local government, since Ayala was known to be "completely insolvent."[36] *El Jaliscience* of November 6 reported on his funeral:

> *Lagos de Moreno.* The funeral was held yesterday for the deceased agrarian leader Macedonio Ayala, in which many noted agraristas participated, among them Sr. José Romero Gómez, who pronounced a brilliant funeral oration asking for justice and revenge for the leader Ayala. The coffin was adorned with the red and black flag.

The agraristas developed several memorials to their fallen leader. A plaque was placed at the site of the attack.[37] The Liga Regional Campesina was renamed the Liga Regional Campesina Macedonio Ayala in his honor. A monument was erected on Ayala's grave by his family and his companions (*"compañeros de lucha"*): a truncated column symbolizing a young life cut short. The ayuntamiento voted after Ayala's death to honor him by paying his widow the sum of 1 peso per day; the pension was discontinued in 1943. Since then she has supported herself by operating a small shop on the main plaza where she sells candies, soft drinks, and cigarettes. She is very bitter about her sacrifices.

The agraristas in Lagos blamed Ayala's death on a plot among the rich people who stood to lose land in the agrarian reform, and on the guber-

---

[35]Six months after his death, Doña Elvira gave birth to Ayala's daughter. The child, who died in 1978, was born with physical and emotional abnormalities which were popularly attributed to the attack on Doña Elvira and the shock she suffered with Ayala's death.

[36]The cemetery in Lagos de Moreno is divided into three categories of gravesites, according to cost and the length of time the body remains in the grave. At the time of Ayala's death, the indigent were buried in third-class graves. The ayuntamiento's decision to provide a gravesite is recorded on the death certificate (*Registro Civil*, vol. U-3, p. 191, #763).

[37]It reads: "Near this place, comrade Macedonio Ayala was assassinated in a cowardly manner by the forces of reaction on October 26, 1934. The agraristas of this region remember him for his untiring and devoted efforts on behalf of the downtrodden classes. On the first anniversary of his death, October 26, 1935."

The tomb of Macedonio Ayala, with two wreaths placed there in his honor on November 2, 1976. On November 2, 1936, two years after his death, the Frente Popular Jaliscience dedicated a plaque at the gravesite which bears the following inscription: "To the memory of our comrade Macedonio Ayala, assassinated by the bourgeoisie in the redeeming proletarian struggle." For many years the older agraristas honored Ayala on the anniversary of his death, standing watch at the gravesite. This practice has declined in recent years, as "the old guard" has been replaced by young men who know little of the early agrarista struggle. In 1976 an honor guard, which was not formally organized that year, was hastily assembled for the photographer.

natorial campaign rally incident at the train station.[38] His widow added that the wealthy landowners were also motivated by the knowledge that Ayala was to be placed in charge of the local government, and that this was more than the rich could tolerate. Doña Elvira insisted, and other informants agreed, that it was common practice at the time for messages to the agraristas to be intercepted at the Lagos post and telegraph offices.

[38]In a telegram dated October 27, 1934, to the Agrarian Department in Mexico City, notifying officials of the attack on Ayala, José María Nares Alvarez also accused the landowners: "[Ayala] was assaulted by individuals sent by owners of properties probably affected by the ejido sought by residents of this town" (expediente ejidal for the Ejido of Lagos de Moreno, ASRA). In interviews with the agraristas, the same names surfaced constantly as the men responsible for Ayala's death. They include two of the then-largest

Doña Elvira Hernández, widow of Macedonio Ayala, in front of her small candy store on the main plaza in Lagos, in 1976.

She maintained that was how the hacendados found out about Ayala's imminent nomination for the municipio presidency. Ayala's assailants were never apprehended, nor was anyone ever charged with the crime. In view of this, when pressed to explain how they knew who was respon- sible, agraristas reply, with an air of disdain, that in a small town there are some things that one simply *knows.*

With the hacendados suspected of ordering Ayala's death, tension mounted in Lagos, and there was great concern about possible reprisals. The newspaper account of Ayala's funeral cited above goes on to report that

> Because of the assassination of this leader, a terrible conflict has intensified between the local agraristas and the large landholders.

landowners in Lagos, and two other men of moderate means who were new and relatively small-scale landowners. Two of them were former administrators of large haciendas who had acquired their own properties; only two of the four were in immediate danger of losing land to the ejidos. There is, however, no way I can corroborate or disprove the agraristas' accusations.

A meeting was held today, convened by the municipio president Jesús Torres Lomelín, to try to calm emotions and to reconcile mutual interests in order to avoid acts of personal revenge.

At this meeting, the local military regiment commander and the municipio president both offered to mediate and urged reconciliation between the contending groups. The agraristas were not persuaded by the hacendados' proclamations of innocence, and redoubled their efforts to secure ejido lands and nominations for agrarista candidates to public office. As one aging agrarista explained, "They had Ayala killed, thinking that in that way the agrarian business would be ended, not knowing that this business [of agrarian reform] wasn't one's own, it was the government's. . . . What could they gain by killing Macedonio, if it all came from above?"

The Land Is Granted

Both national and local events contributed to the improved fortunes of the labor and agrarian sectors in Lagos during the 1934–38 period. Locally, the agrarian movement drew strength from Ayala's assassination. Telegrams and letters of protest sent by the agraristas to officials in Mexico City and Guadalajara at the time of his death attracted outside attention and concern. The surviving band of agraristas in Lagos devoted themselves to the final thrust with renewed commitment. José Romero was still working through the state peasant league in Guadalajara to promote agrarian reform in Jalisco. Francisco Navia, Moisés Pérez, and Miguel Aguirre shared responsibility for guiding the paperwork and maintaining group morale on the home front.

As the local agrarian organization grew stronger, its task was greatly facilitated by the national policies being implemented by President Lázaro Cárdenas. Cárdenas endorsed the principles of land reform, accelerated studies for petitions already under review, and gave courage to groups operating in hostile communities. In his first year in office, Cárdenas quadrupled the amount of land redistributed, from the previous year's 608,000 hectares. In July 1935, he ordered the PNR to begin formally establishing affiliated campesino leagues in every state. These leagues would supersede and incorporate all existing regional, local, and state campesino organizations. Every ejidatario and all agraristas in communities with pending petitions for ejido land automatically became members of the state leagues. Each ejido community selected representatives to attend state agrarian congresses at which the leagues were formed and (in future years) mutual problems would be discussed and political candidates endorsed. In 1938, the new state leagues were united to form the present Confederación Nacional Campesina (CNC), replacing the CCM. The purpose of the new structure of campesino organizations was twofold: to defend the interests of campesinos who had just received land or were still struggling to obtain it, and to support the Cárdenas administration in its struggles with the followers of former President Calles and others opposed to the Cárdenas reform program (Brown, 1979; Cornelius, 1973; Falcón, 1978).

Cárdenas opened up the nation's telegraph lines for free public use during certain hours to facilitate communication with him, and he declared that all correspondence with the Agrarian Department was official and not subject to postage charges. Relieved of the financial burdens of communication, agraristas took their cases directly to the highest authority, often in the most poignant terms. The official ejido archives (expedientes ejidales, ASRA) contain numerous examples of these exchanges. The following communications from Fructuoso Macías, head of the agrarian community of Cañada de Ricos (on the outskirts of Lagos), are illustrative. A letter dated February 22, 1935, to Gabino Vázquez, head of the Agrarian Department, with copies to President Cárdenas and to Graciano Sánchez, Procurador de Pueblos, reads in part:

> The campesinos of this community plead before you that we be granted lands as quickly as possible. It won't be necessary to describe, point by point, the hardships of our people. We earnestly beg you to be frank and tell us when we can be granted lands. The rains are coming. It is time now to till [the fields]. Please answer quickly.

Another letter, to President Cárdenas, dated April 28, 1935, reads:

> The question is quite simple and we want you to resolve it with all sincerity and frankness. Without self-serving statements, please tell us agraristas who await the ejido of Cañada de Ricos, in all frankness, if we are to be granted land or not. We beg that if we are to be granted land, it be granted quickly; and if not, tell us once and for all so that we can give up the idea. We are fed up at being the object of ridicule by the rich [el capital] and even by the government.

The surviving agraristas believe that Cárdenas was personally acquainted with the obstacles to agrarian reform in Lagos, and that he was instrumental in accelerating the final studies for their land grants. They maintain that their protests over Ayala's death, their ties to Margarito

Ramírez, and the fact that José Raimundo Cárdenas, the president's brother, had served as manager of the tax office in Lagos in the 1920s, all heightened Cárdenas' awareness of their problems and advanced their cause. The expedientes ejidales show that the President's office received communications from Lagos and forwarded them to officials in the Agrarian Department, urging their prompt attention with a report back to the President's office. However, there is no evidence that Laguenses received exceptional consideration.

Drawing strength from these local and national developments, the process of land reform in Lagos reached its zenith. Because there was extensive overlap among the properties considered expropriable for the ejidos of San Jorge, Moya, Cañada de Ricos, and Lagos de Moreno, the final studies for these communities were completed together. The presidential decrees for these four ejidos, the first to be granted in Lagos by the Cárdenas administration, were signed on May 14 and 22, 1935. The next step was to survey and take formal possession of the new ejidal lands.

Francisco Navia recalled that when the Agrarian Department engineers arrived in Lagos to implement the presidential decrees, they and the group of ejidatarios who were to receive the lands were confronted by protesters. Led by an hacienda administrator, a large group of hacienda employees and peones descended on the town, declaring that they were the "authentic campesinos" and that they had neither asked for nor wanted the lands. The Agrarian Department officials replied that if the protesters did not want land, they would not be given any. But whether they wished them or not, the engineers were there to give possession of the ejido lands, and they intended to do so even if there were only one or two individuals to accept a community's grant of land.

On June 29 and 30, 1935, extraordinary ceremonies were held in Lagos de Moreno, San Jorge, Cañada de Ricos, and Moya. Witnessing the proceedings, in addition to the Agrarian Department engineers assigned to these cases, were representatives of the Governor and the Agrarian Department. By dusk on the second day, the core group of agraristas in Lagos and the petitioners for ejidos in those communities had attended four formal proceedings which fulfilled the hopes of the agraristas for land and liberty. First, the presidential decree granting each ejido petition was read. The first governing councils for each of the four ejidos were elected by the community's members. The land included in each of the grants was formally measured and marked, and was finally turned over to the ejido communities. Fields which had been planted by the landowners and on which unharvested crops were growing did not have to be turned over to the ejidos until after the harvest; some ejido lands were therefore not available to the ejidatarios for cultivation until 1936.[39]

The leaders of these ejidos recalled that when the engineers arrived for the final ceremonies, some communities had difficulty finding the minimum number of persons to accept the ejido lands. In some cases, the ejidos were given to less than the legal minimum of recipients. In others, such as Ciénega de Mata, the first recipients sent word to families who had been run off the hacienda because of their participation in the ejido petition, and these families returned to join the ranks of the first ejidatarios. Of those who would not accept the land, many did not believe that it really had come to pass, or that it could last; some who were interested feared that the lands would be withdrawn and then there would be reprisals from the former owners. Many were simply afraid of the landowners, or continued to believe that land reform was robbery. Many who later became ejidatarios say that they did not join the initial group of recipients because they considered that economically they would be even worse off as ejidatarios, without animals to till the soil or funds to purchase seeds and equipment. One old-timer who never accepted ejido land explained why he refused to join the ejido when it was created: "What do I gain joining the ejido if I don't have anything to work with? The soil was bad. To work, one needs to have animals, or money, or something else. . . . I didn't like it because one had to move onto lands which weren't one's own."

During the next four years, as President Cárdenas distributed unprecedented amounts of land throughout the Republic, and as they saw that the early ejido lands were not being withdrawn, others who had at first been frightened of agrarian reform filed their own ejido petitions. As an ejidatario in La Laguna explained, "Because we knew from the neighbors that it was an easy matter, because General Cárdenas was distributing a lot of land, we did it [filed an ejido petition in 1939] blindly to see if perchance . . ."

Many of the reluctant began to accept land in the existing ejido communities, although this process took time. As one man recalled, "In the end, when they saw the truth, when they saw that we began to harvest for ourselves, then they began to join us." Some were converted out of necessity, because haciendas such as La Punta lost all of their arable land

---

[39]Expedientes ejidales for Cañada de Ricos, Lagos de Moreno, San Jorge, and Moya (ASRA).

to the ejidos. The owners had no lands left to sharecrop and fewer jobs for their employees. It was not until the 1940s (earlier in the smallest ejidos) that all of the arable plots were distributed to individual ejidatarios. Some ejidos like Comanja and Palomas-Sauceda were not completely cultivated until the 1950s.

In fact, while the ejidatarios felt relieved of the yoke of subjugation as peons on another man's land, during the first few years they experienced severe hardships. The only irrigation dam which might have served the ejidos of Cañada de Ricos and San Jorge was bombed the year after the land was granted. In a few ejidos, such as Lagos de Moreno, the ejidatarios received some loans from the government's Ejido Bank, but only enough to purchase a team of oxen. The agrarian reform struggle had been for "land and liberty"; local reformers did not expect government loans for implements or seeds, nor any technical assistance. Moreover, in the Los Altos region there was no indigenous tradition of collective farming, so the agraristas never petitioned for collectively cultivated lands.[40]

The first ejidatarios made do as best they could, given the particular circumstances of their communities (see Chapter 6). In some ejidos, the land grant also included a share of the calves of the landowners' herd. Some landholders (e.g., the owners of Ciénega de Mata and San Bernardo) were willing to lend animals or plows to the ejidatarios, and a very few provided seed for the first year's crop. In general, the former landowners were more generous in cases where the ejido petition had been initiated by individuals from outside the hacienda. In some of these cases, once reform was inevitable, hacendados urged their loyal workers to accept the ejido lands rather than see the land distributed to outsiders.

In most cases, the first grants to ejido communities left the haciendas

---

[40]Nor was there any large-scale, commercial agriculture in Los Altos de Jalisco, as there had been in regions where the Cárdenas administration established collectivized ejidos to maintain the high production levels and commercial value of the expropriated farms. Cárdenas was the first—and only—president to widely exercise the option of forming collective ejidos, i.e., ejidos with collectively organized labor, marketing, and credit systems. The cotton-growing collective ejidos in the Laguna region of Durango and Coahuila, formed from 150,000 hectares of irrigated landholdings belonging to absentee foreign owners, were created in October 1936. Cotton, rice, and lime-growing landholdings of roughly 150,000 hectares in Lombardia and Nueva Italia in Michoacán, as well as the large henequen plantations in Yucatán, were all expropriated in 1936–37 and established as collective ejidos. Such ejidos were only formed, however, in regions with large landholdings devoted to export crops. See Eckstein, 1966; Glantz, 1974; Martínez Saldaña, 1980; Restrepo and Eckstein, 1975; Senior, 1940; and R. Wilkie, 1971.

Table 3

Ejidos in the Municipio of Lagos de Moreno, 1970

Ejido or Community Name	Total Size (Hectares)	Arable Land (Hectares)	Number of Ejidatarios
La Aurora	596	296	22
Bernalejo	1,492	532	55
Buenavista	934	181	53
Cañada de Ricos	1,250	592	100
La Cantera	1,228	354	73
Cantera de los Torres	378	168	19
El Chipinque	450	169	33
Comanja de Corona	1,764	922	78
Las Crucitas	758	249	24
Cuautitlán o Ledesma	450	377	30
Dieciocho de Marzo (Santa Cruz)	1,432	675	90
La Escondida	1,263	578	82
Francisco I. Madero (Las Cruces)	1,415	1,229	98
Jaramillo de Abajo	485	108	20
Ladera Puerta de Cantareras	352	24	24
Lagos de Moreno	2,319	1,206	158
La Laguna	285	61	19
Lic. Primo Verdad (Ciénega de Mata)	1,472	368	70
Loma de Veloces	588	155	32
Luis Moreno Pérez	509	333	36
Macedonio Ayala (San Jorge)	296	163	26
El Maguey	744	249	46
La Merced	1,052	222	47
Miranda	882	392	48
Moya	1,290	694	100
El Ojuelo	490	96	14
Paloma–Sauceda	2,553	552	95
Potrerillos	950	363	49
Primero de Mayo (Chupaderos)	961	268	48
Puerta de la Chiripa	784	374	41
El Puesto	2,639	1,380	159
La Punta (Los Azulitos)	3,869	2,048	319
San Cristobal	148	148	39
San Miguel de Cuarenta	1,782	1,782	58
Santa Inés o Jaritas	1,516	1,042	62
Soyate	174	48	12
El Tepetatillo (Tacubaya)	2,045	401	50
El Testerazo (Enrique Bancalari)	324	290	27
La Trinidad	498	195	60
La Troje	1,751	540	45
Total	44,168	19,824	2,461

Source: Dirección General de Estádistica, Secretaría de Industria y Comercio, *Directorio de Ejidos y Comunidades Agrarias*; *V Censo Ejidal, 1970.*

with more than the legal maximum acreage.[41] By law, each hacendado retained the main hacienda house and the surrounding grounds. If the hacienda had its own dam, water for irrigation had to be requested by the ejidatarios through a separate petitioning procedure. While the law specified procedures to indemnify owners whose lands were expropriated in the agrarian reform, there is no record that any of the affected hacendados in Lagos were ever compensated for their lands, even though they all filed the necessary petitions. In practice, the government seldom reimbursed owners for expropriated lands, and when they did it was primarily to foreign landowners.

Where possible, each ejido was granted some hectares of valuable irrigated land, some rainfall-dependent farming lands, and several hectares of grazing lands. (See Table 3 for a breakdown of ejido land in the municipio of Lagos by categories of soil quality.) In theory, therefore, each hacendado was deprived of some each of his best, mediocre, and least desirable lands. Although according to the law the ejidos should have been granted lands from among the best available in each category, in practice the hacendados were usually able to retain the lands of their choosing. A comparison of a current map of soil quality in the municipio of Lagos de Moreno with one of land tenure reveals that for the most part the ejidos are located on lands rated as arable only under special circumstances, or as grazing or forest lands.[42] The soil in most parts of the municipio is not very good for farming, but the high proportion of ejido lands in zones of lowest soil quality could not occur only by chance.

Other presidential decrees granting ejidos in the municipio followed rapidly in the later years of the Cárdenas administration. Petitions for original grants to ejido communities, or for expansion through a supplementary land grant (*ampliaciones*), were more quickly reviewed during the Cárdenas administration than during any other administration before or since. This is reflected in Appendix B, Table 3, which reports basic data from the presidential decrees granting ejidos in Lagos de Moreno from 1927 to 1943. For agrarian communities which first petitioned for land prior to the Cárdenas administration, the average length of time

[41]See Table 2 for the largest landholdings in Lagos which lost land in the agrarian reform.

[42]Maps on soil quality and land tenure in the municipio of Lagos de Moreno from Plan General Urbano de Lagos de Moreno, Junta Regional de Planeación y Urbanización del Estado de Jalisco, in Guadalajara.

between the initial petition and the presidential decree granting an ejido was 71.7 months; for those communities which first petitioned for land during Cárdenas' presidency, ejidos were granted, on the average, only 19.2 months after the initial petition.

Arming the Ejidatarios

Opposition to agrarianism did not vanish with the ejido land grants. However, the formalized status of the ejidos, the official sanction of the government, and the establishment of armed agrarista platoons made the agraristas feel more secure and forced the opposition to be generally more circumspect. From the government's standpoint, there were good reasons, both political and military, for arming the agraristas. There was ample precedent for the practice in San Luis Potosí, Tamaulipas, and Veracruz, particularly where brigades of agraristas had been formed to fight during the Cristero uprising. In addition, state power-brokers such as Adalberto Tejeda had employed this as a strategy to control opposition to the agrarian reform while building up their own loyal support groups. By providing arms to campesino communities, Lázaro Cárdenas enabled them to defend themselves against the white guards (Huizer, 1968–69: 127). He also sought to create a paramilitary counterforce which might dissuade the regular military from actively opposing his reforms and his efforts to assert his independence from General Calles (Cornelius, 1973: 457–458). Finally, until Cárdenas began to make his peace with the Catholic Church late in 1935, there continued to be tension and occasional outbreaks of violence between the authorities and supporters of the Church; thus agraristas continued to be used as a counterforce against Church militants.[43]

By September of 1935, the situation in Los Altos de Jalisco provided further impetus for arming the campesinos of that region. Small groups identified as Cristeros had mounted a series of attacks against the army and the agrarian communities. In Lagos, on September 2, 1935, the federal government established and armed groups of approximately 11 men in each interested ejido.[44] In return, the members of these agrarista

[43]As an example of the official sanction of this conflict, El Jaliscience of November 3, 1934, reported that Ing. Jacobo Lomelin, at the time a regional organizer of ejidos with the Agrarian Department, was forming an "agrarian anticlerical front" to combat clerical agitation against Article 3 of the Constitution and to "support the institutions of the fatherland." The report was based on an official circular from the Agrarian Department.

[44]On July 4, 1935, the delegate of the Agrarian Department in Lagos, Ing. David Manjarrez, wrote to the Commander of the Ninth Military Zone in Guadalajara, reporting that on a recent visit to Lagos de Moreno he encountered intense opposition from those per-

squads were expected to attend military drills and to be ready to assist the military authorities in confrontations or searches for Cristeros. The men who were armed warmly recalled that the weapons were small rifles which could easily be shouldered while working in the fields. They also remembered that they were warned that the weapons were for their own protection and should not be used in personal feuds or to extract revenge. After the establishment of the squads, they were no longer afraid and were seldom harassed, because they could defend themselves. But in a way the arms were a nuisance, because their farming was frequently interrupted by calls to form search parties against Cristeros.

Many of the first agraristas in Lagos associate their personal involvement in the armed agrarista-Cristero conflict with the battle of the Mesa Redonda on October 5–9, 1935. They recall that the military authorities in Lagos had received word that there were Cristeros[45] encamped on the Mesa Redonda, a prominent hilltop just outside the town of Lagos (see photo). The agrarista platoon was called up to supplement the regular federal troops. Most of the agraristas recount the story with some boredom or humor, for the three-day siege of the Mesa ended in a few hours of fire when the Cristeros attempted to escape. *Excélsior* reported on October 26–27, 1935, that 31 people died in the battle; but agraristas recall that there were only a few deaths, and that, despite an aerial bombardment by the federal forces, most of the Cristeros escaped.

The armed agrarista platoon came to an ignominious end when the growing use of arms in community feuds caused the government to repossess them from many communities and individuals. The disarmament occurred gradually, and coincided with the national retrenchment against land reform under President Manuel Ávila Camacho (1940–46).

Restructuring the Peasant Leagues

After 1935 there were still a few major political battles left for the "grupo revolucionario" in Lagos. One of these dealt with retaining some auton-

sons most likely to be affected by the implementation of an agrarian reform program: "They have been inciting and even supporting small armed groups which are dedicated to attacking the campesino group in need of lands." He explained that his own personnel—as well as the agraristas—needed more protection if they were to carry out the wishes for agrarian reform expressed by the President and other federal authorities, and proposed that rural defense groups of a specified number of armed campesinos (squads) be established in the following communities: San Jorge (22), Lagos (30), Cañada (15), Moya (15), El Maguey (10), Ciénega (15), Loma de Veloces (15), Puerta del Llano de Miranda (15), Las Cruces (15), Bernalejo (15), and Chupaderos (15). (Expediente ejidal, Lagos de Moreno, ASRA.)

[45]Followers of Pánfilo Limón, Lauro Rocha, and Martín Díaz.

The Mesa Redonda ("Roundtable Mesa"), site of a three-day siege in which armed agraristas and federal troops attacked a small group of Cristero rebels entrenched atop the mesa, near the town of Lagos de Moreno. This confrontation signaled the end of the worst of the armed struggle between Cristeros and agraristas in Los Altos de Jalisco.

omy for the state and regional peasant organizations. When Cárdenas began in 1935 to call for the establishment of a national peasant confederation (the CNC), an effort was made to simplify (and better control) campesino organizing through a series of state-level units with a network of lower-level affiliates. Romero recalled that he opposed this centralization of authority within the agrarian movement. He felt that the regional leagues should become affiliates of the national organization, while retaining their own autonomy. He reasoned that if the central authority were given the task of handling all of the ejido petitions for each state, everything would stagnate. He also feared that such a central organization could become the instrument of political opportunists who would dilute the revolutionary ideology which he felt should be represented by peasant unions such as the Liga Regional Campesina Macedonio Ayala. This latter concern is reflected in Romero's letter to companions in Lagos which he wrote from Victoria, Guanajuato, on July 27, 1936 (AJRG):

Naturally I think it is very necessary to intensify the task of reorganizing the Liga Regional, with all of its rights, since the prevailing mood in Jalisco is Fascism [sic]. Keeping faith with our [class] heritage, we must cast our lot with the Left. . . . We must choose our own battlefield, so as not to be at the mercy of compromises made by the pseudo-revolutionary politicians.

Despite resistance from men like Romero, a national pyramidal structure of peasant leagues was organized. In a letter dated November 7, 1936, and addressed to the president of the ejido council in San Jorge, the Delegate in the Agrarian Department in Lagos outlined this new structure. He explained that following an accord signed by President Cárdenas, the Liga de Comunidades Agrarias y Sindicatos Campesinos de Jalisco had been established in Guadalajara in February of that year. Because the purpose of the organization was to eliminate the regional peasant leagues, his letter was to inform all of the ejido councils that the Lagos branch of the state league would henceforth be known as the Comité Regional Agrario Macedonio Ayala ("in honor of the martyr of regional socialism"), and that all communications bearing any other affiliation or sponsorship would be ignored in Guadalajara and should not be heeded by the ejidos. Thus the local movement began to be forcibly integrated into a national network of peasant organizations controlled by the official party (the CNC became a sector of the restructured PNR, which was renamed the Partido de la Revolución Mexicana in 1938) and the President.

Romero continued to take an interest in the small group he left behind in Lagos, which he fondly referred to as the flock, "*la palomilla*," and his letters to them reflect that he sent money along with his advice whenever he could afford it. But he was correct; the time was approaching when the "pseudo-revolutionary politicians" would appear to claim the fruits of the reformist struggle. The efforts of the agraristas to secure an effective voice in local government were successful only from 1935 to 1939.[46] Even then, there was so much controversy that municipio presidents often changed between elections.

---

[46]Regrettably, there is little written record of these years. There are no copies available of local newspapers printed during the 1930s (if they existed), and all of the books containing the minutes of local government meetings are missing from the municipio archives. I was able to examine one of these books, covering 1936–1938, that is in private hands.

The Agraristas in Local Office

Because of the pro-agrarian national and state governments in the 1934–
40 period, the agraristas were relatively favored by the selection of pro-
agrarian municipio presidents. Nonetheless, even this advantage was
countered by local interests. A brief chronicle of the municipio presidents in the late 1930s reveals the pulling and hauling among competing
interests. More important, these conflicts led to the demise of effective
agrarista participation in local politics.

When Ayala was killed, the wealthy men in town consented to support
Ing. Jacobo Lomelín as municipio president. They did so on advice from
one of his relatives in Lagos who was a politically active small landholder
and former municipio president. However, once in office, Lomelín sur-
prised them. He was the same individual (mentioned in note 43) who
organized a state-level "agrarian anticlerical front" in November 1934.
Francisco Navia recalled that Lomelín subsequently encountered stiff
opposition from the local oligarchy, particularly because of his reaction
to the death of another agrarian community organizer, Jesús Márquez,
who was killed in 1935.

Jesús Márquez had been leading the effort to secure land for an ejido
in Comanja de Corona.[47] When Jacobo Lomelín heard about Márquez'
death, he questioned the two individuals arrested for the murder, and,
according to Navia, they finally admitted that they had been paid by two
landowners whose lands would potentially have been affected by the
ejido. Lomelín had the two hacendados arrested and jailed, arousing the
ire of other landholders, who protested to the Governor.[48] Lomelín was
removed from office.

[47]Comanja is located in the mountains, quite isolated from other localities in the municipio, near the boundary between two of its largest haciendas, La Sauceda and San
Bernardo. The town of Comanja reached its apogee in the nineteenth century, before the
exhaustion of nearby gold and silver mines, a local foundry, and a pottery industry. The
town suffered heavy population losses during the 1910 Revolution and Cristero rebellions,
when its location made it an easy target for rebel groups hiding in the vicinity. Distrusting
and hostile to outsiders, most of the town's residents were owners of very small properties, or self-employed in small-scale trade or charcoal and lime manufacture. As a result,
agrarian organizers found it difficult to recruit supporters there, and it took many years
even after the ejido lands were granted before all of the land was farmed by ejidatarios. To
this day, the ejidatarios of Comanja de Corona do not live in the town, but scattered among
the surrounding hills near their plots of land.

[48]Documentation in the expediente ejidal for Lagos de Moreno (ASRA) shows that a
series of telegrams was exchanged between the Zone Chief of the Agrarian Department,
Ing. Aguilar Gómez, and his superiors in Mexico City in late March 1935, while Jacobo

Lomelín was succeeded by two other pro-agrarista municipio presidents—Carlos Ramos Cuervo and Manuel Camarena—who were sent from Guadalajara and whose tenure was also short-lived. At the time, however, the agraristas had the support of the federal and state legislative representatives for the region,[49] so relatively "liberal" candidates continued to be appointed to head the local government. In 1936, the agraristas succeeded in having Francisco Carrera nominated as municipio president—a friend, though not really an agrarista.[50] The municipio government council that served with Carrera was also composed of men who had been active in varying degrees in the group of agraristas or in the SOV.[51]

For the agraristas and labor union activists, the years 1935 through 1938 provided a brief respite from persecution by local authorities. During those years, more than at any other time in the history of Lagos de Moreno, they *were* the local authorities—serving with friends or supporters in the municipio presidency and as members of the ayuntamiento and employees of the local government. Many of the agraristas report receiving financial assistance from Francisco Carrera while he was municipio president. The reported aid was small—such as occasional purchases of a load of firewood or help in buying medicine for an illness—but an important contribution to individual families in times of stress, and an unprecedented expression of interest from a local government official in the personal welfare of the poor. Even more important, the weight of the police and judicial system was tilted in their favor, and the political system seemed both accessible and interested in their welfare.

Lomelín was municipio president. The telegrams report various threats against Lomelín because of the protection he had given the agraristas. One reads in part: "Zone headquarters [under] my charge fears abuses by hacendados and clergy unified against the municipio president, who gives us protection, since I have learned they plan to assassinate him. The agraristas beg you through me to contact relevant authorities in order to prevent these reactionary elements from obstructing the work I am charged with."

[49]These supporters included Manuel Martínez Valadez, until he was killed in 1935; his successor, Francisco Álvarez (who had been municipio president in Lagos in 1918); and Flavio Ramírez.

[50]Carrera had been an administrator on several haciendas, posts which may have made him appear less threatening as a candidate (under the prevailing national political circumstances) to the Lagos oligarchy. Carrera's son, a physician who practices in Lagos, reported that his father had also been employed "by the government" in San Luis Potosí while Saturnino Cedillo was Governor of that state.

[51]Salvador Martínez, Urbano Esparza, Elías Prado, and José María Romo.

THE PRESIDENT CALLS

The visit of President Cárdenas to Lagos de Moreno on August 4, 1936, was evidence of these political gains and capped the political and economic victory of the land grants. Accounts vary as to the reason for the President's visit; no one knew for sure why or how he decided to stop there. The agraristas recalled that they received short notice of his coming, but that as many communities as possible sent representatives to welcome the President. The large landholders did not appear for his visit. The group of reformists met Cárdenas at the train station and walked back with him to the municipio government building. His entourage included Silvano Barba González, Minister of the Interior, and Gabino Vázquez, head of the Agrarian Department, as well as several deputies and high-ranking military officers.

No one could recall specifically what the President told his hosts, only that he listened to their descriptions of their problems and needs, and that his concern extended to individual problems. The first agraristas recalled discussing with the President which of the haciendas in Lagos had not yet been affected by land reform and which others still had a great deal of land. They also remembered that Cárdenas resolved a dispute over money between two individuals, when one of the men appealed to the President for assistance.

Community petitions for schools and assistance in solving boundary disputes were also heard and recorded. Municipal officials presented a memorandum which contained the following requests: to build a dam for irrigation, proposed since the turn of the century; to build a road connecting Lagos de Moreno with the town of Ojuelos, to the north; to repair the bridge in Lagos; and to provide a few items for the operating room at the public hospital (August 4, 1936, *Libros de Actas*).[52]

President Cárdenas had ordered that an office of the Agrarian Department with the status of *delegación* be established in Lagos de Moreno to handle the basic studies and petitions for agrarian reform in Los Altos. This is an indication of the importance accorded agrarian reform in the region, for at that time delegación offices were located only in state

[52]For an account of another trip by President Cárdenas to a Los Altos community, see Weyl and Weyl (1939: 3–10). They explain the importance of these journeys: "Cárdenas does not conceive of the process of governing as the issuing of decrees from Mexico City.... Distrustful of others, he prefers to cut through the red tape of bureaucratic procedure and make all the decisions himself. He goes personally, whenever possible, to inspect the dams and schools that are in process of construction.... [These tours] serve to break down the barriers of class and language that separate the common people from their rulers."

capitals. Cárdenas designated a large two-story building near the center of town to serve as the House of the Campesino ("*Casa del Campesino*"). The delegación office would be housed there, as would the local office of the state Liga de Comunidades Agrarias y Sindicatos Campesinos.[53] Agraristas might stay there overnight if their business required; they could congregate there freely without fear. It is not clear whether the delegación was already established, or whether it was dedicated during the Cárdenas visit.[54] A simple, hand-lettered cement block in the floor of the patio of the building commemorates the visit. It reads: "The President of the Republic, General Lázaro Cárdenas, honored this house with his presence on August 4, 1936."

ROMERO RETURNS

From 1933 to late 1937, José Romero had been with the state league in Guadalajara, and later served as municipio president in two communities in the adjoining state of Guanajuato. When the next round of elections approached, Romero sought nomination as the federal legislative representative for the district containing Lagos. Finding that the post had already been promised to someone else, he reluctantly accepted nomination as alternate representative (*diputado suplente*), and municipio president of Lagos de Moreno. (The circumstances under which Romero had to leave Jalisco, and how he later campaigned and won elective office, are described in detail in Chapter 5.)

On January 10, 1938, José Romero was sworn in as municipio president in Lagos de Moreno. In Romero's own words, he was seeking "power in the hands of the workers, . . . a complete transformation of my home town." To that end, he appointed men he could trust to leadership positions in the regional peasant league and the local SOV. On March 23 of that year, demonstrations and a general work stoppage were held throughout the Republic to support Cárdenas' expropriation of foreign-owned oil enterprises (Paez Brotchie, 1940: 184). The "grupo revolucionario" was still sufficiently well organized to turn out a large contingent of workers and agraristas for the demonstration in Lagos.

---

[53]Sometime in the 1940s, the delegación status of the office was changed. It is now a regional office, subordinate—not equal—to the Guadalajara office of the Agrarian Reform Ministry. The Casa del Campesino has been reduced to a single room in the building, still occupied by local representatives of the state league and the Agrarian Reform Ministry. The rest of the building is used as a private school.

[54]The earliest correspondence signed by the delegate in Lagos that I have seen is dated October 5, 1936.

Romero's term in the municipio presidency was cut short by a "mini-coup" in which a majority of the members of the ayuntamiento voted to remove him from office. One agrarista attributed the move to Romero's incautious behavior: for example, when Romero called the local land-holders "shameless rich men" at a campaign rally, "Well, he brought the fire upon himself." Romero claimed that the federal deputy engineered his ouster. He contended that in repayment for his position as municipio president, he was asked to pay the deputy and another man out of the public treasury. When Romero refused, a plot was organized to remove him from office.[55] With the support of Margarito Ramírez and the labor unions and agrarian communities in Lagos, Romero went on to become federal legislative deputy for the Lagos district (see Chapter 5).

The Demise of Local Agrarian Power

The beginning of the end of political power for the agrarian and labor reformists in Lagos dates from Romero's expulsion from the municipio presidency and his subsequent withdrawal to Mexico City. By the end of the Cárdenas administration in 1940, the unified agrarian and labor-union movements in Lagos de Moreno had essentially dissolved. Several circumstances contributed to their demise. With the grants of land, the major unifying force was removed. Men whose lives had been consumed by the struggle to achieve economic independence from the hacendados grappled with the burden that their new freedom implied. The agrar-istas had acquired the land they sought, and for most there was no local incentive (nor any state or federal encouragement) to maintain a unified organization. Community leaders no longer gathered together in Lagos de Moreno to discuss each other's plight; each ejido community was involved in its own internal governance problems. The more charismatic

[55]The only documentation of the event is contained in the municipio government minutes in the *Libro de Actas*, in which it was recorded that on August 24, 1938, the government council met in a "special session," from which José Romero was absent. Councilman Aureliano Navarro read a statement allegedly from Romero "in which he asks to be given unlimited leave from his post in charge of the municipio presidency and the ayuntamiento." The ayuntamiento agreed to the leave of absence, and Navarro be-came municipio president. Across this account in the Libro de Actas, José Romero had written that it was not true that he asked for a leave of absence, nor that he resigned: "It is just a wretched maneuver by the discontented councilmen because I did not let them meddle and traffic in the people's money." Other agraristas agreed that the ouster must have been accomplished with the federal deputy's consent, because he never used his power to reinstate Romero (as he might have, had he chosen to do so). They also agreed that the underlying motive was Romero's unwillingness to pay money requested from him.

of the agrarista and labor leaders had either been killed or left Lagos de Moreno, leaving behind men whose concerns were focused on individual (rather than collective) needs. Moreover, after Lázaro Cárdenas, the national political environment was much less supportive of agrarian activism. In fact, Cárdenas' successor, President Manuel Ávila Camacho, strengthened the associations of private landowners (*pequeños propietarios*) which sought to reverse some of the advances of agrarismo under Cárdenas.

Although for a time men of relatively humble extraction led the local government, they do not appear to have used the office to further social or political reforms. Quite the contrary; one of them disbanded the local trade unions[56] and often jailed members of the group of reformists on charges that they were a "tribe of bandits, . . . simple robbers, . . . and scoundrels." In the face of general public hostility and lack of progress in advancing the reformists' cause, Francisco Navia withdrew to the state of Zacatecas in 1943 to continue his work with agrarian communities there (see Chapter 6).

By the late 1940s, the chief executives of the local government were once again members of Lagos' landowning or professional classes. By local custom, two of the six seats on the ayuntamiento have been reserved for representatives of the campesinos, reflecting the official party's reliance on the ejidatarios for electoral support. The agraristas contend that as far as the local power structure is concerned, the same men and their families whom they fought as Cristeros later became supporters of the reactionary Catholic Sinarquista movement in the 1940s and of the conservative Partido de Acción Nacional (PAN) today. While the PAN's candidates for public office do not prevail over those of the official party in Lagos (at least in the official vote tallies), it is well known that many pillars of the local establishment are PAN supporters. One seasoned observer of local politics commented wryly that the PAN is now the fourth sector of the PRI in Lagos. Clearly, the local reform movement has never been as strong—or as radical—as it was in the days when the agraristas held power. Since that time, the municipio has been dominated by conservative elements with an urban bias.

[56]On May 1 of either 1938 or 1939, separate trade unions for barbers, butchers, drivers, porters, tailors, shoeshiners, and millers were established in Lagos.

5

José Romero Gómez:
"The Eternal Rebel"

This chapter presents the political life-history of José Romero Gómez, the master carpenter who became one of the principal leaders of the agrarian and labor reform movement in Lagos de Moreno. As a local leader whose political activism extended beyond the municipio, José Romero's political ideology and experiences are not typical of the surviving ejido petitioners in Lagos. He may have resembled more closely the two other early local leaders, Macedonio Ayala and Aniceto Martínez, whose early deaths have left us to wonder what they might have become. Romero was both privileged and damned in this respect: his survival gave him the opportunity to try to implement his ideals, and to record the struggle as he remembered it; but it also gave him more time to err and to face the judgment of contemporaries. By their deaths, the other two leaders were spared these tests of time.

Romero's story is important because of the differences between himself and the men with whom he joined, but also because of what he had in common with them. Like the others, he professed an independent spirit, a determined desire to be his own master (especially in his work), and a resistance to Church counsel on social issues. In fact, all of the men who were interviewed rejected the authority of the clergy to dictate the morality of agrarian reform. Some came to vaguely question Church theology as well, but generally their posture was more anticlerical than anti-Catholic.[1] Romero was almost defiant in his independence, extending his

[1]This anticlericalism can be partially traced to the strident anticlerical rhetoric of national politicians and leaders of labor and peasant unions during the 1920s and 1930s. However, as we have seen in Chapters 3 and 4, the anticlericalism of most of the agraristas

assertiveness to head-on confrontations with political superiors. Even if his recounted conversations with such persons are not totally faithful to the historical record (they may be exaggerated, but seem to be generally accurate), descriptions of him by former companions, documentary evidence in his personal archives, and photographs of him during the critical years portray a man of combative spirit.

This contentious independence was one reason why he was not politically successful within the Mexican party-government structure. He seems never to have adopted the "smoothness" such success required. Several times during my interviews with him, Romero described confrontations between himself and political superiors to illustrate his independent political activism. He analyzed the consequences of his behavior as follows:

> I was extremely radical, a complete radical. You know, Margarito Ramírez called me "the eternal rebel," because I was always in rebellion. I didn't have a political career because of this, because I never went around brushing off anyone's shoulders. I would arrive, and whatever their rank, I would speak clearly and forcefully. I wouldn't do any ass-licking or anything. I'd state my business and wasn't servile to anyone. . . . What need did I have to go around bowing and scraping for a job? It would have been enslaving myself, seeing as I was so free. So I never had a job I got through influences, because I always knew that I did know how to work [as a carpenter].

By all accounts, Macedonio Ayala had a different personal style, a manner which endeared him to politicians, while at the same time he expressed the ideals and compassion which made campesinos trust him. Romero's experience illustrates how the political advancement of local leaders in Mexico can be blocked when they refuse to play politics by the traditional rules of the game.

Many of the surviving community leaders of Lagos' agrarian reform were articulate men with a flair for words and dramatic recall. This may be a facility they developed as local spokesmen in the early years of agrarian struggle, or an ability cultivated over a lifetime, or it may be part of a set of characteristics which set them apart from other campesinos in their villages and was thus a factor in their selection as commu-

---

in Lagos stemmed primarily from personal involvement in conflicts between agraristas and the federal government, on the one hand, and priests, the landed aristocracy, and Cristero rebels, on the other.

nity leaders. Whatever the reason, among these survivors were a few whose recall of dates and sequences of events was more precise than Romero's. Some of the others matched Romero's gift for stage-setting and detail. But none of the other men interviewed conveyed the same ideological quest and conviction—nor, with two exceptions, did they trace their inspiration to the printed word.

Most of the surviving agraristas spoke of their hopes for *"tierra y libertad,"* for land reform and the freedom not to have to work for others, for higher wages for laborers, or for the right to have their voices heard effectively in government. Romero's goals were much more socially and politically radical, far more elaborated, and with a vision that extended beyond Lagos and the individualistic benefits of reform.[2] Many in the generation of reformers said that Romero shared this vision of extensive change with Martínez and Ayala. They claimed, convincingly, that Martínez came to his ideas by instinct, and Romero by self-education, but that Ayala was *"más preparado"* (had more formal schooling).

Romero was never a tiller of the soil; neither were the other two leaders. Nor did any of them aspire to become ejidatarios. Romero's participation began in the labor movement and May Day celebrations. For him, agrarian reform became the logical extension of the goal of freedom and justice for workers, and a vehicle for building additional support for his cause: *"el poder en manos de los trabajadores"* ("[political] power in the hands of the workers"). This urban craftsman or laborer's background was a characteristic Romero had in common with other survivors of the early local trade union, but it is something which distinguished him from the other agraristas.

On three other points, Romero's life diverged from the lives of most agraristas: he received some formal schooling (others taught themselves to read and write); he never went to the United States, nor had he worked outside of Lagos de Moreno before joining the reform movement; and he achieved higher elective office, had wider political contacts, and acquired more detailed political knowledge than the remainder of his companions.

Romero's political life-history is told here largely in his own words. It has been chronologically and thematically reorganized from nearly eight hours of taped interviews, edited to delete redundancies and interviewer questions. These interviews have been supplemented where

[2]This judgment is supported by interviews with other agraristas, all of whom agreed that if they personally (or the bulk of the reformists) were not completely radical, José Romero—"now *he* really *was* a revolutionary."

noted by documents from Romero's own archives, as well as information from interviews with other informants and other document collections. In the translation I have tried to duplicate the style and emphasis of the original Spanish, using colloquial or formal expressions to parallel the speaker's words. The eloquence is Romero's own, not an artifact of the translation.

José Romero was candid in response to probing questions, proud of his accomplishments and still committed to the ideals of his youth. If at times he claimed too much personal credit for the movement's direction, these are only occasional slips; he was usually careful to credit his collaborators (for he saw them in those terms), and urged me to be certain to mention everyone else who also contributed to the local movement.

At the time of the interviews, Romero lived with his youngest son and his family in a sparsely furnished three-room cement-block house on an unpaved street in Ciudad Netzahualcóyotl, one of the poorest sections of Mexico City. He spent most of his time in bed, or dressed in a green cap and khaki bathrobe, sitting on the bed playing with his grandchildren. He was tired, annoyed by the infirmities of age, and frustrated by the inconvenience his continued life posed for himself and his children.

In his late eighties, Romero was a small, stooped man, slightly less than five feet tall, whose fading eyesight denied him the pleasure of writing to friends and reading the books which lined two small wall-shelves in his house. He had long, thick, curly white hair and a full white beard. His torso reflected the hard physical labor of his youth. He moved slowly, and at rest one could tell that he was indeed tired and aging. Yet, when he began to talk about the past, about his ideas and his struggles, his memory and mind were sharp, his voice strong and clear, and the words tripped across each other—racing—as he transported himself and his audience to another time.

Child to Man: Learning a Trade and Independence

Sometime between 1891 and 1893, young, unmarried Luciana Romero left Lagos de Moreno for León, Guanajuato, where she gave birth to her son José Romero. His paternal grandfather, a Señor Gómez, was manager of an hacienda of moderate size located between Lagos and San Juan de los Lagos. "Because of that, my father lived a carouser's life. He got together with my mother, and I came along."

Romero was raised by his mother and her family, in a completely devout religious environment. "My mother, poor thing, knew nothing

José Romero Gómez, photographed in his son's house in the Ciudad Netzahualcóyotl section of Mexico City, in 1976. He was using the bent construction rod in his hand as a cane.

else. I was not aware of what I was. I was an acolyte, with sons of another family." Until 1905 he attended Mariano Pérez' school[3] in Lagos, where he learned to read and to do basic arithmetic. He could not afford to

[3]The Colegio Particular Guadalupano of Mariano Pérez Oropeza. Romero completed the primary schooling of the time, probably three years.

continue his schooling at the Liceo del Padre Guerra, even though the classes were free, because "I had to go to work to earn my expenses." When he finished school, a priest friend and counselor of his mother's asked "that I be given to him so he could take me to Guadalajara to study the priesthood." Having been raised in that environment, Romero "of course" wished to go with the priest.

"At that time in the family there was an uncle of my mother's whose name was Andrés. Having been a Juarista, a soldier in Juárez' time of the Reform,[4] he had his ideas. Because of that he was a liberal of the time. Not like now. Then it meant to think freely, and to act freely, without subjection to the advice of the clergy, who ran everything. He was a stonecutter; he worked in *cantera*,[5] and he traveled from Lagos to León, to Guanajuato, wherever there was cantera construction. That's why he was in Lagos. My mother told him that I had finished school and that the priest had asked 'to take him to Guadalajara so that he can study to be a priest.' And just like this he answered: 'How cute! That priest will take him and who knows what he will do with him! He should learn to work, to take advantage of his schooling and of what he knows. He should learn to have an independent life.' My mother repented, and did not send me with the priest, because in those days uncles had a lot of influence and were respected by their nephews and nieces, and because she didn't know about anything—didn't even begin to have an idea. She was an uneducated person—she could barely read and write.

" 'Put him to work,' he told my mother, and she said, 'I'll let him become a store clerk.' He said, 'A fine thing he will become! The same slavery. No, he should learn to be a free man. Have him learn a trade.' And her uncle went away and the matter was left like that. My mother told me, 'Uncle Andrés says I should put you to work at a trade,' and I told her 'Carpentry.' " Romero chose carpentry because on his way home

---

[4]The period of the Reform lasted roughly from 1855 to 1876. Benito Juárez served as President of Mexico during part of this time; the Constitution of 1857 was promulgated during his term of office. Juárez' name and the Reform are associated with many liberalizing policies, including limitations on special rights (*fueros*) of the Church, the military, and groups legally identified as corporations. Nineteenth-century liberals were anticlerical: they denied the Church and its corporations (including religious orders) the right to own property, restricted the civil rights of priests, and limited the jurisdiction of Church courts to ecclesiastical issues (see Bazant, 1977: 62–94; and Brandenburg, 1964: 188–189, 351–353).

[5]*Cantera* is a stone widely used in Jalisco and Guanajuato for construction and architectural ornamentation. Cutting and sculpting of this stone require fine workmanship, so Romero's uncle would have been a skilled craftsman.

from school he used to pass a carpentry shop, stopping for hours to watch the men work. "Surely, that had some influence on me."

After a false start as an apprentice in a wheelwright's shop, where the work was difficult and he was treated harshly, Romero moved to a shop where he studied carpentry and cabinet-making under another uncle, a master carpenter also named Andrés. Romero learned his lessons well, taking a craftsman's pride in wood-finishing as well as in special skills such as making spare piano parts. "I ended up [also] in piano repair, a skill I know completely, everything, including varnishing the piano by hand. They would end up looking like mirrors, and there were no little machines then [to do the work] like there are now!"

Romero was still an apprentice when the Revolution of 1910 began. The first two years of the armed conflict had little influence on his life. In the following years of civil unrest, however, Romero's life changed significantly, although not as a result of the Revolution. Romero recalls that Lagos suffered through a typhoid epidemic in 1912,[6] in which the master carpenter died. "The shop was left headless, the widow couldn't manage it, and we were left without work. I left, well-known as a good carpenter and varnisher, and started to work in shops. Some said, 'José Romero only does fine work,' and I went to make coffins!"

During the years of civil and political turmoil which followed, Romero remained in Lagos, picking up odd carpentry and varnishing jobs. Later, the manager of the local electric plant invited Romero to become master carpenter at the plant, offering to pay him a peso and a half per day in "valid" currency (gold).

About 1922, Romero opened his own carpentry shop. During these years when unrest and economic disruptions produced heavy out-migration from Lagos to other towns and to the United States, Romero never left. "I never wanted to go anywhere. I worked, I had my future assured. The shop gave me good returns. As I say, I was very competent. In Lagos, there was a time when I was the one who made the furniture for the young people who were married there. I made everything, everything for the house. I had commitments for at least three pieces of furniture, in addition to occasional individual pieces they'd ask me to make. . . . I never had the urge to travel. I was independent, a master carpenter, and all."

        [6]He may have meant 1911, when such an epidemic could easily have been caused by a severe flood. Other respondents reported a typhus epidemic in 1916–17.

Ideological Growth

It was during his apprenticeship in his uncle's shop that Romero was first exposed to radical ideas and anticlerical literature, beginning his ideological awakening and laying the foundation for his later struggle for labor reform. Throughout his adolescence and young manhood, he sought out diverse ideas which had in common only the fact that they contrasted sharply with prevailing social thought in Lagos. This willingness to challenge local doctrine led enemies of the reform movement to brand him a communist.

Even today, "communist" is a label freely applied in the Los Altos region to individuals who espouse unorthodox views (by community standards), who ask strange questions, or who are inclined to question the authority of the Church and its ministers. Locally, the agraristas were often accused of being communists, partly because they sought agrarian "communities," but largely because they questioned or rejected the authority of Catholic priests, particularly when the priests preached against land reform.[7]

Did Romero consider himself a communist? "I was a communist. I still am. Only, not with the communism we began with. You know, every beginning has its errors. In communism, there were errors which to date have neither been remedied nor overcome. We were Leninist communists, because we, I, am a communist following upon the communist movement in Russia. Initially I steeped myself in the libertarian ideas of Ricardo Flores Magón. I was one of the major *Floresmagonistas* of that area.[8] I must have been about 11 years old, still hadn't passed my 12th year, when I began to read *Regeneración*[9] of Ricardo Flores Magón, because the master carpenter where I was learning the trade received *Regeneración*. He was a Floresmagonista, not committed, not what we could call ideologically [committed], not openly. In that town of Lagos de Moreno, who could be open and aboveboard? After all, it was a com-

---

[7]See Chapter 3, section on "Bitter Enemies: 'El Clero and 'El Capital.' "

[8]This transformation from Floresmagonista into communist or agrarian activist has been found elsewhere in Mexico during the same time period. See, for example, Friedrich (1970: 64–67).

[9]A newspaper published intermittently between 1900 and 1918, mainly in the United States, by Enrique and Ricardo Flores Magón. The Flores Magón brothers, who helped to organize the Mexican Liberal Party in 1906, advocated radical programs of economic and social reform, and anticlericalism. They were heavily influenced by the Spanish anarcho-syndicalists (see Bartra, 1977; Gómez-Quiñones, 1980).

pletely monastic town. Why, even the liberals who appeared at the time were seen as heretics, and they were liberals, just liberals, who were no danger to society! I was influenced by many of them. There was a group of liberals headed by Dr. Agustín Rivera y Sanromán and Ausencio López Arce, a poet who started *El Defensor del Pueblo*, a newspaper of more-or-less liberal ideals of the time. I was influenced by them—still a kid, except that I liked to read.

"My master received the Flores Magón newspaper, *Regeneración*. In those days they distributed the poison [the newspaper] in little rolls, almost clandestinely. . . . But I, curious as always about books, would go and look for that newspaper. The master wouldn't read it, and I would. He'd leave the newspapers laying around, and I'd go read them. But by then my interest was instinctive, and it seems that I absorbed what I read by the Flores Magóns, so clear, so concise, so radical. So, that's how I began to get the idea of the freedom of the workers, to seek the freedom of the workers. Of course, from [the paper] came the news about the Chicago martyrs. All of that influenced me to continue the struggle. That's why I was prepared. Later, [in the 1920s] there was a newspaper in Tampico, published by Librado Ribera, called *Sagitario*,[10] and it was a paper of completely open ideas, entirely anticlerical and socialist ideas. So, with all of that correspondence, and all of my reading, I developed a more independent spirit—aside from the fact that I think I was born with a more independent spirit. Because I didn't like to be controlled by anyone or anything.

"Look, I made the organization of reformists a completely radical movement, which was my orientation ever since I came to know the Flores Magóns—that is, their literature, which regularly reached me. That's how I developed the idea of an organization that would be entirely anticlerical, in those days. Anticlerical because, well, because there was no other solution, because the clergy was the major opposition. The clergy, during these struggles, right from the pulpit would accuse So-and-So and Such-and-Such of being enemies of God—really laying it on, as they say."

Romero began to express publicly some of his ideas in support of the rights of workers, as early as 1925. These ideas are reflected in a speech

[10]*Sagitario* was published between 1922 and 1927 in Tampico, Veracruz. It was founded by Librado Rivera, an old Flores Magón supporter. See *Regeneración (tercera etapa)*, nos. 56–27 (1961), 67–68 (1962), and 88 (1965).

he delivered in the Rosas Moreno Theatre on May Day of that year,[11] a handwritten copy of which is preserved in Romero's archives. It reads as follows:

Compañeros, I come not with florid language, nor with elegant phrases, to address you, my brothers in oppression, my companions in the struggle for the vindication of the worker; I come only in these moments with the dictates of my heart and faith in the ideal to render sincere homage to the most noble and largest of sacrifices. Why are we here? Why have we come to this hall, neither in jubilation nor to clap our hands with glee, but with our hearts banded by sorrow? We come to commemorate a day of mourning and of glory in the annals of the universal proletariat. Thirty-nine years ago today, May 1, 1925, the first martyrs of liberty, those who opened the glorious epic [sic] that would make the capitalist bourgeoisie of the world tremble, fell, cut down by the bullets of Yankee-land in the city of Chicago.

We recall that tragedy today, not as a vain memory nor in a spirit of impotent resignation, but rather as a day which marks a necessary stage on the ascending path of workers' vindication, on which one looks back to contemplate the road traversed, where shreds of the people's soul—the blood, flesh, and heritage of poverty—have been left behind. That began the gigantic struggle which has cost so many tears and heroic sacrifices. For us, the irredentists, the pariahs, who hunger and thirst for justice, the blood of our brothers spilled in Chicago has nourished fighters and martyrs; and each day we see that the struggle grows, gets larger in the whole world. The assassins who thought they were killing the idea in order to continue at their leisure the exploitation of the oppressed, to replenish their coffers with gold while the laborer grew old at the foot of the machines in the factories and shops—leaving his wife and children in the most frightful misery—they saw with fear that quite to the contrary, the blood that was spilled became wisdom that fertilized the idea. The workers of the world stubbornly threw themselves into the struggle with greater tenacity. Unions and re-

---

[11]Such a radical speech was possible, despite intense local conservatism and opposition to worker organizations, because the state and local governments then in office were supportive of labor organizations. José Guadalupe Zuno was Governor of Jalisco (1923–26), and in 1925 Susano Castañeda was municipio president in Lagos. During both men's tenure, six of the seven earliest petitions for land reform in the municipio of Lagos de Moreno were submitted to the state government, and the local labor union (the Unión de Obreros Libertarios) applied for official recognition.

sistance leagues were formed, governments were pressured and recognized the right to strike, and the eight-hour day became a fact in the whole country to the north [the United States]. Later here in Mexico the proletarian struggle began, a terrible struggle that has required gigantic efforts to secure rights. And here, too, there have been martyrs, but there also are fighters who do not retreat, and the struggle continues. It will continue until a complete victory is achieved for our social and economic well-being, until the capital is divided among the productive forces, the workers.

There you have the reason why we have dedicated this day to the commemoration of the first martyrs of that beautiful idea. Workers of the world, united in this moment in fraternal embrace by means of a single sentiment. We protest such an abominable crime before the oppressor bourgeoisie; and you martyrs who, from infinity, now contemplate the fruit of your sacrifice, see how your brethren the oppressed have come to your aid in the struggle. And I, along with all of the oppressed of the world, pay homage to you with these mournful, plebeian thoughts and in my sad memories.

Romero's May Day speech delivered the following year dwelled entirely on world history, tracing the development of slavery, capitalism, and the resistance to oppression from the cave-men through Spartacus to Rome and Europe. The speech concluded: "Workers, in the name of all the Anarchists of the world, of whose ideals I am the bearer, I greet you on this day dedicated to work."

Both speeches reflect the influence of Romero's reading of *Regeneración*. By the time they were written, he may also have been exposed to the Communist Party's *El Machete*, to *Espártaco* (the railroad workers' union paper), and to *Sagitario*.[12] As early as 1923, he had expressed to a friend from Lagos his desire to see other radical publications. In a letter to Romero from Mexico City dated June 24, 1924, Pedro Moreno Mitre indicates that during the previous year and a half he had been sending the "propaganda" Romero had requested. This may have included some of the publications just mentioned or other literature which influenced Romero's ideological formation.

Always open to new ideas, Romero turned eagerly to opportunities to formulate and test alternatives critical of the status quo. By the mid-1920s, his radical reputation (within a small circle), his political

---

[12]He referred to all of these publications by name, but could not recall when he first read them. All of these newspapers would have reinforced the ideas expressed in Romero's speeches.

contacts, and his contacts with the electric plant manager opened up a peculiar new alternative: Freemasonry.

"I was even a Freemason in Lagos. There were about 16 of us. There were Masons of conviction and Masons of convenience. . . . All of the politicians [in Lagos] who had ambitions sided with Susano Castañeda. So Castañeda—I don't know at whose suggestion—set himself to making a revolutionary movement in Lagos, and organized the so-called Masonry.[13]

"I familiarized myself with the Masonic movement, partly just to learn about it. That's why I joined the Masons. . . . But there was no place for the revolutionary movement in Masonry, because the Masons were made up of people who didn't yet have completely revolutionary ideas. They were just Masonic ideas . . . there were no ideas to nourish the workers, nor any movement to help them. One night they even told us that we'd have to deny the workers the help they asked for, because Masons couldn't help a labor movement because it was a radical movement. So I, who was a radical, began to see Masonry not as an instrument to continue the revolutionary movement, but just as a refuge for chatting and all. . . . Inside of myself, I didn't commune with the Masonic ideas, because I was an enemy of what they said—useless things, like that business of initiating one blindfolded, and things which just didn't set with me. So, I began to distance myself, and then later Castañeda left, and everything fell apart. By the time I left for Guadalajara [in 1933], the Masonic Temple was no longer in use."

At about the same time, late in the 1920s, Romero met Bernardo L. de los Ríos, who was an instructor with the army regiment in Lagos. "De los Ríos was a theosophist. He inculcated in me many ideas of theosophy, very attractive ideas. He was very outstanding, well-versed in theosophy, and he gave me many lessons in it and taught me many things which, speaking honestly, I later found were of no use to me in the movement I took part in."

During this period of ideological exploration, Romero also tried his hand at poetry, including among his ambitions the publication of a book

---

[13]Jean Meyer (1976: 27–28) contends that Governor Zuno propagated Freemasonry in Jalisco through municipio presidents and teachers. See Brandenburg (1964: 191–204) for the most extensive discussion of the checkered history of Freemasonry in Mexico and the involvement of Masons in national politics. In Mexico, Masons have been regarded as anticlerical (see also J. Meyer, 1976: 25–30). With the Constitution of 1917, and the enforcement under President Calles of constitutional limitations on the Church and its priests, individuals with political ambitions probably became involved in Masonry as an expression of support for the government's policies toward the Church.

of his own verses. At that time there were various poets in Lagos, and Romero knew many of them. Were they also supporters of his fight for change? "No, in truth, they weren't. But I settled for their friendship to enlighten myself, to make myself more at home in the arts. There were even times when Robles, Pepe Becerra, and others would gather at my shop and we constituted what we called the Cenáculo, since everyone recited. I would even throw in my two cents. But I picked up something of their lexicon, of their language. It was useful to me for cultural growth, and they would gather in my shop because they were comfortable there, no one bothered them; each one brought his bottle, and so would I. I wasn't always an angel, but I never let myself go. . . . I never lost control or consciousness. But I did drink a lot."

By all accounts Romero read voraciously and eclectically. His conversation was sprinkled with references to plays he had read or seen produced in the Rosas Moreno Theatre in Lagos, and to books, including those of Ricardo Flores Magón and Emile Zola. Even though he could not complete his schooling, "I read the French classics, the Spanish classics, . . . I read them all, I understood the idea of them all. But not because I studied them at the University, no. Just for the pure love I had of reading, that's why. I would take advantage of Sundays to spend the whole day reading. I'd leave my house—at the time I lived in La Otra Banda [one of Lagos' poorest neighborhoods]—to go to a tree-lined avenue. I'd sit in the shade of a tree, and spend the whole day devouring the books that reached my hands.[14] When I learned the trade, when I began to work, I bought as many books as I could find, and which I could read. I got myself a library, [with] books like the dictionary published by García Cuyas—encyclopedic, alphabetical, very good. Then a history of Spain, printed in Spanish type with illustrations, all wood engravings."

Even before he formalized his reform efforts, Romero was subjected to criticism and name-calling because of his ideas, especially his anti-clericalism. "People would get things mixed up. They called me Protestant, Bolshevik, Mason. They called me all of the epithets to say that I was anti-religious. True, I was a radical, and I did not try to hide my anti-clericalism. My poor mother, she suffered a great deal because of me. . . . She saw how they scorned me, and she herself suffered because she was perfectly religious."

---

[14]A local newspaperman in Lagos retained vivid memories from his boyhood of José Romero wandering and reading in the park. Other agraristas confirmed that Romero read a great deal.

The local persecution of Romero for his ideas did not stop at name-calling. He had a family, "from when I was quite young, before starting the revolutionary movement. I was still in the [carpentry] shop. I met a woman in Lagos, and we had three children. . . . I didn't marry her. . . . Her family was simple—*rancheros*.[15] One of the priests [in Lagos] began to persuade some relatives of theirs, and they knew I lived with Luisa. These relatives, influenced by the priest, began to say that I was a Protestant. And then they managed to get this girl, who already had children and everything, to leave me. Because the priest told her mother, 'If Luisa, your daughter, marries that man, she'll be damned.' Since they were, of course, easily influenced that way, they made her leave me. . . . In spite of the fact that I had contacts in the municipio government, they couldn't be found anywhere. Her flight with the children was secretive, and only later did I find out that an aunt took them from Lagos, by night, to Guadalajara. I called in the police, sent notices to Aguascalientes, but they didn't show up anywhere. Finally, I was young—well, so okay, they're lost, what can be done? I continued on my path, kept working, still didn't throw myself completely into the [reform] struggle. But I already had my ideas; I was already a Bolshevik."

Leading Local Reform

A great deal of José Romero's life after the mid-1920s is intimately bound up with the history of the local labor and agrarian reform movements. Early on, his involvement in campaign politics won him a position on the ayuntamiento as a labor representative during José Guadalupe Zuno's term as governor (1923–26). Romero also served as Secretary of the Board of Conciliation and Arbitration[16] for the Lagos region, before becoming involved in the agrarian reform movement.

When Romero's carpentry shop was located across from the Fábrica La Victoria, Nieves Ortiz, Aniceto Martínez, Fabián Espinoza, and other employees who disagreed with the orientation of the Sindicato de Obreros Católicos used to come to his shop and discuss their hopes for change. "All of us, those with similar ideas, naturally sought each other out to organize and do something. That's why they would come to me. I was educated because I read a lot. I had read the work of this Frenchman, Emile Zola, the one who wrote the book called *Works*, and I had

[15]A term used to describe someone from a ranch or small rural community, and also to connote rustic behavior or simple thought.

[16]See note 45, Chapter 3.

more or less guided myself by that book; and besides, I belonged to the
school of thought I told you about, of Ricardo Flores Magón. I had
already read a lot of Flores Magón. So I was prepared to undertake the
struggle we were going to begin." When the reformist leaders at the
factory despaired of any leadership from the Catholic union for the
improvement of wages and working conditions, they formed (in 1924)
the Unión de Obreros Libertarios (UOL), with Nieves Ortiz serving as its
president. José Romero was drawn into its activities, without joining the
union.

Sometime between late 1924 and 1926, the factory closed permanently and the workers dispersed to hunt jobs in other cities. Later, when
support from local and state authorities declined, the UOL slipped out of
formal existence. Nonetheless, Romero and the workers who stayed in
Lagos, joined by a few agraristas, continued to meet surreptitiously during the years of the Cristero rebellion. At some point during the Cristiada,
definitely by 1930, Romero, former members of the UOL, and other
interested parties formed the Sindicato de Oficios Varios (SOV), and
began to talk first of labor reform and then of agrarian reform. Their
ranks increased after 1930 and 1931 with men who had been working in
the United States but, faced with high rates of unemployment during the
Depression and with the repatriation of Mexicans, returned to their
home communities. Although many of the men may only have been
interested in higher wages and the redistribution of land, for Romero the
union and the reforms were really a means to a larger political end:
"Power in the hands of the workers."[17]

By December 1931, the group interested in agrarian reform had
grown sufficiently to support its own organization, which they called the

---

[17]A letter in Romero's file confirms that some of the local leaders discussed agrarian
reform as a step toward other objectives. Undated, it must have been written sometime
between late 1931 and late 1934, when Romero had his most frequent contacts with its
author. The letter, from Captain José Vallarta to Romero, reads in part: "LET US BE
REDEEMERS WITH THE MASK OF PHARISEES. The greatness of the fatherland and
the pressing welfare of its children demand that we not interrupt the struggle, that we use
'Camouflage' so that, blending into the environment, we do not frighten our enemies, and
[so that we] can, step by step, take each of the redoubts until we reach our goal. . . . Our
most efficient course is to require legal compliance with the solution of the Agrarian
Problem. Let us earnestly continue the task of organizing the campesino mass, their
communities [the ejidos], Cooperatives, and Schools. Let us today be the Apostles of the
Ejido, so that our actions, backed by the law, can become translated into immediate
benefit to the campesinos; so that, persuaded of the goodness of our methods, they will
have complete confidence in us—because only that way (take careful note) will they
follow us everywhere tomorrow." [Emphasis in original.]

Liga Regional Campesina Magdaleno Cedillo. José Romero was named Secretary-General, a capacity in which he served until 1938, according to letters in ejido files in the Ministry of Agrarian Reform. Aniceto Martínez and Macedonio Ayala also shared leadership responsibilities. The local league became affiliated with the Liga Nacional Campesina Ursulo Galván, and Romero and others kept abreast of developments in national peasant and workers' unions through correspondence and publications of the Liga Nacional and its affiliates.

As membership in the labor and agrarian movements began to grow and to receive encouragement from leaders in other states, the local opposition increased its persecution of the reformers. At the time (roughly 1929–33), the movement in Lagos was receiving little or no encouragement from the Jalisco state government—much less from the local government—and the personal risks to the reformers increased. Even the federal military authorities in the region harassed the agraristas.

To illustrate the persecution by the authorities, Romero described several instances in which his own life was threatened. "They almost killed me . . . I don't know how I am still alive. Sure, escaping from street to street, block to block. Once, hoping to do me in, they latched onto a mistake of mine and used it to set up a case against me. On Sundays, the campesinos would get together in my shop, for us to handle their correspondence and to see what steps had been taken on their petition for lands. . . . Well, once Macedonio Ayala was typing the correspondence that had to be handled, and suddenly some campesinos from the hacienda Las Cruces showed up. It was an *hacienda intervenida*,[18] and the federal government rented it [to a private party]. But we had already set up a community there, and there was already a petition for the hacienda's lands. The fellow who was renting it of course opposed the campesinos who were seeking lands. So he began to harass them. He took away the water from the campesinos, and they had chile plots already planted, so they came immediately to the Liga to complain. Since it was a government-administered hacienda, the one who managed it in Lagos for the federal government was the man they called the Administrador de Rentas del Timbre [the tax officer]. . . . So then I told Ayala, 'Write a letter to the Administrador de Rentas del Timbre, asking him to order the man who runs Las Cruces to give water to the campesinos.'

[18]An hacienda administered by the federal government, in this case after the owner (a priest) died.

Instead of saying 'We beseech you,' he put 'You are ordered.' It was a stupid mistake—I could not order the local representative of the President of the Republic [to do something]. I didn't notice, nor did Ayala. I signed. Time passed, and about 20 days later I received the court summons already marked with the charge 'Usurpation of duties: ordering the President's representative.' Well that was what they called 'usurpation of duties.' So with that, right away, an order for my arrest. But it wasn't that; rather, they just wanted to get me out of the way.

"They put me in jail. The municipio president, an enemy;[19] the judge involved, an enemy; I was strictly among enemies. Well, there were some friends, among them Dr. Camarena.[20] I became ill in jail, because they were punishing me there, they were trying to make me give in, and I got sick. . . . I got an intestinal fever, and became very ill. . . . So Dr. Camarena told the municipio president, 'If you don't order them to take Romero to the hospital, I will hold you responsible, because there will be an epidemic in the jail and you are the authority, and later you'll have to answer for the epidemic that develops.' And the municipio president ordered me to be taken to the hospital; I wasn't even conscious. . . .

"I was sent to the state prison in Guadalajara. It was to my advantage, because I was in terrible danger of being killed in Lagos. In Guadalajara, I fell into prison among the group of revolutionaries who were in jail there, for being revolutionaries. Then I was among my people. . . . I spent three months that way, and here in Lagos, all of the enemies who thought they had a right to judge me said, 'Romero won't be back, because they are going to leave him in Guadalajara, so he won't be causing trouble around here.' And imagine their surprise when I returned to Lagos! In Guadalajara, friends told me, 'Don't go to Lagos, they've got it in for you.' And I said, 'No, I'm going to Lagos; that's my battleground, I'm going.' And I returned."

On another occasion, not long after the events just described, Romero had to flee Lagos under circumstances which finally· won him some grudging support from state officials. Friends of Romero's overheard some army officers discussing a plot to kill him. They ran to warn Romero to flee his carpentry shop and to seek protection from Margarito

[19]José María Padilla was municipio president in 1930–31. Every other agrarista interviewed agreed with this characterization of Padilla, who was a small landholder and came from a humble branch of one of the older and wealthier families in Lagos.

[20]Two other agraristas independently confirmed that Dr. Salvador Camarena had once saved Romero's life when he was in jail. The physician, now deceased, did not belong to the group of reformists; he was respected by wealthy and poor alike.

Ramírez, a former governor of Jalisco; they also sent a message to Ramírez. Margarito's answer: 'Tell Romero that the day after tomorrow at 9 in the morning we'll pass through Castro.'[21]

"Margarito Ramírez and the whole delegation were on their way to Aguascalientes with General Calles to form the PNR.[22] Sure enough, the next day at 9 a.m., there came the presidential train, and passing through Castro, out comes Margarito Ramírez to one of the windows. 'Come on, get on,' Margarito says to me. And I got aboard. Manlio Fabio Altamirano was already there, with other deputies of the legislature from Guanajuato, Aguascalientes, and Veracruz. Manlio Fabio Altamirano already knew me, and so did Carolino Navia[23] of Veracruz. They welcomed me; Margarito Ramírez said, 'Well, come here and let's hear how this business is in Jalisco.' The next day Margarito Ramírez told me, 'You're going to introduce yourself to General Calles.' . . . So then we passed into the reception room, and they announced, 'Margarito Ramírez and his companions,' and General Calles said, 'Compañero,' like that, 'Compañero,' and he hugs me. General Calles! He was like that with all of the workers. . . . And he says, 'I already know about your struggle, that the government of the state gives you no protection [*garantías*], not just you, but the state government has been obstructing all over the state, wherever there are revolutionaries.' I told him 'That's right, General, what they've told you is true. In fact, I was in jail for such a time. I just got out of prison.' So he says, 'Summon General Allende.' Allende was a General, and Licenciado, and Governor of Jalisco.[24]

'General,' [Calles said to Allende], 'I am very sorry to have to reprimand you because the revolutionaries of Jalisco have no protection un-

---

[21]A train stop northwest of Lagos.

[22]The train's passengers presumably included the entire delegation from Jalisco to the official party convention, among them deputies and senators from the federal legislature. According to Romero, the purpose of the entourage's trip was to participate in the formation of the Partido Nacional Revolucionario (PNR). However, the organizing convention for the PNR was held in Querétaro in 1929. There was a party congress in Aguascalientes in October 1932, to formulate party policy on the principle of no reelection (Osorio Marbán, 1970: 299–336). Given the timing Romero describes, and the persons involved, the encounter probably occurred on the occasion of the 1932 party congress.

[23]Altamirano and Navia were both figures in Veracruz state politics and active in the first national peasant organization, the Liga Nacional Campesina Ursulo Galván (Falcón, 1975; Fowler, 1970; [Fowler] Salamini, 1978). Altamirano also served as a senator from Veracruz and was on the organizing committee for the first conference of the PNR (Osorio Marbán, 1970: 46ff.).

[24]Sebastián Allende was Governor of Jalisco from April 1932 to February 1935. *Licenciado* is a title conferred upon completion of a university degree in law or the liberal arts.

der your government.' 'No, General, what do you mean they don't?' 'Well, the compañero here has suffered this and that.' So, Allende had no alternative but to charge that we ran to San Luis Potosí to protect ourselves, that we didn't seek out the [Jalisco] state government, but rather sought help from the government of San Luis Potosí or Guanajuato,[25] and that we didn't recognize the government of Jalisco. So Margarito Ramírez tells him, 'But if in the government of Jalisco they don't have protection, then they must seek it where they find it. So that's why with good reason they seek the protection of General Cedillo or of Melchor Ortega [Governor of Guanajuato].' Calles said, 'No, General [Allende]. From today on, you answer to me for this compañero's life. Anything that happens to this compañero, you answer to me for his life and for that of the other compañeros in the state, who are not here but who I know are persecuted.' Later, when I returned to Lagos, they didn't want anyone to even look at me, so that nothing would happen to me!"

As a result of his prison sentence in Guadalajara, Romero had established contacts with members of the state agrarian reform movement and the state peasant league. These contacts, the growing strength of the Liga Regional in Lagos, and the increasing importance of worker and peasant groups as potential support bases for the presidential candidate to be selected by the official party in December 1933, all coalesced to catapult Romero into the state organization. Romero led a delegation of 36 men representing the agrarian communities that belonged to the Liga Regional in Lagos to the state congress held in Guadalajara in March 1933, at which he was named the Jalisco league's Secretary of Lands and Waters, a capacity in which he served from March 29, 1933, until March 1, 1936. Subsequently, because of his official position and his increasing visibility, Romero attended the national campesino congress in San Luis Potosí in June 1933 as a delegate from Jalisco. The Confederación Campesina Mexicana (CCM), forerunner of the present Confederación Nacional Campesina (CNC), was established at that meeting, partly to serve as a campesino support group for Lázaro Cárdenas' election to the presidency the following year. In January 1934, Macedonio Ayala and José Romero also served as Jalisco delegates to the national labor convention (Cámara Nacional de Trabajo) in Mexico City.

Although he achieved some prominence within the state agrarian

---

[25]This refers to the advice and protection that Romero and the local organizations had sought from General Saturnino Cedillo and his campesino army in San Luis Potosí, and from the governors of the adjoining state of Guanajuato.

movement, Romero claimed that he was constantly in trouble in Jalisco because he persisted in challenging the governor's authority over the state league. Romero favored a campesino union which would be independent of state authority, and he claims to have tried to handle his relationships with agrarian communities and national peasant organizations as though the state league were independent and not subject to gubernatorial control.

Lean Years in Exile

"I found myself in a desperate situation because I could be neither in Guadalajara nor in Lagos, because I was an agitator, always bothering— or rather, I bothered the government because of the demands I made for the communities of the region. . . . The governments of the time, in spite of being revolutionaries and everything, couldn't get onto the idea of agrarianism, and they were always looking for a way to persecute us, to put us in the service of the large landholders." Under these conditions, the agraristas in Lagos had made an important miscalculation in supporting Silvano Barba González as the candidate to succeed Governor Allende in 1935. As things turned out, the official candidate selected was Everardo Topete.

That error, Ayala's assassination, and the continued persecution of reformers before Lázaro Cárdenas had consolidated his power and was able to begin intensive organizing of campesinos and urban workers, all combined to produce the "desperate situation" in which Romero found himself. He left for Mexico City, where he searched for work and took an interest in the labor-organizing efforts in the capital. His personal circumstances and his thinking at the time are eloquently captured in two letters which he wrote back home, of which he retained copies in his files. The first, to his friends in the reform movement, reflects his understanding of the national political scene and his suggestions for a local political strategy. The second, to his mother, even more vividly captures his sense of mission and purpose.

> April 20, 1935
> Sr. Francisco Navia
> Lagos de Moreno, Jalisco

Dear Comrade:

More than personal, this letter is for all of you, for Urbano, Salvador, Martín, Exiquio, Barbosa—in sum, for all of you who in these moments have passed a new and difficult test. But comrades, this involves a new experience in our field of battle, and I must tell you that I almost expected it, since one could not expect anything else from the GOVERNMENT OF JALISCO, OF GENUINELY LATI-FUNDIST[26] AND CLERICAL EXTRACTION AND WORTHY SON OF THE PNR, which is nothing more than the protector of the large interests of Mexican capitalism, and thus the enemy of the working classes, which it hopes to break up and take into a "FASCISTIC" [sic] state, in the manner of Hitler and Mussolini; the PNR, detritus of ill-omened Callismo which is laying waste to the workers of Mexico.[27]

I have not communicated with you because with Miguel's [Miguel Aguirre Salas'] letters I was kept informed of the course of events in that homeland from which I have been in exile for so long, and also because, since this is like a burning volcano, I was waiting to give you some guidelines. . . . I think the time has come to act and to return to our burden as in our best times of struggle, since my energies have not abandoned me and I think I can still attack head on and make the enemy squirm, as we did not so long ago. . . .

The formidable strikes of the last few days, the unrest which reigns in all sectors of the workers, reveal to us that something is being readied for a not-too-distant time, it's just a matter of further loading the barrel. The already bare-faced accusations being made against the government, of betraying the workers' cause; the terrain which Cardenismo is daily losing, . . . while Cárdenas remains imprisoned in the claws of Callismo; the Callista mafia, drawing its strength only from the high bureaucracy, which does not wish to release its prey; and many other details which it would take too long to enumerate—suggest that there will be a fight.[28]

Don't have illusions that you will win the new [municipio] elections. The charade they have prepared for you will be like all the rest—even though you might have a majority, the game will be the

[26]Large landowner(s). Emphasis in original.

[27]Former President Calles had begun with a radical and combative program. However, by 1935, Calles and his followers had grown more conservative: they no longer supported labor strikes nor extensive land redistribution. The Callista-dominated leadership of the CROM, the first national labor union to be organized in Mexico, had grown corrupt, and the labor movement had split into factions (see, for example, Weyl and Weyl, 1939: 228–240; Cornelius, 1973: 405–406, 418-419).

[28]Romero accurately anticipated the confrontation which erupted in June 1935 between the newly inaugurated president, Lázaro Cárdenas, and his former mentor, General Calles, who was attempting to control Cárdenas and to obstruct his reform program. Cárdenas had encouraged organized labor to strike for the full benefits promised in the 1917 Constitution, and during his first year as president the number of strikes trebled over the previous year's (see Cornelius, 1973: 443-455).

same as always. When you present your candidates' platform, do so only with the objective of not leaving the field to them entirely without a fight, but there will be no good outcome. (Ask yourselves this: If the government of the state had wished to leave the situation to us, why take it from us when we had it in our hands? Consider that.) So then, for this new battle tactic, communicate with General Cedillo, since he has always been our friend, tell him the situation we are facing, but do not do this in the political party's name, but rather in the name of the Liga [de Comunidades Agrarias Macedonio Ayala], with all the members signing in the absence of the Secretary-General [José Romero]. . . . From the political side we must expect nothing; our blow resides in the social issue [land reform].

After the agrarian congress in Morelia, we shall have something new and new guidelines for our struggle. Soon we shall be matched, gentlemen latifundists of Lagos and of the entire country. I am getting deeply involved in the CGT [General Confederation of Workers] and the PC [Communist Party], and in the committee against the imperialist war and fascism; in sum, we are seeking ties everywhere—with the streetcar drivers and the railroad workers, taking note of the social movement. I am sending you these circulars so that you can send them to the communities, and in Lagos, as home of the movement, put them into practice. . . . If you celebrate the first of May, don't forget the dead and have an impressive demonstration, without songs and . . . dances, but a protest demonstration. Don't show the red and black flag, just the RED.

I cannot be with you because of my economic circumstances, but it doesn't matter. From here I shall be the eternal rebel, just as when we were together. Take heart, comrades, and to the struggle—the future is ours.

With a fraternal embrace for everyone, in the name of our cause.

José Romero Gómez

May 14, 1935
Sra. Luciana Romero
Lagos de Moreno, Jalisco

My dear Mother:

I am notifying you that on the 15th of last month I established myself definitively in the offices of the Labor Department; it being impossible to return to Guadalajara, I have decided for the time being to remain here. Since I have not had a fixed abode, I have been wandering from one place to another, and for that reason have been unable to tell you with any certainty where I would be residing. By no means have I forgotten you, it is just that the difficult situations I had to go through and the continuous struggle to push forward require that I forget everything except the struggle against the powerful ones. You must understand that men like myself are not our own masters; we belong to all of humanity, and we must even sacrifice our lives if it is necessary.

Soon my efforts of so many years of struggle against the capitalists of Lagos will be crowned—soon the papers for granting lands in Lagos will be signed by the President of the Republic, soon the engineer will be out to give those lands which were so impudently stolen, leaving the communities in abject poverty. But the hour of Justice draws near, and those who called me mad will see that I have defeated them.

Perhaps I may not enjoy the benefits of the lands, but I will live with the knowledge of duty fulfilled and of having done the land which saw my birth the greatest service of liberating it from the claws of the robber landowners. I will continue my pilgrimage, struggling where there are injustices to be righted, struggling for social vindication until this regime of oppression which weighs on humanity is toppled—or I shall fall in the struggle, as so many have fallen before me.

It is possible that I may go there when they grant possession [of the ejidos], since I am determined to be present when the papers are signed and to have the satisfaction of seeing my efforts crowned. . . .

Say hello to Chano, and receive the affection of your son who hopes to see you soon. Don't worry about me. Remember what I've told you before: I came to the world with a mission, and I must fulfill it for the good of humanity.

José Romero Gómez

A year later, Romero was still worried about "fascism" in Jalisco and the consolidation of peasant unions into a national peasant organization (the CNC). He opposed the centralization of the peasant movement, reasoning that if the work of handling ejido petitions and complaints were effectively centralized at the state and national levels, land reform would be allowed to stagnate. Like other radical agraristas with roots in local movements, (see Brown, 1979), he also feared that a central union could become the home of political opportunists who would dilute the revolutionary ideology which he felt should be represented in peasant and worker organizations. Some of this thinking is reflected in a letter to the

Lagos agraristas which he wrote from Victoria, Guanajuato, on July 27, 1936: "Keeping faith with our [class] heritage, we must cast our lot with the Left. . . . We must choose our own battlefield, so as not to be at the mercy of compromises made by the pseudo-revolutionary politicians."

While Romero was in Mexico City casting about for a job and unable to return to Jalisco, an old political acquaintance came to his aid. This friend, Luis Romero Gallardo, had collaborated with the Laguenses on agrarian petitions and was serving at the time as an assistant to the Governor of Guanajuato. "Luis told me, 'You come with us to Guanajuato.' Well, I was living from hand to mouth, I had no work or anything, and I couldn't go to Guadalajara or Lagos because we were enemies of the gubernatorial candidate who was running at that time.

"In Guanajuato, I had many privileges. Mainly, the Governor appointed me as a member of the Local Agrarian Commission, which at the time operated in each state, in charge of the agrarian movement of the region. Governor [Enrique] Fernández Martínez entrusted me with the task of organizing the communities in the north of Guanajuato: Dolores Hidalgo, San Felipe, all of those. I organized them so they could be given arms. It was necessary to arm the agraristas so they could defend themselves against the assaults by the white guards, who at the time were still encouraged by the haciendas and were responsible to instructors or [military] officers of the federal government. . . .

"I was sent to Victoria, Guanajuato, to a terrible situation there, because it was way up in the mountains, and, well, isolated, and in the middle of Cristero revolutionaries who roamed the hills. I lasted, endured really, three months in Victoria. . . . The Cristeros slept there, and from there would go out to the hills. And there I was—I had no more than 25 men as the local garrison. For the municipio presidency I had only four carbines, just that, with a very small quantity of ammunition, and I could pay only two police. It was a terrible situation. I went because I had an obligation to Fernández; besides, I wanted to see what there was there. It was my nature to go and make the revolution wherever I was. . . . On September 28 [1936] the Cristeros who were roaming the hills attacked me. I defended myself as best I could, and was able to get out. Three or four days later, I came to [the city of] Guanajuato, to see Fernández Martínez, and told him that I couldn't stay there, there was no money, nothing, not even anything to survive on there. And I went to Luis [Romero Gallardo] and told him, 'They don't even give me money to be able to stay there, and anyway there's no reason to be there—there's nothing to organize. The ejido communities are very far away and belong to [the municipio of] San Luis de la Paz. I can do nothing there.' "[29]

As a result of these problems, the Governor transferred Romero, sending him to serve as municipio president and trouble-shooter in Romita, Guanajuato. Romero spent several months in Romita,[30] and then the campaign for governor and federal deputies in Jalisco began, and he returned to his native state.

Seeking Local Office

While still serving as municipio president in Romita, Romero decided to seek the nomination as the candidate for federal deputy from Lagos de Moreno. "Politics then was handled on the basis of personal arrangements between one another. Silvano Barba González was the *tejemaneje* [power-broker], the one who nominated everyone, which was the custom then, as it still is.[31] So, when I went to see him I told him that I was about to launch my candidacy. 'Well, yes, there's no problem, I know that you are in command of the situation. But it turns out that I gave that district to my *compadre*,[32] Luis Álvarez del Castillo. You know, he has helped me a great deal with my campaign [for Governor].' He had already given it out! 'I gave it to my compadre. So I'll put you in as the alternate.'[33] No, I became indignant! I had a short fuse. They called me the eternal malcontent, the eternal rebel, because I didn't yield easily to

[29]In a letter written to Moisés Pérez, Francisco Navia, José García, and Salvador Torres Villa, in Lagos, dated July 27, 1936, Romero described his situation in Victoria as follows: "There is no point to this sacrifice of being cut off from the field of useful battle, since in this town one cannot even dream about the revolution, since there are no useful people nor any material for struggle. If there were any chance, of course, I would gladly sacrifice myself with the hope that in time something would be done, all the more so if I could earn something decent to have something at my disposal to help our movement; of course then I would sacrifice myself, but under the circumstances it serves no useful purpose."

[30]Romero kept a frayed photograph of his inauguration in Romita. The negative was dated November 22, 1936.

[31]Barba González, a native of Jalisco, was then president of the official party. He served in that capacity from August 1936 until April 1938. He was also the official candidate for Governor of Jalisco. The nomination practice which Romero described is still generally in effect: the President of the Republic selects the gubernatorial candidates, who then dispense federal legislative positions among their confidants, who then select from their associates the nominees for municipio presidents.

[32]A close friend through fictive kinship (*compadrazgo*).

[33]In Mexico, there are two categories of legislative deputies, *"diputados propietarios"* and *"diputados suplentes,"* both popularly elected, the former actually holding the legislative appointment. The *suplente* is entitled to occupy the post in case of the death, or resignation, or election to another office of the *propietario*.

the caprices of the politicians. I addressed them all as 'tú.'[34] I told him, 'No, no, not the alternate.' "

When Romero returned to Guanajuato, Governor Fernández Martínez had heard about his disappointment over the nomination and called him in to his office. "So I went to see Don Enrique, and he told me, 'No, Romero, you must accept the alternate post, because if you don't, you'll be completely left out of the party, and out of the district. Don't you see that what they want is to get you out of the movement, they want to get you out of Jalisco, and mainly they want to get you out of Lagos, because you will hinder Silvano. Silvano is afraid of you, because you'll make revolutions against him there.' Since Don Enrique was one of the most astute politicians there in Guanajuato, one of the most experienced, I followed his advice. . . . I accepted the alternate deputy post.

"Afterwards I ran into Margarito [Ramírez] at the party [PNR] offices. 'What's new? What happened? Is everything arranged for Lagos?' I told him, 'No, the situation is like this.' [He answered] 'Accept the alternate position. The thing is, you shouldn't leave there. But have a talk with the deputy-to-be and extract some deals. Have him give you the municipio presidency in Lagos, and whatever municipios that you want, to run, wherever you have organizations. They should be given to you.' Margarito had told me, 'You tell him that you are the strong one—that's where the strength is to help him. He has to depend on you because—on who else? Politically, to handle the politics, he must have a show of support.'

"So I went to Luis Álvarez del Castillo. I extracted an agreement that I would be the municipio president, which would help me to continue the revolutionary movement, since he knew nothing of the revolution. He was one of the millionaires—what was he going to understand about the revolution? It wasn't even to his advantage. But for political convenience he said, 'You take charge of organizing for the elections, take charge of the political party.' Because at that time one didn't demonstrate throughout the municipio, one just mobilized the municipio capital for the [election] rallies that were held in the park. A huge crowd of people would attend the demonstration to support the candidates. . . . It was necessary to mobilize the campesinos from the most distant municipios of the [legislative] district, from Ojuelos, Unión de San Antonio, San Diego de Alejandría. They had to gather in the center of Lagos for the demonstration. . . . So Luis Álvarez del Castillo says to me, 'What will the

---

[34]The familiar form of address in Spanish.

Campaign rally in late 1937, organized in support of the slate of candidates for municipio office headed by José Romero. The banners included the insignia shared by the regional and national campesino organizations.

campaign cost?' I knew he was a miser. 'Look, Don Luis, that campaign can be done with no less than 15 or 20 thousand pesos.' 'Okay,' he says, 'Can I count on all of the support you can give me?' 'Yes.' "

Romero commuted back and forth between Lagos and Romita. "I would see to the business of the municipio government in Romita, and then move on to Lagos to continue the campaign. Don Luis stayed in Guadalajara, and me out here working on the campaign. . . . But since all of the campesinos were my friends, neither the campaign nor the arrangements cost me anything. Fernández Martínez gave me what I was able to spend.[35] Then, with only three or four days left until the demonstration, I really got things mobilized. . . . For example, the people from Ojuelos, you know how far it is from Ojuelos to Lagos [68 kilometers], well in those days they made the trip on horseback. The people from Ojuelos, all of them came. And they paid their own expenses, feeding their horses and all."

Once Luis Álvarez del Castillo was elected federal deputy, he kept his promise and Romero was nominated, and elected, municipio president of Lagos in the next local election in Jalisco. In the same election, Álvarez

[35]Fernández Martínez had given him 3,000 pesos, upon hearing that Alvarez del Castillo had not contributed any money to the campaign costs.

During his tenure as municipio president in Lagos, Romero was photographed with Luis Romero Gallardo (on the left), his friend and supporter in the state of Guanajuato, and Francisco Navia (standing behind Romero), in the agraristas' meeting room secured for them by an employee of the Agrarian Department when General Cedillo was the head of that agency.

del Castillo ran for head of the city council in Guadalajara. Both men took office in January 1938.[36]

"They were terribly afraid of me in Lagos—the rich people, whom I was already making poor, their haciendas were being divided. . . . When I was about to become municipio president, there was a terrible campaign against me. 'No, who knows what Romero might do, that Protestant, he'll throw out the priests.' Once they falsely accused me of something—they said that I had said that I would hang the black and red

[36]When Romero became municipio president, the Liga Regional received letters congratulating it for succeeding in electing a member of its own ranks to that office. The letters were replies to an announcement sent out by the Liga when Romero took the oath of office. Romero kept copies of such letters from the Jalisco branch of the Communist Party; the national executive committee of the Young Socialists of Mexico; and the central executive committee of the CCM.

flag between the steeples of the Church. I never thought of doing it, but that's what they attributed to me.

"Well, I already had administrative experience, by instinct, and because I'd already been municipio president in Victoria and Romita, Guanajuato; I had already run large groups in Guadalajara, and I had experience in dealing with people. I already knew which way I had to go with my radical thoughts. I was no longer moving blindly. Especially among the women and the Church, they were terribly afraid of me. The day came when I took charge of the [municipio] presidency, and after the festivities I called Miguel Aguirre Salas and told him, 'Look, Miguel, sit down at the typewriter and type what I dictate.' And I dictated a manifesto to the people of Lagos, calling for their help to carry forward an administration for all, without distinction. I gave it to them gently: everyone would have their rights protected, we were all going to work for the people. I bore no grudges, nor did I intend to favor any group. I was there to serve the people, whom I loved and intended to serve. It was published; whether they read it or not, it softened the propaganda against me.

"Then the next night I called a meeting of all the agrarian communities in the Lagos district. I told them, 'Compañeros, the struggle we have long sustained to get power has fallen into the hands of the workers. I am a worker, as you know, the only difference is that the government is in my hands, and the government is each of you, because here everyone has his place. I am no longer the workers' leader, nor am I the party president, or anything. I am a citizen in charge of the municipio government to protect the interests of my community. And we are this community. . . . Here each of us will take the path that belongs to us. You, Navia, are president of the SOV. You, Moisés Pérez, are president of the Liga de Comunidades Agrarias—you run it. And you, So-and-So, are such-and-such, and I gave them all a task. . . . Some of you don't need to think that I will give you jobs, because I don't have jobs for everyone. I will give jobs here to those who need them and who are capable. I am not going to give jobs out of favoritism.' And with that I began as municipio president.

"I'd been in the presidency about two months when Álvarez del Castillo called me to Guadalajara. Do you know what he wanted me for? To tell me that out of the municipio funds I was to send him 400 pesos per month for his expenses on behalf of the municipio. As a rich man, not needing it—damn him, he's a millionaire, he has three or four pottery factories in Guadalajara! It's that he's ambitious. And then he tells me,

'And you will also send me 200 pesos for a good friend of mine.' A vagrant, assassin, an evil man. [The friend] was in León because he couldn't be in Lagos or Aguascalientes, because he had committed some crimes. He had been made out to be a gunman for Don Luis. 'Listen, Don Luis. Do you think that I will sacrifice the people of Lagos to send money to that vagrant? To that evil man? No, don't expect that from me, nor the 400 pesos that you want me to send to you.' 'What do you mean, no, when I made you municipio president?' 'No, you didn't 'make' me, I became president because I had to be. And I didn't become deputy because I left the field to you.' From that point on, precisely because I refused to send him the money and because I put myself in direct opposition to him, he brought all of his power to bear. That's when he called in all of the members of the [Lagos] ayuntamiento and began to work on them to remove me from office. That's how the coup [*cabildazo*] went. . . . He managed to get a majority over me in the ayuntamiento."[37]

While he was away investigating an urgent complaint about water rights in a distant ejido of the municipio, the members of the council who sided with Álvarez del Castillo accused Romero of abandoning his post without receiving permission from Guadalajara, and they expelled him from the municipio presidency. "I was going to fight in the council, but I found myself without support. So what was I going to fight with? I had no money; I grabbed my library, took down my books, wrapped them, stacked them in the middle of one room, and then my bedroom furniture and my tools, and I called one of those men who buys anything one sells, and he bought everything from me and gave me 300 pesos for all of that."

[37]Three other agraristas independently reported the same reasons for the coup. In addition, a letter from Ramiro Baranda V., secretary of the local railroad workers' union in Irapuato, Guanajuato, to Deputy Álvarez del Castillo, dated August 25, 1938 (AJRG), supports Romero's account of this affair. Baranda demanded to know from Álvarez whether the "coup" against Romero in Lagos was accomplished with his knowledge and consent and with the knowledge of Silvano Barba González. He criticized the members of Lagos' municipio council who participated in deposing Romero, and openly threatened both Álvarez and Barba González with withdrawal of support by the groups which, under Romero's guidance, had helped to elect Álvarez deputy. Baranda's letter bears out Romero's contention that he was deposed because of his unwillingness to relinquish funds for illicit purposes: "It was with great displeasure that I found out today when I arrived in Lagos that the vilest of the members of the local governing body in this town agreed to depose from his post as municipio president the honest compañero and true revolutionary José Romero Gómez, for the sole crime of not permitting public funds to fall into the hands of these voracious scoundrels and bad servants of this miserable town which you honorably represent."

Deposed from the municipio presidency on August 24, 1938, Romero concluded that he could no longer remain in Lagos, and so made his way to Mexico City. Strengthened by his ties to the CNC (by then a sector of the official party), he decided to fight to have himself appointed as a regular federal deputy, replacing Álvarez del Castillo. He felt justified in his bid to move out of his alternate status, because Álvarez had been elected to head the city council in Guadalajara and was simultaneously holding two elective positions. "He already had another elective post, and he no longer had a right to be in the legislature, according to the constitutional rules and to the rules of the legislature as well. Well, no sir. He came and went from Guadalajara to attend the legislative sessions [in Mexico City]. So when the CNC found out, . . . they began to pressure the standing body of the legislature to call me to take the post of regular deputy. When the organizations saw that there were obstacles to my entry into the legislature, all of them took action, mobilized themselves.[38] But at the time, the legislature was in recess, and they were very long recesses. . . . The whole year passed, because the legislature wasn't in session."

When it finally did convene, the legislature voted to award Romero the regular deputy's seat, and he served out his term in the 37th Legislature. But problems continued for him. "When I left Lagos to come to Mexico City as the deputy, I came determined to be influential in the municipio of Lagos and in all of the other municipios in my jurisdiction. I went to Silvano [Barba González], who was already Governor,[39] and told him to leave me the [reform] movement in the municipios of Ojuelos, Lagos, and Unión de San Antonio (which were the ones that interested me, where there were the most agrarian communities). Those were the municipios that I wanted to run, to put in trustworthy people so that the revolutionary movement could continue. Silvano told me, 'Fine,' but he said it without meaning it. He told me to reach an agreement with the president of the party [the PRM] in Guadalajara, so that action could be taken in Lagos. But it was a lie; Silvano did not keep his promise.

"I took to the party officials the names of my candidates—the people I considered most resolute, the people I considered it advisable to have

[38]Romero saved copies of letters written on December 18 and 19, 1938, to the President of the Cámara de Diputados (the Chamber of Deputies in the federal legislature) from a local union, the Sindicato de Trabajadores y Trabajadoras de Molinos para Nixtamal, in Lagos, and from a nearby ejido, El Chipinque. Given the local labor and agrarian leadership at the time, these are probably only two of many such letters sent to Mexico City to support Romero's bid for the regular deputy's post.

[39]This dates the event as occurring after March 1, 1939, the date that Barba González took the oath of office as Governor of Jalisco.

stay on in the municipios to give life to the [agrarista] organization. They said yes, but when . . . I went to see how the elections had turned out,[40] I found out that all of my candidates had been rejected [by the party leadership]. The people chosen were the ones that Luis Álvarez ordered—that is, completely rightist people, strictly enemies of the organization and my personal enemies. So I went to the government palace in Guadalajara, found Silvano, and got into an argument with him.

"I, who was not diplomatic, spoke to him about what he'd done to me, that he betrayed me. 'Why?' Naturally, I refused to give him an out, because I was very blunt. He was Governor then, and he said, 'It's all done, the party did this, nothing can be done.' So I said, 'I'm going to Mexico City, and from there I am going to move things to change this situation.'

"I went to Mexico City. I was walking near the Alameda, and I met a friend who had been a compañero in Lagos from the Romo-Cuéllar struggles,[41] José Rodríguez Reyes. He had been head of Alfredo Romo's campaign in Lagos. I was on my way back from Guadalajara, where I'd fought with Silvano, and out comes my *tocayo*.[42] We greeted each other, he congratulated me, and I told him that I had come to fight Silvano, that I could count on the support of the deputies from Aguascalientes, Guanajuato, and Veracruz, and that I was going to start a movement to take away Silvano's influence and to change things in the municipios. My tocayo listened to me, and then he said, 'Oh, Tocayo, when will you give up being a dreamer? Why are you dreaming about the municipio council? Why are you dreaming about the organizations? Look, they're not even going to remember you! Why are you fighting for that? No, look, you'll come up against the Governor, and think about who the Governor is: right-hand man of [President Lázaro] Cárdenas! The deputies from Aguascalientes and Guanajuato won't help you. When they see it getting rough, they'll close their eyes and they won't help you. They're not capable of opening their traps to say you're right. Why are you going to fight for people who later won't even remember you? Why, you're wretchedly poor, you're dying of hunger.' And, in fact, I was living like that, without a penny in my pocket. Sometimes Margarito Ramírez was the one who supported me; sometimes he'd give me 30 or 60 pesos. That's how I lived in Mexico City, and I still hadn't found any job. 'Take advantage of the few cents you will earn in this [legislative] session, and start living.'

[40]He had been in Mexico City attending the legislative session.
[41]An intensely contested gubernatorial election in Jalisco.
[42]A nickname for someone who shares the same first name.

"In sum, he brought me up short—and just in time. Because if he hadn't, I would have made the asinine mistake of fighting with the Governor, raising a scandal in the legislature, something that wouldn't even have made it to a scandal. Because, like my tocayo told me, 'You'll see, those representatives will shut their traps and not talk.' So I started thinking, maybe he's right. And I established myself in Mexico City. . . . I looked up Lombardo [Toledano],[43] talked with other leaders there. For a while I kept up with the [agrarista] organizations. I continued as a representative member of the CNC, and they gave me a few assignments [*comisiones*] here and there, but very occasionally. I no longer participated actively in the struggle. . . . I didn't see it any more as suited to my radical ideas. The organizations weren't fighting any more the way we had."

Romero finished out his term in the 37th session of the national legislature, coinciding with the end of Lázaro Cárdenas' presidency. He supported Manuel Ávila Camacho as the succeeding President, since Cárdenas had selected him. When Ávila Camacho assumed the Presidency, "Don Manuel said, 'All of the [legislative] representatives who want jobs, who want work, and have collaborated with me, fine.' Naturally, I wasn't in very good circumstances. 'Yes, I wish work.' After a lot of struggling, I acquired a job as administrator of public markets in Mexico City—not my preference, but I needed to work. I had to struggle to support my children, which I had by then. But I quit government work because I was opposed to Alemán.[44] When they fired me from the markets, precisely for being an opponent of Alemán, I already had a piece of land with a house, and I took out my nails, my tools which I had lying around—I had my property, and I set myself up to work. There was always something; I did not return to government. I never went back."

Retirement from Politics: The Twisted Revolution

When Romero withdrew from politics he was about 55 years old. He had a second family of three children in Mexico City, in addition to his first family in Guadalajara. Except for a brief period when he returned to Guadalajara to work and live, Romero lived in Mexico City after his

---

[43]At that time Vicente Lombardo Toledano headed the Confederación de Trabajadores Mexicanos (CTM), the largest national labor organization in Mexico.

[44]Miguel Alemán Valdez, President of Mexico from 1946 to 1952. He is generally regarded as the country's most conservative post-Revolutionary president.

political retirement. He remained an astute observer of the national political scene, with firm opinions about what had happened to the Revolution after his struggles ended.

Romero began to withdraw from politics even before he was removed from the government for his opposition to Miguel Alemán's presidential candidacy. After the coup against him in Lagos and the rejection of his proposed slate of candidates for local offices in the municipios in which he had been most involved, Romero abandoned the reform movement in Lagos.[45] The advice of his friend on the futility of battling Silvano Barba González and the rightward drift in national politics also contributed to his political withdrawal. "I grew tired. . . . On May Day, when I saw the castration of the workers, I said, 'Now the revolutionary workers' movement has hit bottom.' I could hear only praises for the government, only thanks for the benefits [it provided]. There wasn't anything any more."

Was he disillusioned when he retired? "Almost disillusioned, because I saw that the movement was very twisted. They no longer had what we did when we formed the workers' groups, when David Alfaro Siqueiros[46] was beginning in Jalisco." How did it become twisted? "The current leaders corrupted it—Fidel Velázquez,[47] the one who's now eternal president for life [of the CTM], a bunch of corrupted people. They took over the movement, became millionaires, and there you have them, still entrenched in the labor organization, running the workers. That's how it is. When we took the organization [the CROM] away from [Luis N.] Morones,[48] a corrupt leader, we built a movement in which I took part from Jalisco. . . . All of us—revolutionaries, who saw the corruption of the CROM, that it no longer responded to the workers' needs; it was a completely political organization. That's when Lombardo [Toledano] formed the CTM. [Later] the corrupt ones and their followers left the CTM because of ideological dissent . . . and the rest of the group stayed with Lombardo Toledano. Lombardo imposed on the organization a completely radical movement. [The old-line labor leaders] had to have disagreements with him, because they were moderates who did not want to

[45] The unified agrarian front in Lagos de Moreno had essentially dissolved as an independent group by the end of the Cárdenas administration in 1940. (See "The Demise of Local Agrarian Power" in Chapter 4.)

[46] A world-famous Mexican muralist and early member of the Mexican Communist Party.

[47] Mexico's principal labor leader and head of the CTM since 1941.

[48] Head of the main, government-backed labor organization, the CROM, from 1918 until 1936.

take the movement into radicalism, and he wanted to turn it into a social-ist movement. So disunity and disorganization of the workers followed.

"The workers today have lost the love for the struggle, because they have already achieved what we struggled so long to attain, which was the improvement of the workers' conditions, and now many say, 'Well, I earn so much, I live well; no, why should I get involved in that?' And the bureaucratization of the workers has hurt the movement. I have a son working in Mexico City, and I told him when he started to work, 'Orga-nize a movement there, mobilize the workers in this way and that.' He started, and a little while later the company calls him in and says, 'Why are you doing this? No, we'll make you a supervisor, you'll earn so much.' They gave him a 15 or 20-peso raise, made him a chief supervisor, and goodbye to the movement—he forgot it. He forgot his father's begin-nings. 'I earn more now, I'm a supervisor.' And for what? Corrupted! And those who haven't had those advantages are the ones who continue to suffer. It's fine as an improvement for some workers, but not for all. . . . But now with that business of collective contracts and all that, they've paralyzed the truly radical revolutionary movement.

"The same thing has happened to the agrarian movement. There have been campesinos who have raised themselves up, have made themselves bosses—more accurately, have become *caciques* [political bosses] in their own ejidos—and that has also damaged the agrarian movement. It took away their ideals. And now, with the bureaucratization that's being imposed on them, it's going to be worse. They have killed the camp-esino's fighting spirit, his love for the land. Now, if the campesino works the land, it's because he knows they [the government] will give him money [loans]. . . . When the Banco Agrario[49] was founded by General Cárdenas, we knew that campesinos would go, take out the money, and get drunk, and that finished the money. If they're still following that path, it's corrupting them further, and it's money that comes from the people, on top of it all. . . . I see the movement [today] as very different from the one we began. We followed the precept of Flores Magón: 'Land for all, the land belongs to the tiller.' . . . Now they give campesinos land in the form of community parcels, but they really aren't—they make them [individual proprietors], without a conscience.

"Look, I believed in the revolutionary sector of the campesinos. But

[49]The Banco Nacional de Crédito Agrícola was originally established under the terms of the agrarian law in 1926 as a government agency to provide credit to ejidatarios. It was subsequently reformed by changes in the Agrarian Reform Law in 1931 and during the Cárdenas administration.

One of the first May Day parades in Lagos de Moreno which involved public-school children (ca. 1935). The largest banner reads: "The Red Shroud of the Chicago Martyrs Covers the Hopes of the Laguense Worker." The PNR banner behind it calls for "Open Struggle for Vindication of the Workers of Countryside and City."

now I see it corrupted. How can a faithful, completely different movement come about? Perhaps a socialist movement within the bureaucratic revolution, just to maintain their wages, their strikes. . . . But a radical movement that would completely transform society, well, I don't see it near, because the worker's fighting spirit is gone; he no longer needs to struggle as much, nor would he risk it, because he would say, 'Why should I? I'm eating well.' And there you have it—the belly is what rules."

What would he do if he were young? "If I were, say, 40 years old, I think I would [pursue] the radicalization of property, the system of [individually farmed] ejido plots, because it is a way of not giving complete freedom to the campesino, since the campesino is in no condition to receive it. If I still had the fighting spirit, I think I would fight for the land, without [individual] plots—the collectivization of the land. I think that movement is already underway.[50]

[50]A reference to then-President Luis Echeverría's policy of promoting the collectivization of ejidos, a move strongly resisted by ejidatarios in the Lagos region.

"But there's no radical movement to speak of now, like that time I came here from Guadalajara, with David Alfaro Siqueiros at the head of a Communist Party demonstration. What fiery speeches they all gave! What a movement! The President of the Republic, there on the balcony, and us down below, screaming and demanding—not asking but *demanding*! Many times they would machine-gun us; many times they would shoot at us in the street. In Lagos I organized the first demonstrations to celebrate May Day. And we had some May Days—it was as though we were in Russia!

"In politics I had belonged to the Partido Nacional Revolucionario, but without leaving the Communist Party.... With Cárdenas it was more or less all right to collaborate [with the official party], but the [Communist] Party didn't surrender completely. But General Cárdenas did give the CP a lot of support.[51] It even happened in those days that at any public festivity or celebration of civic holidays, they would play *The Internationale*. And it was sung! The greeting was still with a fist in those times. Political passions and the passions of ideas, invading humanity. That's what the Cárdenas period was like."

---

[51]Cárdenas did recognize the Communist Party in Mexico, and allowed its members and sympathizers to participate in peasant and labor organizations. He also appointed CP members to important positions in the national Ministry of Education. After 1938, however, the influence of the Communists in the Çárdenas government, and in Mexican politics generally, declined markedly. The CP was badly split and differed strongly with Cárdenas over the Hitler-Stalin pact and the issue of providing asylum in Mexico to Leon Trotsky (see Calvert, 1973: 278–279; Schmitt, 1965: 16–20). Moreover, a strong rightist reaction to Cárdenas' agrarian and labor policies had developed, culminating in an armed rebellion against the central government led by General Saturnino Cedillo of San Luis Potosí (now opposed to Cárdenas' policies), and a nationwide electoral movement headed by General Juan Andreu Almazán, the conservative candidate for president in 1940. Responding to these and other developments, the Cárdenas administration during its last three years shifted its policy emphasis from the deepening of labor and agrarian reforms to consolidation and national unification. For further anàlysis of the relationship between the Cárdenas administration and the Mexican left, see Anguiano et al. (1975), Córdova (1975a), and Velasco (1975).

6

"La Vieja Guardia": Foot-Soldiers of Agrarian Reform

In the preceding chapters, attention has been focused primarily on the genesis and evolution of the agrarian reform movement in Lagos de Moreno, in which the thoughts and actions of key leaders such as Macedonio Ayala, Aniceto Martínez, and José Romero were of central importance. In this chapter our attention shifts to the second echelon of reform leaders. They are the old guard, *la vieja guardia*[1]—men who promoted the creation of specific agrarian communities and/or were among the first recipients of ejido plots in their communities. More than Ayala, Martínez, and Romero, these were the foot-soldiers of agrarian reform in Lagos de Moreno.

An initial hypothesis of this research was that the first agraristas, having participated together in the reform movement, would regard themselves as a generation whose membership was defined by the shared experience of the movement.[2] This hypothesis was amply confirmed by the research. All of these men not only identified themselves as part of the cohort of first agraristas; they also perceived latecomers to the movement and second-generation ejidatarios as forming another, "out" group. They maintained occasional social contacts with each

---

[1] *La Vieja Guardia* is the name of a national organization to which early agrarian reform leaders can belong. It functions primarily as a mediator to which old agraristas can turn when they encounter problems within their ejidos. It is part of the government-sponsored national campesino organization, the Confederación Nacional Campesina.

[2] This view of a "political generation" as being defined by common experiences at a given moment in history is similar to the concept of generations developed by Karl Mannheim in his classic essay, "On the Problem of Generations" (1952).

other, and tried as much as possible to help each other whenever one had problems with "newcomers" within his ejido.

The First Agraristas: Shared Attributes

The individuals discussed in this chapter were born between 1886 and 1915. Ejido files in the Agrarian Reform Ministry indicate that, according to censuses conducted as part of ejido technical-planning studies, signatories of the first petitions in the municipio of Lagos de Moreno ranged in age from 18 to 44 at the time of the census. Nevertheless, in my interviews with them, the agrarista community leaders reported that they and *most* of their associates were roughly between 25 and 30 years old when their involvement in the movement began. They were also married men with young families.

United States Experience

The single most distinctive characteristic shared by the majority of the first agraristas is that they had worked in the United States before becoming ejidatarios, usually even before joining the agrarian reform movement.[3] This is true not only of the majority of the early agraristas who were interviewed for this study, but also of deceased agrarian activists such as Moisés Pérez and Urbano Esparza, who were active in the Liga Regional Campesina. Romero was a notable exception to this pattern; the widows of Ayala and Martínez did not know if their husbands had ever worked in the United States.

Temporary migration to the U.S. has become so common in the Los Altos region that today in many communities over 50% of the men have worked at least once in the United States (Cornelius, 1976, 1981). However, between 1917 and 1930, the period when most of the agraristas interviewed for this study had been in the U.S., northbound migrants were a much smaller proportion of the Alteño population. Unfortunately, it is impossible to determine in retrospect whether the individuals who migrated north during these early years were predisposed by personality to be open to new experiences, to challenge the established order, and to be willing to take risks, or whether their experiences in the U.S.

---

[3]This pattern has been reported elsewhere in Mexico, particularly for men who became campesino leaders at the state or regional level. Primo Tapia, a state agrarian leader in Michoacán, had spent 14 years in the U.S., during which time he worked with the Flores Magón brothers and the Industrial Workers of the World (IWW) (Friedrich, 1970: 64–70).

may have been primarily responsible for producing these traits. The same set of traits would seem to have facilitated both migration and participation in the early phase of the agrarian reform movement.[4]

Why did they go to the United States? They were not political refugees: none of the agraristas reported leaving because of participation in the Revolution of 1910, nor in any of the revolutionary groups involved in the civil disorder which followed. Only two claimed that they left because they were persecuted by Cristeros (in the 1920s) for their agrarista sympathies, and the dates mentioned by one of them are sufficiently contradictory to raise some doubts about this claim. With differing emphases, the major explanation for their departure was "economic necessity." Either they were dissatisfied with the local wage scale, or they could not find work, or the pressure of too many sharecroppers on too little land led to their departure. All of them went with friends or relatives, or went to meet someone they knew who was already living in the U.S.

Working in the United States seems to have contributed to agrarian activism in three principal ways. First, it was, quite simply, an awakening. Men who had been to the U.S., whether they worked in agriculture or on the railroads, were exposed to very different working conditions and wage scales compared with their experiences in Lagos de Moreno. All of them reported higher take-home pay for tenant farmers, more generous crop-sharing—advantages never qualified by any mention of the higher costs of living in the United States. They also cite better living conditions and more agreeable relationships with supervisors and owners. José Romero recalled that he sought returning migrants as recruits for the reform movement because they were not willing to return to the old system of wages and labor relations.[5] As one of these recruits

---

[4]Manuel Gamio (1930: 161–162), the principal Mexican scholar studying Mexican migration to the United States during the 1920s, argues that the agrarian movement in Mexico "probably was imported from the United States to Mexico by the repatriated immigrants." In defense of this hypothesis, Gamio cites "the fact that until the immigration to the United States began to develop on a large scale and, in consequence, the repatriation of immigrants became great, the Mexican revolutions had a social, economic, or political character but never one fundamentally and exclusively agrarian. On the other hand, the revolutionary movements which succeeded, and coincided with the great development of immigration [to the U.S.] were chiefly characterized by their agrarian tendencies." However, Gamio's study was based primarily on one-shot interviews with Mexican immigrants who were living in the United States at the time of the research. His conclusion that migration to the U.S. led to agrarian activism is, therefore, entirely speculative.

[5]In his interviews with Mexican immigrants in the U.S., Gamio (1930: 161–162) found that "the circumstance of American social life which impressed the Mexican immigrant most was the existence of the homestead and the contrast between the comfortable and

explained, "Here they have always paid really miserable, very low wages, and so those of us who were accustomed to earning more money there [in the U.S.], and to another life, well, how could we come back here to work the same way [as before]?" A related observation made by some interviewees about the U.S. was that there "everyone works"— women, children, and men—and that even the well-to-do get their hands dirty at least occasionally. Clearly, returning migrants perceived prevailing working relationships in Lagos as more exploitive than those they encountered in the U.S., or they were at least more open to reform leaders' arguments to that effect.

A second major consequence of the U.S. experience is suggested by the agraristas' statements that they were "more liberal" or "less fanatical" (in religious terms) than other residents of their communities when they returned from the U.S.[6] Again, it is difficult to know whether this willingness to question orthodoxy of religious belief and practice was a function of a more open personality, whether it emerged from exposure to alternative religious beliefs and authority systems in the U.S., or whether it followed as a consequence of the local priests' criticisms of land reform. Most of the agraristas reported that they went to Mass more often or were more devout before they went to the U.S. than after they returned. Some recalled criticisms of Catholicism which they heard from U.S. citizens. Most of them mentioned Protestant sects or the beliefs of other faiths when discussing their impressions of the U.S. As one agrarista explained, "In the United States there is a lot of love, a lot of respect,

---

quiet life of the American workman and his own of perpetual misery and servitude upon the great haciendas, where he never realized the ancient and traditional desire for the possession of a piece of land of his own."

[6]Other observers of Mexican migrants to the U.S. returning to their homeland in the late 1920s and early 1930s have noted the same phenomenon. Gamio (1930: 116–117) notes that "the burden of fanaticism which the immigrant carries from Mexico little by little slips away [during residence in the U.S.] and often leaves him entirely. . . . One of three things happens: He becomes a normal, non-fanatic Catholic; indifferent or an unbeliever; or a Protestant." Paul Taylor, who studied returned migrants in the Los Altos municipio of Arandas (south of Lagos de Moreno), cites "a common observation [in the municipio] that the active adherence of the Mexican immigrants to their Catholic faith was weakened by the migration; this was true apart from, and in addition to, the proselytizing efforts of some Protestant denominations." But he also notes that many of the returned emigrants of Arandas "slipped back readily into the old ways" of religious practice (Taylor, 1933: 58). Nevertheless, even today, many local community priests in the Los Altos region oppose emigration of their parishioners to the United States—even for short periods—on the grounds that their religious beliefs are "diluted" or "corrupted" by the U.S. experience. In practice, this often means that returned migrants—like the agraristas of Lagos in the 1920s and 1930s—are less willing to pay tithes and to obey priestly authority in general than they were prior to migration.

there are all kinds of religious beliefs. I know evangelists. In the U.S. we would go to cultural temples, to evangelist churches, to Masonic temples, to the other Protestants." In the U.S. they were also released from home communities and their pressures to conform to local religious-observance practices. The combination of U.S. exposure and separation from the home-community environment may have weakened the authority of the Catholic Church and its priests. Whatever the cause, however, this greater "liberalism" was a critical factor in reducing the credibility of the local priests' threats of eternal damnation for those who petitioned for lands belonging to others.

Finally, the experience of being in the United States, far from home, induced them to develop basic literacy skills or aspirations for self-education. Of the eight individuals whose life histories are profiled below, only one of the men born in rural communities had received any formal schooling, and he was raised in Lagos town. For the rest, in quite a literal sense, the U.S. was an educational experience. Most learned at least some English, and those who did proudly recalled certain phrases, even after 45 years with little use of the language. More important, however, they all reported embarrassment at being unable to read their letters from home. This gave them the incentive at least to begin learning to read and write. Most of them became only functionally literate in the U.S.—but even functional literacy would have placed the returned migrant among the educated elite in his home community.[7]

Literacy also provided the aspiring agraristas with a skill which was critical to the success of the reform movement. Being able to read and write, they could sign petitions (not just mark thumbprints), which would itself have marked them as candidates for leadership positions. Many were able to compose their own messages to government officials and agencies. They were also able to read newspapers and political newsletters or flyers. This ability was, of course, particularly important in an era when television was nonexistent, radio and telephone communications did not yet penetrate into the countryside, and travel to large cities was difficult and costly. Thus all news about the agrarian reform movement in other parts of the country, as well as petitions for land redistribution, had to be conveyed by word of mouth and the written word. It is difficult today to appreciate what a boon basic literacy skills

[7]Official census data for 1930 show that only 28% of the males aged 15–29 and 31% of males aged 30 or more in the entire municipio of Lagos de Moreno knew how to read and write. The proportion of literate men in *rural* areas of the municipio was undoubtedly much lower.

were in rural Lagos de Moreno of the 1920s and 1930s. The results are reflected in numerous laboriously written but eloquent documents in the ejido files of the Agrarian Reform Ministry.

For most of the agraristas interviewed, their U.S. experience did not include any strictly political activities. Three of the men profiled below belonged to a labor union while in the U.S., two of them for only part of their stay. But only one of the three reported any participation in strikes, and none were elected to union positions. Agraristas who had worked in the U.S. did remark that they had observed more cooperative work patterns there and had learned about vaguely-defined benefits of organizing to achieve a goal.

The agraristas who worked in the U.S. reported a variety of reasons for returning to Mexico. None of them, however, claimed to have been among the more than 400,000 Mexicans who were deported or "voluntarily" repatriated between 1929 and 1935.[8] Some gave family reasons, or cited unemployment and Depression conditions in the U.S. as their reason for returning to Mexico. All but one claimed to have known about the land reform movement in Mexico before they returned, and to have had an interest in "seeing if it was true" so that they might benefit. But only one had heard about the small amounts of land being distributed by the Mexican government specifically to returning migrants from the U.S., in Jalisco and several other states (see Carreras de Velasco, 1974: 115).

Participation in the Agrarian Reform Movement

The men whose life histories are recounted below participated in the agrarian reform movement in slightly different ways. Some lived in or very near Lagos and participated actively in the overall reform effort, coming to know many agrarian communities and their leaders, even though they themselves were not necessarily among the first petitioners for an ejido. Others worked primarily toward the formation of their own ejido community. Some were not among the original petitioners, but were part of the small groups of first recipients of ejido lands and later became leaders in their communities. All of these men were knowledgeable about the general reform movement based in Lagos under the leadership of Macedonio Ayala, José Romero, and Aniceto Martínez. All of them knew Ayala and Romero, but only Francisco Navia recalled personal contacts with Martínez.

[8]The most detailed studies of this mass return migration from the U.S. to Mexico are Carreras de Velasco (1974) and Hoffman (1974).

Remarkable similarities emerged in their accounts of the agrarian reform movement and their participation in it. Every *agrarista* interviewed was asked why he had participated in the agrarian reform movement and what he had hoped to achieve. Philosophical or ideological motives were reported almost always as a second reason, and then only in very general terms. Other than José Romero, only Francisco Navia first attributed his initial interest and involvement in the reform movement to the appeal of its *ideals*. When cited, these ideals were: "land and liberty," "land belongs to the tiller," "to help poor people live better," and "to be our own masters."

In almost every case, the *agraristas* explained that they first began to consider joining the reform movement because of their own poverty and a desire for independence. Redistribution of land was viewed as a pragmatic solution to a basic problem—one for which they could find no other solutions. For the town-based laborers, represented by José Romero, Francisco Navia, Salvador Martínez, and Ernesto Rodríguez, the goal was to collectively secure a fair price for a man's labor:

> For them [the workers] to make good on their work, to make their labor worth more. Because here [in Lagos], if the price of anything rose, [wages did not also rise].

> It was our nature to work, to continue struggling, somehow, with the unions so that they might achieve an improvement, rights, all of those things which we had never had.

For the men who hoped to become ejidatarios, land reform was a way out of hunger, enabling them to keep their entire harvest and to have something left over to buy basic necessities:

> My ideals, which came naturally to me, were to be able to eat enough to be full. . . . Because to live in complete poverty is something, well, very harsh.

> I would see stacks, stacks of maize that we picked. And with any little debt that my grandparents owed, they [the hacienda] would take it all. Nothing was left.

> I was already married [and had children]. . . . We didn't have enough. You can't imagine, you just can't imagine. . . . In our house, we never had a bench on which to sit. We had no bed to sleep on, just a straw mat. [We were] nearly naked.

As the following statements attest, the aspiring ejidatarios also wanted to be their own bosses, to dispose freely of the fruits of their labor and to be responsible only to themselves:

> Those of us who were used to agricultural work, we hoped to own a piece of land, to protect ourselves against having to do other people's work.

> [The goal was] to have a piece of land to work individually, that is—to be free from slavery.

> On the hacienda, as sharecroppers, it was work from 6 to 6, all day behind the plow or wherever.... When the plowing was finished, there was always work on the hacienda. And that was from sunup to sundown. Frankly, I was tired. . . . In the ejido, well, it's different.

These motives all came together and propelled the reformers forward, as one of them explained:

> If you enclose a piglet in a small corral and he doesn't like it, of course he tries to get out, right? Or to find a way to feed himself and not be there, right? In view of the wages that the rich paid and the oppression that we faced—we couldn't even gather firewood. When they would see us go for firewood, or whatever, they would take our axes, take away our burros, the ropes and everything. Well, they make one explode, right? . . . When I learned about the [land reform] laws—because I could read and had a good memory—I said, well, here there's no other way except for the village to explode, and let's take something from them, so that we can at least have someplace to farm.

To be sure, there may have been other motives for seeking agrarian reform. For example, one agrarista reported that the men who filed the petition for his ejido were peons and servants who had been dismissed by the owners of the hacienda from which the land was sought. Possibly, then, revenge or resentment may have played a part in the decision to petition for that ejido, and this motive may have influenced individual participants in other communities. Nevertheless, while the men I interviewed expressed general dissatisfaction with the treatment they or others received from the hacendados, revenge was not a dominant motive for sustained participation in the movement.

Similarly, political mobility—either individual or collective—does not seem to have been a primary concern. Most of the agraristas who hoped that the campesino class might come to play an important role in politics, or that they themselves might gain employment in local government, acquired such aspirations only after they became ejidatarios. While leaders like José Romero viewed the agrarian reform movement in part as a vehicle for building a constituency for more sweeping political and social reforms, there is little evidence for such objectives in the case of most agraristas.

All of the agraristas identified the clergy, rich people ("el capital"), and the Cristeros as the principal opponents of agrarian reform. The following statements are typical:

> The real enemy we have had is the clergy; they have always been on the side of the rich.

> The clergy have always been allied with the rich, and here in Mexico . . . it has always been that way. It is an inheritance the Spanish left to us.

Four of the agraristas interviewed had been sought or physically attacked by bands of Cristeros, and all of the others spoke about a close relationship between rich landowners and the Cristeros. In general, they attributed some peasants' siding with the rich and the Cristeros to religious fanaticism and fear. Two of them described the origins of the relationship, as they understood it:

> Look, I understand how they took advantage of a person's ignorance, foolishness, and hunger. They offered them any little thing, and gave them a few centavos—to persecute their own [social] class. That was promoted by all of the rich landowners.

> The rich would tell their own peones acasillados, "You go, I'll give you money, a weapon, support for your family. How can these shameless people [the agraristas] do this and leave you without a roof, with nothing? Because they'll take our land and where will we go? . . . Don't let them do this to you. Look, they don't believe in God. We must stop them. Here's some money."

When asked why they had not believed the priests' threats against agraristas when nearly all of their neighbors did, some simply shrugged and commented on their own daring. Others described themselves as being "more liberal," or having been raised in a "liberal environment."[9]

Given the opposition of the clergy, an economic boycott by landowners, local opposition from other community residents, and the dan-

---

[9]See Chapter 2, note 13, for local usage of the term "liberal."

ger of attack by Cristeros and white guards—why did they persist? Each time this question was posed, the agraristas would pause, shrug, and smile. Some referred to their own stubbornness or foolishness, but most explained their behavior as a matter of necessity. As one agrarista put it, "Oh, Señora, it's that hunger is unbearable."

Most of the men described in this chapter were given arms by the Cárdenas government in 1935 and participated in the campesino para-military units organized by the government during the 1935–38 period. Some agrarian communities in Lagos were issued weapons even before their land grants were finalized. All of the men who received rifles viewed the weapons as essential for self-defense against the Cristeros and white guards. Their sentiments were expressed most pointedly by a frail, aging agrarista in the ejido of Ciénega de Mata, who reported: "After they gave us arms in Lagos, we lost our fear."

All ejidatarios whose life histories are presented in this chapter also served in the municipio government in elected or appointed positions, but only one of them during the period since 1940. They have been loyal supporters of the official party, the Partido Revolucionario Institucional, most of them having served as PRI representatives at polling places for various elections. They have joined or organized community petitions to government agencies for services (piped water, electricity, etc.) for their communities. Particularly when dealing with the Agrarian Reform Min-istry, and especially with regard to problems which they or their friends (rather than the entire community) have encountered, they often work through representatives of the government-backed national campesino organization, the CNC. In short, they remain squarely within the official political establishment in Mexico, however critical they may be of the regime's performance during the post-Cárdenas era.

The First Agraristas: Individual Profiles

Francisco Navia

Among the prominent early participants of the reform movement in Lagos, Francisco Navia is the only survivor who continued to participate formally in administering agrarian reform after 1940.[10] In 1976 he was a government employee in charge of one of the offices of the Agrarian Reform Ministry in the state of Zacatecas. He had a quiet yet forthcom-

[10]In fact, Navia, Moisés Pérez, and Miguel Aguirre were the only agraristas who re-mained active in agrarian reform in any capacity after the early redistribution of land in Lagos (i.e., after 1940). Pérez and Aguirre, deceased respectively in the 1940s and 1950s, were involved in the movement as local officers of the state branch of the CNC.

ing manner in dealing with the endless stream of ejidatarios (each of whom he addressed as "compañero" or "compañera") who approached his desk with problems relating to their individual land-tenure rights or the governance of their communities. Because of his official capacity, he was well informed about agrarian problems in Zacatecas, and on changes in the agrarian law over the years. He continued to visit relatives who still lived in Lagos, but had distanced himself from agrarian issues there since his departure in 1943. He was, however, eager to help write a history of the past and willing to speak freely of his involvement in it. His recollections as well as his correspondence with Romero have been cited several times in earlier chapters.

Francisco Navia was born in 1910 in Lagos de Moreno, where he completed his primary schooling while working part-time in the Rizo de Oro barbershop, shining shoes. His father had worked for a time with Nieves Ortiz at the Victoria textile mill, but later acquired four looms of his own on which he, and later his son, wove blankets. Navia senior and Nieves Ortiz together helped to encourage residents in the community of Buenavista, near Lagos, to petition for ejido lands; Buenavista subsequently became one of the earliest ejido communities in the municipio. Francisco Navia's father probably also was involved in the early Unión de Obreros Libertarios. Throughout their participation in the agrarian and labor movements, both Navias retained their "laborer" status, continuing to weave blankets (although they were sometimes boycotted) and never seeking land for themselves. Navia explained that he did not accept an ejido plot "because the motto was that 'land belongs to the tiller,' and I was not going to work it, because my nature, and my circumstances, were different—[those] of a laborer."

In his late teens, Navia became one of the founders of the Sindicato de Oficios Varios. In a photograph of Lagos municipio employees taken in the late 1930s, he is easily identified not only by his youth but by his distinctive attire—a leather waist-length jacket, riding pants, and boots. Macedonio Ayala's widow recalled that Navia began in the movement as an errand boy. He soon rose, however, for he appears in later photographs (one of them reproduced in Chapter 4) of the Jalisco delegation to the national labor convention held in Mexico City, in January 1934. As the movement progressed and prominent senior members died or left Lagos, Navia advanced within the organization. It was he who received the news when President Cárdenas approved the first ejido grants in 1935; and it was he who organized the community groups to receive the ejido lands and arms from the government later that year.

A photograph of Lagos municipio employees taken in the late 1930s. Francisco Navia is seated, far left; Salvador Martínez is standing, second from left.

Navia joined the reform effort, he explained, because he enjoyed listening to his father and Nieves Ortiz talk about their involvement with Buenavista, and he agreed with their ideas. Aniceto Martínez was his friend, and he convinced Navia that they should work for the people:

> I began to talk with Aniceto. I liked his ideals, his thoughts, his action. He said, "Look, here we are screwed. We live here, completely isolated, without rights, without this, without that. Okay, I believe it is more just that we organize ourselves to work for the people. We're going to organize ourselves a union.

By establishing a labor organization, they hoped to achieve through unity what they had been unable to secure individually. Whether he approved of them or not, it appears that Navia understood more about the potentially socialist directions of the national agrarian and labor reform programs of the Cárdenas administration than any of the other surviving agraristas, with the exception of José Romero.

After the ejido grants began, Navia continued to weave blankets and to work with the local labor and campesino organizations. He became an officer of the armed agrarista reserve regiment, participating in the climactic "battle" with the Cristeros on the Mesa Redonda in 1935. He won a seat on the Lagos ayuntamiento during the administration of Francisco Carrera (1936–37). Navia continued, however, to be threatened because of his political views, and he recalls at least three face-to-face confrontations with local landowners.

In the early 1940s, the political climate shifted once more against the reformers. Navia recalled that when Luis Nungaray was municipio president (1943–44), and Manuel Ávila Camacho was President of the Republic, an "emergency salary" (possibly in response to World War II) was made available to the workers. At the time, Navia was working on the construction of the Nestlé factory in Lagos, with promises from Guadalajara that he would become Secretary-General of the union in that factory once it began operations. At the same time, he was working with employees of the potable water plant, who sought through him to petition for their rights under the emergency salary decrees. When he went to the municipio government building, the local chief of police cornered him and offered him a choice between leaving Lagos and being killed if he continued with his union activities. Also received badly by the Nungaray (widely acknowledged to have been hostile to the reform movement), Navia left Lagos. His sister had moved to Zacatecas in 1939, because as a teacher in Lagos she had been persecuted for trying to implement the federal lay-education reforms. So in 1943 he and his family left for Zacatecas. They have not returned to live in Lagos.

Ernesto Rodríguez

For years he was known around town by his nickname, "Muerte" ("Death"), referring to his stark features and thin frame. By 1976, reliance on a walking cane and shoulders bent by his 77 years had reduced Ernesto Rodríguez' stature, but his eyes still sparkled with the mischievousness of a boy. His picaresque expression (partially captured in the photograph of him) was easily triggered by a piece of social gossip or political news.

Rodríguez was born in a small settlement in the state of Zacatecas, at the turn of the century.[11] He was the youngest of 12 children born into a family of agricultural day-laborers. When he was about 7, his father lost his job due to the death of the landowner, and they moved to the town of Lagos de Moreno to join an aunt and an uncle who was serving as priest

---

[11]His birthday was November 7. As he told me, this was "the anniversary of the Revolution—not the Mexican Revolution, the Russian."

Ernesto Rodríguez ("Muerte"), in 1976.

in the area.[12] The family lived near the edge of town; and while his father sharecropped, Rodríguez attended school, completing his primary education.[13] The master barber and owner of El Rizo de Oro, the barbershop serving the wealthy men in town, was a neighbor who urged Rodríguez' father to let the boy work in the shop. Rodríguez recalled that even before the 1910 Revolution, he listened in the shop as some of the rich "liberals" in town discussed the need to limit the authority of the priests and to enforce constitutional limitations on religious celebrations held outside of Church buildings. During the Revolution, federal troops were garrisoned a few doors away from the barbershop, where young Ernesto often played pranks on them. From the shop, he overheard the soldiers' conversations critical of the Porfirio Díaz regime and, later, speculations about the government of Francisco I. Madero.

As he grew older, Rodríguez rose from odd-job boy to apprentice in the shop. In 1920, as a journeyman, he opened his own small barbershop. Most of his clients were employees of the local textile mill, the Fábrica La

---

[12]There were several priests and nuns among his sisters, nephews, and nieces. Rodríguez' father wanted the boy to become a priest, but Ernesto quit school early, rebelling against the discipline he resented.

[13]Probably three years of school, although he was inconsistent on this point.

Victoria, some of whom were already talking about labor reform. However, he did not participate in the UOL, and knew José Romero only casually.

Late in 1922 it became apparent that the factory would close and that Rodríguez—along with the workers who were his clients—would face dire economic problems. So he closed his shop and, with a friend, left for the United States. At first he traveled around a great deal, working for the railroads and in agriculture near Los Angeles, Butte, Portland, Salt Lake City, Ogden, Las Vegas, and Reno. He met a friend who had been to Idaho, and since Rodríguez had a brother living in that state, they decided to go there. Early in 1924 he arrived in Pocatello, Idaho, where he lived for the next seven years.

He began working as a barber in the two shops which served the Mexicans in Pocatello. There was a substantial seasonal fluctuation in the Mexican population, increasing at harvest-time and declining in the slack agricultural season. The more-or-less stable population of Mexicans (estimated at less than 50—primarily men without families) consisted of men who had been brought in as strikebreakers to work in the local steel mill. Some of them stayed on to work after the strike, plus a few agricultural workers who stayed during the winter, living in shacks along the railroad tracks where they could "secure" charcoal from the railroad cars to heat their homes. During the off-season there wasn't much activity in Pocatello, so Rodríguez and others spent their time playing cards and pool in the billiards hall where the Mexicans congregated, and at the movies, which provided inexpensive entertainment. "I sometimes went three times a day to the movies. There was nothing else to do." Rodríguez learned much of his English from these films.

After some time in Pocatello, a Greek barber hired him to work in a "white people's" shop serving the steel mill and railroad crews. He was asked to join the barbers' union. "Because I had already seen in the United States that everyone was united and I didn't want to be on my own, I immediately joined the barbers' union. I could have worked independently [outside the union], but no, I took the qualifying examination." The union was formed as a means of insuring some uniformity in prices and wages. A local barbers' school, eager to process as many graduates as possible, was turning its students onto the market and they had been charging lower prices. Rodríguez recalled that the union served its purpose well. Although he paid his union dues for four or five years, he neither attended any meetings nor served as a union official.

Together with a Mexican friend, he helped to dispatch crews of Mexican agricultural workers to the potato, sugar-beet, and pea harvests in parts of Idaho, Wyoming ("near Yellowstone Park"), and Montana. He recalled having to help out in the field kitchens, and occasionally traveling with the workers to work-sites in the area. He also sometimes sold bootleg liquor and marijuana. During his stay in the United States, he kept informed about events in Mexico through a subscription to *La Prensa*, a newspaper which was written and published by Mexican exiles in San Antonio, Texas.

Rodríguez decided to return to Mexico late in 1930. As he explained, "You can wander, wander, but a penny doesn't stop being a penny even if it rubs around with quarters or gold coins." This sentiment, together with the Great Depression ("in Hoover's times—God, it was hard!"), led to his decision to return home.

During his absence from Lagos, an older brother, Juan (whom Rodríguez described as "a revolutionary") had participated in an electoral campaign[14] for José Guadalupe Zuno and had been named to a local judgeship. In that capacity he had tried to foment redistribution of land in the municipio of Lagos, and as a result in 1924 or later he had been run out of town. This brother moved to Aguascalientes, where the agrarian movement was stronger, becoming secretary of the ayuntamiento in the state capital and participating in redistribution of the lands of the hacienda Pabellón. The remainder of the family followed Juan to Aguascalientes.

Because these members of his family had moved to Aguascalientes, Rodríguez settled there upon his return from the United States. He tried to make a living as a *colono* (a private small landowner benefiting from a limited agrarian reform) from late 1930 until 1932. In 1932, relatives still in Lagos notified him that an established barbershop site on a corner of the central plaza was available to rent. These relatives offered to set him up in business if he would train their sons as barbers. So in 1932 Rodríguez returned to Lagos after a nine-year absence.

He found the local economy in terrible straits; no one could find work. The SOV was already operating as a union of agraristas and craftsmen working together to promote agrarian reform and higher wages for laborers. He joined the SOV, prompted by his experiences in the U.S. and his own disquietude:

[14]Rodríguez recalled that he met Zuno during this campaign in 1922, just before he left for the U.S. Since Zuno became Governor of Jalisco in March 1923, it probably was the gubernatorial campaign.

> I have always had [leftist ideas]. Ever since I was in school there were many things I did not like. Then I went to the United States and I saw that everywhere there were unions, workers met together everywhere, so I began to be more concerned about that. I had already been a friend of Romero's [and others].

Although he joined the SOV, he never discussed his politics with his clients at the barbershop, for fear that it would have negative consequences for his business. But he recalled that the reformers and sometimes a group of Freemasons would meet in the central plaza during the midday meal hour, when the streets would be deserted.

Except for brief periods in Guadalajara and Mexico City, where he lived with nephews and nieces, Rodríguez did not leave Lagos de Moreno until his death in 1979. He never returned to work in the United States. He continued his local activism in the SOV, becoming president of the local barbers' union when the labor movement became large enough in 1938 or 1939 to permit division of the SOV into separate trade unions. He remained a fiercely loyal friend to José Romero, strongly supporting him in his political travails. He kept abreast of local political developments, maintaining friendly relations with lower-echelon politicians. He himself never took an active role in local electoral politics. He was ardently anticlerical, a religious skeptic, and a believer in equitable treatment of urban and agricultural workers.

Salvador Martínez

Salvador Martínez was known as "El Charro," in recognition of his dapper dress in his younger years (somewhat subdued in the photograph shown earlier, where he appears with Navia and others). Until his death in 1975, he continued to work in the municipio treasury office, where he had been employed with few interruptions for nearly 40 years.

Martínez was born in about 1886, the only son of a relatively well-established muleteer who made his living transporting crops on consignment between Ojuelos, Lagos, and San Juan de los Lagos, and occasionally to adjacent states. Martínez often accompanied his father on these trips, or had to go in search of him when his return to Lagos was delayed by bouts with the bottle. The elder Martínez must have fared well, for he left his son a small plot of land and a multiple-room house on the edge of town which the family continues to occupy. Martínez was also sent to primary school, where he learned to read and write and mastered basic mathematics. In 1900, unable to afford further schooling, he turned to carpentry, regarding it as a more secure occupation than being a store clerk or another kind of employee. In 1909–10 he spent a year in Mexico City ("just to take a look"), working as an assistant carpenter. He returned to Lagos just before the outbreak of the 1910 Revolution. His father subsidized the cost of establishing a carpenter's shop, which Martínez operated for some 18 years. During the turbulent years of the Cristiada, Martínez sided with the government, explaining, "I was always with the government."

With the onset of the Great Depression, he fell upon "very difficult times; there was no work, and furthermore, all of the rich men wanted one to work for them very cheaply. . . . I had to pay journeymen, and help them with the work, to meet my obligations." When José María Padilla was municipio president (1930–31), he commissioned Martínez' shop to make some doors for the municipio government building. From that time on, Martínez was involved in politics and left his carpentry shop to be managed by others.

The agraristas all agreed that Martínez joined forces with the reformists, participating in the SOV and the agrarian reform; but they always described him as one of the few whose participation was motivated by political patronage. Martínez himself admitted, "To be sure, I worked with the agraristas, because that was what we had to do to be in with the government. . . . We took charge of organizing [agrarian communities] on government orders." He claimed a leadership role in the movement, explaining, however, that he did not wish to be at the head, "because they [the principal leaders] were the ones they shot at."

When land was finally granted, Martínez accepted a plot in the ejido of Lagos. However, he never farmed it himself; a neighbor sharecropped for him. He continued to work in the municipio government, serving as treasurer under three different local administrations, and as an elected member of the ayuntamiento under Francisco Carrera. He said that he spoke with the municipio government for the agraristas when they encountered problems, helping them through his contacts in the administration. He also put up bail and loaned money, initially through contacts with a deputy in the legislature who had money; this would have been a lucrative business. After portions of his plot were taken from him by the ejido community, he withdrew from the cause, calling the agraristas "ungrateful" and "envious."

From his vantage point as an employee of the municipio government and an active member of the official party, Martínez observed local and national politics for many years. The earliest party membership card he retained was dated 1931. He recalled, however, that he first participated

Arcadio Amézquita, photographed on his ejido plot, in 1976.

in a political campaign when Daniel Benítez was elected governor of
Jalisco (in 1927). That year, he went as part of a local delegation to
Guadalajara to support Benítez' candidacy. He remained a wry and inter-
ested political observer until his death.

Arcadio Amézquita

Appearing frail of frame and health, Arcadio Amézquita in his 75th year
regretted that "I can take the downhill path more easily than the in-
cline." Yet in 1976, one could still find him on his ejido plot, unshaven and
in tattered clothing, denims rolled up to his knees, planting tomato seed-
lings in the mud, tending irrigation ditches, and observing his successful
experiment with lentil cultivation or his less felicitous venture into fruit-
growing. Although it was hard work, he took pride in his occupation as a
farmer: "Our life is pleasant, preferred by many who do not know much
about it. . . . [Here] it is peaceful, but it is hard work from sunup to

sundown." He had an almost anthropomorphic view of the land, and his speech was distinctive in its rustic poetic imagery:

> I prefer to be a son of the soil and not of a good employer. Because the land, if I work it, says to me, "Eat." If I don't work it, it doesn't give me much. "You didn't work me well, I won't give you [much]." . . . The land doesn't say to me, "Where were you yesterday? Where did you go?" . . . I told you [the author] that I was coming today [to the author's residence, to be interviewed], but first I had to go around and do everything that had to be done [on the ejido plot], so that the land would not be left wanting. Because the plants are family, too. At least, that's how I feel, they are my family. I have to feed them, give them water, soil.

Amézquita was born in 1900 in the small settlement of San Jorge, nestled among several large haciendas and ranches near Lagos town. His grandfather purchased about 8 hectares in the nineteenth century, when land was cheap; of these, Amézquita's mother inherited approximately 4 hectares, including a small adobe house. The Amézquita family farmed about 2 hectares of the land—not enough to support the 10 children. So his father worked as a mule-driver, carting firewood from the mountains into Lagos town for sale, and as a sharecropper on several haciendas. When he was about 12, Amézquita began to work for his father.

Between 1919 and 1921, Amézquita worked in the United States, part of the time on the railroad, but mostly in a meat-packing plant in Kansas City. The work was initially exhausting, but soon he grew accustomed to the schedule, and he found that he could earn 30 dollars a week in the U.S., compared to 17 or 18 pesos every two weeks in San Jorge. While in the U.S. he learned to read, so that he wouldn't be embarrassed by having others read his letters to him; he didn't like the readers to learn that he was being scolded by mail before he could hear the letter. In 1921[15] his shift at the plant was reduced to seven hours per day. Feeling tired and knowing that his take-home pay would be less, he returned to Mexico for a vacation, with his employer's promise to finance his trip from the border back to Kansas City when he returned to the U.S. However, in 1922 he married and his father expected him to stay at home. He never went back to the U.S.

---

[15]A recession year which also witnessed a resurgence of anti-Mexican nativism in the U.S. (see Cardoso, 1980: 97-99).

Amézquita became involved in the agrarian reform movement slowly and reluctantly. When municipio president Susano Castañeda was promoting petitions for land reform, Amézquita never heard about it. "Then, we were very distant from the government. There was a government—[and] we didn't even know [the officials'] names." When a man from Aguascalientes came to the hacienda San Bernardo in 1927 and urged Amézquita and his father-in-law to join the agrarian movement, neither of them was interested. During the Cristero rebellion of 1927–29, Amézquita was "also with the rich," not as a resident laborer on an hacienda (peón acasillado), but as a sharecropper. He lived in the small house his mother inherited, farmed some of her land, continued to collect firewood, and worked occasionally on the nearby haciendas. He was never a peón acasillado, because "I never wanted to serve anyone."

Amézquita described himself as "very timid" before he joined the agrarian reform movement. "Yesterday, I was afraid of everything. Today, I'm not even afraid of the President of the Republic." He recalled one specific example of his timidity. In 1928 or 1929, the tax collector in Lagos called a meeting in San Jorge to announce the availability of land for ejidatarios. This was the first he learned of any petition for land for the community of San Jorge.

> He told all of us, 'I have come to tell you that the lands are available to give to you. Let's see who wants them.' But there were some [hacienda administrators] there, with pistols that looked bigger than I was. And they would adjust their pistols upward on their hips and say, 'Who wants [land]?' Well, nobody did!

Although at the time he was afraid to express an interest in ejido land, Amézquita was dissatisfied with his situation, and in the year or two that followed, conditions worsened. In 1930 he lodged a protest against the administrators of one of the haciendas on behalf of his father, who was unwilling to protest himself. His father had planted "*a la cuartilla*," an arrangement in which the laborer supplied only his own labor and that of another person to plant, while the owner of the land provided the land, a plow-team, plow, and seed, in return for which he took three-quarters of the harvest, leaving the remainder plus a payment of 210 kilos of maize to the laborer. That year, although his father had supplied the plow-team, hoe, plow, and seed, when the harvest division was made, the hacienda kept the same three-quarters of the crop. Once he protested, Amézquita did succeed in getting some additional corn back from the hacienda, but in the process one of the employees of the hacienda suggested that, given the unfair treatment, he should petition for ejido lands.

During this period, Amézquita owned five burros, two calves, and a team of oxen. He tried to find a place to sharecrop where he might also pay a fee to pasture his animals. But the landowners would only accept workers who were willing to give up their own animals and come to live in hacienda houses—i.e., they would give him work only if he became a peón acasillado. It was a strategic ploy by the landowners, Amézquita claimed: "That way they could destroy [a land reform movement] if there were anyone who would ask for land."[16] Under these circumstances, Amézquita tried late in 1930 to keep his nine animals corraled, feeding them as best he could. "And it rained, continuously, through December, January, and February."

Every week he would travel to Lagos to go to Mass, and then wander the streets asking if anyone knew of work or a place to sharecrop. In one such encounter, a man from the community of Buenavista told him that his community was an ejido, but that he would be welcome there. The work terms were 15 percent of the maize and forage harvest paid to the community leader, with free pasture for the animals. At first he worried because no one liked the agraristas, and his father opposed the ejidos. But he concluded that, after all, the people who hated the agraristas would not feed his family when they were hungry. Given the hunger of his children—which he feared might force him to kill someone else's animals for food—becoming an ejidatario seemed preferable to dying in jail for theft. After thinking it over, he, a brother, his father, and his father-in-law spent a year farming on the ejido land in Buenavista. Later, he also farmed briefly in other ejidos, while awaiting the grant of land in San Jorge.

Very early in 1931, he began to attend meetings of the reformists in Lagos and, with his relatives, to pursue the petition for an ejido in San Jorge.[17] He spent the next five years, until 1935, struggling to secure ejido land for San Jorge and nearby communities. Sometimes he would ac-

---

[16]At the time, peones acasillados were ineligible to petition for ejido land (they became eligible in 1934), so the landowners' policy of forcing agricultural workers into hacienda housing would effectively have aborted a land-reform drive.

[17]According to documents in the expediente ejidal (ASRA) for San Jorge (now called Macedonio Ayala), the petition for an ejido was signed on May 25, 1931. The head of the petitioning committee was Aniceto Amézquita. Arcadio Amézquita's name first appears in the record in January 1932, as the community's representative for the agrarian census. He was elected on December 6, 1936, as president of the first ejido governing council, the day that the land was formally turned over to the ejido.

company Macedonio Ayala on his visits to rural communities, trying to convince others to join the movement.

He recalled the reform as a slow process, involving great personal sacrifice. He would go into Lagos to inquire about progress on their petition, only to be told by Romero or Ayala, "Well, man, nothing. Forgotten by God and man." Often during these years, while he farmed in other ejidos, he could visit his family only on weekends. He claimed not to have slept at home more than five nights during those five years, "not so much out of fear [for his own life], but so that they [the Cristeros] wouldn't hurt the little ones. For five years I never used a blanket, just a jacket [as a cover]." He recalled that "my wife was very young, and I missed the flower of her youth."

In about 1931, José Vallarta came to San Jorge looking for relatives of his young fiancée. Amézquita was the closest relative, and soon they fell to discussing the reform movement in Lagos. Amézquita introduced Vallarta to José Romero. On a later visit, Vallarta told Amézquita that he hoped that General Lázaro Cárdenas would become the new President of the Republic, and invited him to join the Cárdenas camp. Amézquita was told that if Cárdenas succeeded, the land would be granted; and if he did not, agraristas would have to take up arms. Amézquita agreed to join the Cárdenas supporters.

Cárdenas did win, and he signed the presidential decree granting the land to San Jorge on May 14, 1935. That September, Amézquita became the leader of the 17 men in San Jorge who received arms from the federal government. A few weeks later, Amézquita fought, together with the other agraristas from San Jorge, in the battle between the Cristeros and the federal and agrarista troops at the Mesa Redonda. "We thought we would be killed," he recalled. "We didn't even know how to use the rifles."

The first year as an ejidatario was still a year of hunger and suffering. Amézquita remembered gathering seed pods from the mesquite trees and stuffing them into his jacket for his midday meal.

> It was a shame, enough to make one scream. The kids didn't eat, we didn't eat. . . . We had nothing. We were in the depths of poverty; there was no one to give us even a tortilla. . . . We didn't have time [to beg]; we had to work. The first year was rough, but later there was enough for everyone.

Amézquita attended several state congresses of agrarian communities in Guadalajara, the first in 1936. He served at least three different terms as head of the ejido governing council of San Jorge, now renamed in honor of Macedonio Ayala. In his position as ejido official, Amézquita taught himself to write in order to make out official correspondence. He also served as representative of the PRI in local election booths.

Although Amézquita succeeded in making a living as an ejidatario, there was scant evidence of prosperity about his person or his home. His small, sparsely furnished adobe house lacked windows, and its dirt floor was muddy during the rainy season; chickens and turkeys wandered through the kitchen. His family wore simple, threadbare clothing. His wife, in fact, complained about how little money he had given them over the years for clothing and household expenses. Yet his 8-hectare plot had three kerosene-powered pumps which he had purchased over the years to supply a system of irrigation ditches he had dug. He grew small quantities of various crops to supply his numerous grandchildren and for his home consumption. After all the effort that he had put into clearing, cultivating, and maintaining his plot, he valued the land highly: "I really cherish this piece of land. If they gave me 100,000 pesos [for it], I wouldn't take it." And he was proud of his contribution to the agrarian reform: "I am not [only] the father of sons, I am the father of a village."

There was, however, dissent within his family and tension in his community. With the product of his ejido land, he purchased some 45 additional hectares of land, 25 cows, and a small truck. All this he gave to his sons to manage, and they sold or exchanged it for inferior property. He also had recurrent problems with the local ejido leadership. The ejido is small—26 men. As a leader of the community, Amézquita was permitted to select his own parcel when the ejido was granted; he chose 8 hectares of rainfall-dependent land (*tierras de temporal*).[18] However, since he had introduced his own well-pumps and irrigated his land, the ejido leadership tried to repossess half of his plot, claiming that he was entitled to only 4 hectares. Amézquita appealed to the Vieja Guardia and the CNC in Mexico City. He won his case, but Amézquita anticipated that when he died, his wife and granddaughter would be forced to move off the land.

He was also angry and scornful of recent ejido officers for their lack of attention to communal tasks and responsibilities. He noted that no one even remembered or celebrated any more the date when the land was

[18]Ejido plots in Lagos were generally limited to 8 hectares of rainfall-dependent soil, or 4 hectares of irrigated land. Irrigated land was defined as land which had access to water supplied from dams, not as land individually irrigated by well-water.

granted. "They have lost their hunger." He worried because he was the only survivor among the original agraristas in San Jorge: .

> There used to be a good harmony before, but born of necessity. Not now. We had a brief time when they had something to eat, to wear, and even to go out on. . . . [But] instead of benefiting, or of making their lives better, they squandered it, and they'll end up in the same jam: in need.

By his own admission and his wife's complaint, Amézquita learned to drink quite heavily when he began to keep company with the agraristas. He used to get drunk "and even to go after women." Because of the priests' opposition to the movement, for 30 years he never went to Mass or to confession, saying prayers to himself whenever he felt the need. But a few years ago a friend persuaded him to see a priest, who did not reprimand him for his sins, as he had expected. At the same time, he gave up drinking, in part because of doctor's orders. Through it all, he developed his own brand of religion: "This soil we walk on—there is some spirit which had to form it. Let us not doubt it: Jehovah exists, but we don't know where. We say he is in Heaven. . . . But I know He is here."

Arcadio Amézquita died in 1978.

Cipriano Barbosa

Very short, nearly bald, and approaching 88, Cipriano Barbosa was a rover most of his life: "I was an adventurer in life. . . . One gets used to wandering. My ambition was to see the world, but I didn't have enough time or money." Even in his old age, he moved often between the homes of his children and other relatives, out of habit and also because of family squabbles deriving from his wife's strong character and his own fondness for liquor.

Barbosa was born in 1893 on a small ranch which his grandfather rented in the northern part of the municipio of Lagos de Moreno. There his father (who could read and write) supervised field laborers on some 20 hectares which he worked in a sharecropping partnership with an employee of the Hacienda El Tecuán. When Barbosa was about 7 or 8, the family moved to El Crespo, a large ranch where his father began as foreman and later became a sharecropper. About 10 years later, just as the Revolution began, Barbosa left the agricultural fields and began a series of odd jobs. He worked for six months in 1911 as a house and errand boy for one of Lagos' major landowning families. He earned 5

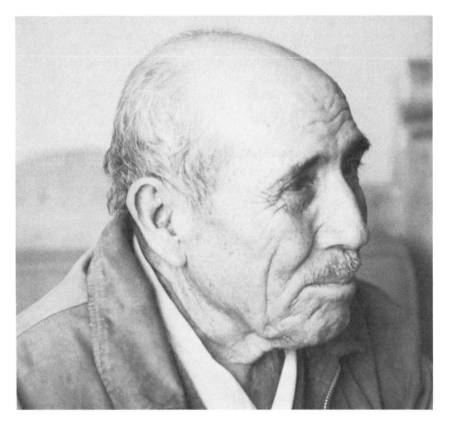

Cipriano Barbosa, in 1976.

pesos per month, plus room and board. But he quit when the señora scolded him for breaking some inexpensive pottery water-jugs, the cost of which she planned to deduct from his wages. ("Although I had no schooling, I was always a little touchy, even when I was young.") In the same year, he worked with Aniceto Martínez in the Fábrica La Victoria. He also briefly managed a small ranch and learned barbering in Lagos in the years that followed. Early in 1918 he was hired as a milk-carrier for an hacienda where he was paid 15 centavos and 3 liters of maize per day to leave the hacienda at 4 in the morning and deliver the milk in Lagos by 7. ("A salary like that doesn't compensate [for the job].")

Later in 1918, an older brother who was then working at a sugar mill in Utah sent Barbosa 30 dollars, which was more than enough to pay the train fare to the border. His departure for the United States marked the end of his services to the wealthy families of Lagos. "Since I went north [to the U.S.], I haven't worked for them even a single day." He lived and worked in the U.S. from 1918 to 1930, returning to Mexico for two brief periods (of less than one year), when he worked in a barbershop in Lagos and on the docks in the port city of Tampico.

In the U.S. he worked a variety of short jobs in 14 different states, changing seasonally from the railroads to agricultural harvests. He found that railroad jobs were plentiful; workers simply presented themselves at railroad offices to be sent wherever laborers were needed. He was never a union member.

> The U.S. government took over the railroad companies during the war [World War I]. Then they didn't repair the tracks. They were badly damaged; there were a lot of "wrecks" and derailments. So they hired lots of people, mostly Mexicans. . . . They preferred to hire the Mexican because he goes all out in work. They paid very low wages; at the end, the Union Pacific paid 40 cents an hour, with $3.20 for meals discounted from the wages; but the charge was reasonable. The worker was still left with something.

Barbosa and others found agricultural and service jobs through the U.S. Department of Labor's branch offices. In general, he had little difficulty finding employment, although during the recession of 1921, "when Woodrow Wilson turned over office" to the new President, "people were jobless, dying of hunger. We went six months without work, those of us who worked in the fields." The following year, Barbosa and 3 or 4 other Mexicans were part of a group of 15 taken to a roundhouse in Texas as strikebreakers.

In 1925, while working in Nebraska, he heard about the petition for ejidos in Lagos. "We knew everything. . . . [The news came from] our fellow workers, the friends who went from Lagos [to the U.S.]. Also, my relatives would write to me." Barbosa explained how men who had worked in the U.S. became ejido activists in Mexico by comparing working conditions in the two countries:

> The large landowners [in Lagos], what they wanted was to have people enslaved. To have them work for nothing, and to be hungry. Lots of people claimed that if the poor laborer, the field worker were hungry, he would work more. But in the U.S. one learned that a man with a full stomach and clothing to protect him from the cold works willingly if he is paid for his work. In the U.S. they don't trick people with their wages. When they see that someone is not doing his job, they act as they should—take out the record, the pencil, and

make out their time, as they say there, and they give one a piece of paper, "Go to the office and collect."

He also explained why, in his view, he and other men who had worked in the U.S. became more "liberal" and were not frightened by the priests' threats against the agraristas:

It is a freer country [there] than here, because there are different religious beliefs, right? People are a little more aware than those of us who go from here. . . . There, the law is what rules. In the schools, they never teach them religious doctrine, right? They teach the laws of the land, which is what everyone obeys there. It is very different [in the U.S.].

Look, many norteños adopt new ideas and leave the old religious beliefs. . . . Some do [change religions]. Others become liberals, because that's something else. Liberalism is not accepting any religious creed, because everything in life is just a business. Without understanding much, in the U.S. I noticed many things. In other faiths, at least, there is some help. For example, the evangelists treat each other like brothers; they give up some vices.

Let me tell you about the Methodists. We went to work with a man who was a minister at a [Methodist] church in Nebraska in 1923. [After greeting them, the minister's wife asked about their religion, and on hearing that they were Catholics, said]: "The Catholic religion is very corrupt, very dirty. Look. Because he depends on going and confessing and telling the priest everything, the Catholic thinks he is cleansed. Not so. The Catholic has many defects: he is a drunk, a womanizer, a bandit, and a killer. And relying on his confession and the priest forgiving him everything, well, that's why he makes those mistakes. In this world, no one forgives. Only God is authorized to forgive. A band of lazy men in the seminaries, getting ideas on how to extort the poor, to live off people who work." She disabused us of our illusions in one blow. . . . And the Presbyterians are different, and the Pentecostals as well. I learned a lot.

Barbosa also recalled with great emotion the way he was treated by many of his employers in the U.S.: comfortable beds in tidy rooms, "without saints' figures, just plain painted pictures of trees and birds, better than a hotel"; consideration and concern from small farmers who worried about paying him, despite their own precarious finances; and generosity at meal time:

They let me use a new little wooden house, with its little stove. I ordered five dollars' worth of provisions, and never once turned on the stove. In the mornings they would send the little girl with a jug of coffee and milk and a piece of bread, and with that I was off to work. At noon they would feed me. What good people!

Barbosa returned to Lagos de Moreno for Christmas in 1930, and never went back to the U.S. The previous year, while working for the railroad near Gillette, Wyoming, he was taken ill during a very bad snowstorm. He and his co-workers had been put on 20-hour shifts to clean switches, clear tracks and fences, and keep trains moving. A year later, Barbosa was still not strong enough to compete successfully against other workers in the sugar-beet harvest, which provided the most lucrative work. In addition, a physician had advised him to change climates because his "blood was drying up" from the cold. So, thinking it best to die at home, he returned to Lagos.

In 1931, he began to work in a small barbershop in the Pueblo de Moya, adjacent to Lagos town. There, he learned about politics and agrarian reform from a friend who also introduced him to José Romero. Barbosa remained a barber for five years, while the final grant of ejido lands to Moya was pending. He was interested in becoming an ejidatario, because as a barber in a poor, third-class shop, he was paid only 20 centavos for giving a shave and a haircut. "We were really destitute. And I, accustomed to another way of living, to other wages and all [in the United States]. . . ." Having sworn when he left Lagos that he would never again work for the rich, becoming an ejidatario was Barbosa's most attractive alternative to barbering.

Once he made a commitment to the agrarian reform movement, Barbosa became an active participant in the core Lagos group. He attended the monthly meetings of the Liga Regional Campesina Magdaleno Cedillo. He came to know Captain José Vallarta, whom he respected as "righthand man of Lázaro Cárdenas." In 1934 he joined in common-law marriage with the widow of Aniceto Martínez, Doña Carmen Casillas.

When ejido lands were granted to Moya by provisional gubernatorial decree in 1933, Barbosa received one of the 2-hectare plots. On September 2, 1935, the same day that arms were being distributed by the government to ejidatarios in Lagos town, Barbosa was assaulted by a small group of Cristeros while gathering firewood. The Cristeros knew him and also knew that he was an ejidatario. They briefly hanged him by the neck from a mesquite tree, releasing him only when he promised (falsely) to turn over the rifle scheduled to be given him later that day.

By 1976, Barbosa no longer cultivated his own ejido plot, leaving it to

Juan Oliva and his wife, Trinidad Guevarra de Oliva, photographed in the patio of their house, in 1976.

the care of a son. But the memories of the first years of struggle were still quite vivid for him. He recalled that credits were made available to him and the other ejidatarios of Moya in 1936, but that they could only borrow 100 pesos, with which he bought plow animals and a plow. Through a friend who was administrator of the town slaughterhouse, he purchased two burros on credit at 4 pesos apiece, and with them was able to bring firewood into Lagos to sell every third day. Each load sold at 35 centavos. The money was used to purchase maize for home consumption until the crops were harvested. He recalled that on one occasion Francisco Carrera, the first native-born, pro-agrarista municipio president in Lagos (1936–37), helped him out by purchasing a load of firewood for use in the women's jail. That day he was able to bring a special treat—20 centavos' worth of sweet rolls—to his young daughters.

Barbosa served three times as an officer on the ejido governing council in Moya, and once as treasurer of the ejido. He represented Moya at the state agrarian congress in Guadalajara in 1936. While he had been an ejidatario for most of his life, most of his sons and sons-in-law have not. Taking note of their situation, he worried about the current and future status of agricultural wage-laborers in Mexico:

Here, we are starting the Porfirian system again. What slavery exists here for the field worker, the salaried [landless] worker, now that they have him on a short leash! May God forbid it, but the time will come that they will nearly kill him from hunger.

Juan Oliva

Although he was nearly 90, one seldom found Juan Oliva at home. He and his wife, Doña Trinidad (8 years his junior), lived in Lagos in an adequate house purchased for them by their sons, who live in Monterrey and Mexico City. They occasionally traveled to the capital for medical care and to visit, but they preferred to reside in Lagos, where they were among friends and could live self-sufficiently. In the evenings they watched television, fortifying Oliva's ardent curiosity about all manner of current events both in Mexico and the United States. He still read, especially the Bible and magazines.

Oliva was born in 1890 to parents who had worked on various haciendas belonging to the González family in the municipio of Lagos. His father sharecropped, and was a paid laborer for the planting and harvest of wheat on hacienda property. In addition, he had some burros which he used to purchase pottery in Guanajuato, selling it in Lagos, Tepatitlán, or Aguascalientes. As a result, Oliva's father was financially more independent than many campesinos, and only once fell into debt.

Oliva began to work as a planter, dropping seed behind his father's plow, at the age of 4. By the time he was 7 or 8, he joined four older brothers in the fields, using both hands to plant maize and beans, for which he was paid half as much as his father's daily wage of 12 centavos—minus the ration of maize. At 11 he took up the plow and team. At 19, for a combination of reasons ("the hard life, wages at rock-bottom," and a girlfriend whose hopes for marriage he did not share), Oliva and a cousin left the hacienda. After walking for 17 days, they reached Torreón, where they spent a period weaving reed baskets to sell in the market. Subsequently, they were employed on vast haciendas owned by Spaniards in Torreón, Linares, and Monterrey, where they worked in the cotton harvests, transported silage, and built irrigation canals and earthen dams.

Oliva and his cousin found that in Mexico's northern states the wages and working conditions were much better than in Lagos. Pay scales ranged from 1 peso per day to 3 centavos per kilo of cotton (the best pickers could earn up to 6 or 7 pesos daily), compared with wages of 12 centavos per day and 4 liters of maize in Lagos. Living costs were lower, the work easier, and no letters of reference were required to change employment from one hacienda to another. In the north, agricultural laborers talked often of Francisco Madero, hoping that a successful Maderista challenge to Porfirio Díaz would improve their situation.

In 1911, when he heard that his former girlfriend had married, Oliva returned to Lagos to work as a sharecropper, but he found that he "no longer liked the pattern here, the slavery." He spent a brief time in the ranks of the Villista troops during their victorious drive southward. After he returned to Lagos, the situation on the hacienda became intolerable. Oliva resented the crew foreman's paternalistic control over the workers. Oliva himself had numerous girlfriends, but incurred the enmity of the hacienda manager and the local police when he asked permission to marry the manager's niece. When a friend—a widower with two daughters—who had worked in Texas and Los Angeles suggested in 1917 that they go to the U.S., Oliva went enthusiastically.

Four men left together for the United States, taking with them the widower's daughters, one of whom later married Oliva in Madisonville, Texas. They worked in Oklahoma and Texas on a variety of short-term agricultural jobs. Then Oliva was employed on a railroad track crew out of Normangee, Texas, for five years. He belonged to a union during these years, but he was never an activist. Agriculture was a more attractive occupation to Oliva ("I worked less and it suited me better"), so he left the railroad and moved to North Zulch, Texas, where he became a sharecropper. "I saw another life there, very different from the agriculture here [in Lagos]." In Texas he worked under an arrangement where one-third of the cotton harvest and one-fourth of the corn harvest went to the owner—considerably better than the 50–50 split which prevailed under the most favorable arrangements in Lagos.

Five of the Olivas' 12 children were born during their stay in the U.S., from 1917 to 1932. These children began their schooling in the U.S., and all of them continued when they returned to Lagos. Three of Oliva's four surviving sons are professional men (engineers and a topographer), whose education was financed in part by scholarships first made available to sons of ejidatarios by the Cárdenas administration; the three surviving daughters finished primary school.[19]

Oliva himself learned to read and write while in the United States. On the haciendas, there had been no schools "because it wasn't to [the

[19]Although other agraristas expressed belief in the importance of education, the Oliva children received more formal schooling than those of any other agrarista interviewed.

owner's] advantage." He began to learn in Torreón, hoping that he could write home without bothering anyone else, but he did not learn properly until he lived in the U.S. It was also in Torreón and the U.S. that Oliva became "more liberal,"[20] because he "saw things differently, . . . in a new light." In the U.S., his liberalism and interest in agrarian reform were kindled by two friends he met, natives of the state of Guanajuato. An ejido had already been established in their home community, and they received photographs of the fields and the stacked harvest. They began to talk among themselves "of what it must be like," and became interested in the redistribution of land.

In 1932, the Oliva family returned to Mexico. Oliva insists that the U.S. policy of repatriating Mexicans did not contribute to their decision to return, because people in their Texas town assured them that hard-working Mexicans like themselves would not be expelled. Although it is unlikely, given the date, Oliva contended that they returned to Mexico because he could see war on the horizon, with all the jockeying between Germany, Russia, and others, "during Hitler's time." "And I had my sons, they were growing. And I thought, later, what will they do here [in the U.S.]? After they grow up, they won't want to leave; or if they come of age, they will want to go to war. So we returned, and I put them in school, so that they could have a career." Although they were offered land in the state of Coahuila on their way south, Oliva decided to return to Lagos, despite the rumor that central Mexico was in ashes after the Cristiada. "This is my homeland," he explained. "I came back to see what was left."

At first, he rented a very small vegetable plot on the edge of Lagos and sold produce in the market. Nieves Ortiz was a friend of one of the Olivas' neighbors, and after some conversations about land reform, Nieves took Oliva to one of the reformists' meetings, where he met Ayala, Romero, and the other early labor and agrarian activists. He joined the group, as a petitioner for land in the ejido of Moya, adjacent to Lagos, and began to work toward achieving land for other communities in the municipio.

When Moya received some lands by provisional gubernatorial decree in 1933, Oliva was among the first recipients. For two decades thereafter, he and Doña Trinidad and their children lived near their land and worked on it. The first years were difficult. He served as a squad leader in the armed agrarista regiment and participated in two skirmishes with the Cristeros in 1935. He was able to acquire some burros to help with the

---

[20]Oliva says that he used to be a religious "fanatic," but that in the U.S. and northern Mexico, people are more liberal; "here in the center [of Mexico], it is the cradle of the Inquisition."

plowing, and after two or three years the family began to fatten hogs for sale to supplement their income. Later they acquired some cows and sold milk. Although he sometimes borrowed seed for planting, he never received loans from the government. He was able to irrigate his land after the federal dam at Cuarenta was completed, benefiting parts of the ejido of Moya.

From 1938 to 1941, Oliva served as an elected representative on the Lagos ayuntamiento. During those years, he worked in the municipio slaughterhouse, issuing permits for the sale and transportation of animals, while he continued to cultivate his land with the help of his sons. This work provided him with additional income, contacts for renting animals when he needed them on his land, and assistance in securing scholarships for his sons' secondary-school studies. Oliva also served as treasurer of the ejido of Moya, and represented the ejido on three trips to Mexico City ("where there is the key to everything") during the Cárdenas administration, to resolve some boundary disputes. Although the Cárdenas election was the first time he participated in a political campaign—indeed, the first time he and the other agraristas had voted—he subsequently served as a poll-watcher in many elections, and always voted with the official party. In his 80s, he maintained an interest in politics and attended all local election rallies, but doubted the sincerity of politicians' promises.

At the age of 65, Oliva ceased to cultivate his ejido plot himself, entering into sharecropping agreements with men who had no ejido land (an arrangement permitted under the Agrarian Law for older ejidatarios and widows). Finally, in 1975, he gave his plot back to the community of Moya for reassignment to another ejidatario, explaining that there was too much work and too many headaches involved in trying to hold on to it.

Víctor Reyes

Ruggedly handsome, fastidious about his appearance, twenty years older than he looks, though slightly stiffened by rheumatism, Víctor Reyes was one of the best-known early agraristas in the municipio. He was among the first recipients of ejido land in the village of La Escondida, and he gave support and encouragement to agraristas in other communities. He is best known, however, as an agrarista who miraculously survived a vicious attack by a band of Cristeros.

La Escondida ("the hidden one") is a small community, accessible only with great difficulty via a rocky, boulder-strewn, badly eroded dirt road. Although only 26 kilometers from Lagos as the crow flies, it has always been very isolated. Nestled among several large haciendas, the residents of La Escondida traditionally have owned their own house-lots and, in some cases, small subsistence plots under 5–10 hectares. Most residents were employed by, or sharecropped on, one of the haciendas, retaining their own residence in La Escondida. Before the agrarian reform, Reyes recalled, "We supported ourselves, you might say, like Indians, doing what we could and never eating enough." Today, the land around the village is eroded, full of boulders, rocks, and ledges. Even in the 1930s, one engineer estimated the topsoil at only 10–40 centimeters.[21]

Víctor Reyes was born in 1906 in La Escondida. As he was growing up, he never worked for any of the hacendados. Instead, he wove ropes, harnesses, and other house and farm materials from *ixtle*, a fiber derived from maguey plants. Occasionally, he sharecropped with a small landowner. In October 1923, "hunger and nakedness" forced him to leave home with a cousin. Together they took a train to El Paso, Texas, where Reyes' aunt and her family were living. He lived with his relatives and, although he was quite young, went to work at the lumberyard where his uncle had a job. He had had no schooling "and I didn't know what a circle [an 'o'] was called." On payday, "I was very embarrassed because they all signed their paychecks, and I had to mark an 'X.' And I would break out here [the forehead] in a cold sweat. I would look all around and I felt that only I had made the 'X.' " In order to avoid this shame, he asked his cousins to teach him to read and write.

In the U.S., his ideas changed.

> You see, there is precisely something about the United States which awakens one. . . . We saw in the United States that progress comes from work. Because there we have seen men or families that are very well off, who have money, [still] working. And we remembered that here, the rich men don't work, they just exploit the poor. There, women and children, everybody—to work. Also, they teach people to save money in the bank, as little as a dollar, from the time they are young. They teach them to start those savings accounts. And here, we didn't even have a bank.

While in the United States, he also heard about agrarian reform:

> I was thinking of coming back, and I kept hearing about the government program, that they were going to give us land, and

---

[21]Report of Ing. Enrique Macías, October 26, 1935, in the expediente ejidal for La Escondida (ASRA).

that's what I planned, to ask for land, to see if it was true that they were giving [land] . . . and it was true!

A petition for an ejido in La Escondida was filed in February 1925, while Reyes was still in the U.S. He returned to La Escondida in December 1926, but he was pursued by the Cristeros because of his agrarian sympathies, and he could not remain. After a few months, he returned to the U.S. and stayed for a year working in the beet and lettuce fields of Montana, Oregon, and California.

After returning to La Escondida in 1928, he married and started a family. In about 1930, when the members of the original petitioning committee for the ejido of La Escondida—confronted by local opposition[22] and the slowness of the grant procedures—began to weaken, Víctor Reyes assumed a leadership position. His enthusiasm for reform had increased since he could read newspapers and flyers, and he attended meetings of the reformists in Lagos when possible.

At some point during these early years,[23] a band of 42 Cristeros descended on the community in search of agraristas. They opened Reyes' house, ransacked it, beat him so severely that he was left for dead, and branded him and six other men for life by cutting off the tips of their ears, as can be seen in the 1976 photograph of him. His wife, frightened and more religiously devout than Reyes, took their three children and left him because he refused to give up his agrarista sentiments. His father also disagreed with the idea of land reform. Reyes subsequently took a second wife, with whom he had eight more children. All but two children from both unions have left the community and scattered, some in Mexico and some in the United States.

Reyes spoke of the effect on his religious views of the Church's opposition to land reform and the attack by the Cristeros:

> That's why one sometimes doesn't know whether to believe in religion or not. Because I do not think their way of thinking [the priests'] about that [land reform] was fair. Because I believe that the land belongs to everyone. We all have a right to it. No, they didn't like me [in La Escondida] for a time, supposedly because I

---

[22]The expediente ejidal for La Escondida includes several statements by agrarian engineers assigned to do studies for the land grant, about the especially difficult situation in La Escondida created by the recent "fanatic rebellion" (the Cristero revolt). The engineers noted that local "fanaticism" reduced support for land redistribution.

[23]Reyes recalled only that it occurred "during the Cristiada." Reports of other agraristas indicate that the attack probably occurred in 1934 or 1935.

Victor Reyes, photographed in front of his house in the ejido of La Escondida, in 1976.

didn't believe in God, because I didn't believe in the faith. . . . I have noticed that in Catholicism there is a certain selfishness which one cannot sometimes understand.

In November 1930, President Pascual Ortiz Rubio granted land to the ejido of La Escondida. Reyes was secretary of the first ejido governing council. The first recipients (captured in a photograph taken the day the land was given) were 20 men who were granted only grazing (not arable) land. In Reyes' words, "They gave us something just to shut us up, a piece of hillside." Recognizing the inadequacy of the grant, Reyes urged the community into a second petition in July 1934, for an expansion of the ejido. That expansion, the only one successfully sought by the community, was granted by President Cárdenas in 1937, bringing with it the only irrigated land in the ejido.

After his experiences with the Cristeros, whom he regarded as lackeys of the rich, Reyes was eager to accept arms when they were distributed to ejidatarios by the Cárdenas administration. He became a squad leader of the agrarista troops. This association with military authorities continued into the 1970s, through relationships with officials in Lagos who were associated with the Vieja Guardia. For this reason, Reyes worked as

A group of agraristas photographed in front of Víctor Reyes' house in the ejido of
La Escondida, probably on the day when the ejido lands were turned over to the
community after the final presidential grant in 1930. Pictured in the front row,
from left to right, are: an unidentified agrarista, Enrique Bancalari (an engineer
with the state Mixed Agrarian Commission, who completed many of the preliminary studies for the ejidos in Lagos), Macedonio Ayala, and Víctor Reyes.

readily through military as agrarian authorities when he encountered a
personal or community problem.

Reyes was an important figure during the agraristas' heyday in local
politics. He was among the officials of the Liga Regional Campesina, and
José Romero vaguely recalled that he had tried to nominate Reyes to a
municipio or regional elective office. Reyes claims that the campesino
sector of the official party nominated him to run as its candidate for
municipio president in the mid-1930s. By his own account, wealthy local
opponents of his candidacy conspired to charge him as a cattle thief. He
was sent briefly to a military prison; but even though the charges were
eventually dropped, they had succeeded in obstructing his candidacy.
This experience, Reyes said, left him "incapacitated" and disillusioned
about his participation and about the role allotted to agraristas in local
politics.

That disillusionment stopped me completely from approaching
people who are involved in politics. Now, when they invite me and

ask me to go, I tell them, "No, I don't understand such things." "No, but you can help us." "I can't any more because the Cristeros beat my head a lot and now I'm not fit for anything."

Nonetheless, Reyes remained for many years a leader in his community. He served three times as president of the ejido governing council, and helped to petition for local improvements such as a small earthen dam or well. Occasionally, he still used whatever contacts and affiliations he had (he was still a member of the Vieja Guardia) to help others. But he felt that his leadership was no longer respected within his own community by the "newer people" who have inherited ejido plots from the original grantees. Because his rheumatism made him unable to work in the fields, he had put someone in charge of farming his ejido plot on a sharecropping basis. Still, he kept close watch on the crops and carefully followed plans for community improvements.

Nicolás Domínguez

Proud, robust, and wily, Nicolás Domínguez lived in El Puesto, one of the largest, most factionalized, and generally inhospitable ejidos in the municipio of Lagos. In the last century, El Puesto was one of the haciendas forming part of the empire of the Rincón Gallardo family, whose vast holdings at one time extended into contiguous portions of five states. When Domínguez was born in 1905, El Puesto had been separated through inheritance from the larger Rincón Gallardo estate and encompassed some 7,400–7,600 hectares. The ejido community of El Puesto has grown up around the old hacienda headquarters (chapel, main house, granaries, and peons' homes), now mostly in ruins. Except for the area adjoining a narrow stream whose shallow flow skirts the town during the rainy season, the community is barren, dusty, and desolate. The photograph of the author and Domínguez, taken beside one of his plots, captures the landscape of the ejido.

When Domínguez was six months old his father was widowed, so the child was raised by grandparents who lived and worked on the hacienda. Domínguez was the only agrarista interviewed who (until his young manhood) was a peón acasillado—an hacienda employee, sharecropper, and occupant of housing provided by the hacienda owners. From these inauspicious beginnings, he made himself one of the most prosperous ejidatarios in El Puesto. In 1976, his adobe house, facing the old hacienda main-house across the village square, had several rooms, some of them with cement or tile floors. He and his sons had a 20-year-old car and a

The author and Nicolás Domínguez, on one of his *parcelas* in the ejido of El Puesto, in 1976.

newer truck, and he was co-owner with other family members of a tractor. With his sons, he farmed a total of 10 ejido plots—5 of these owned by them, and an additional 5 which Domínguez farmed for other people under various arrangements. He traveled regularly to Aguascalientes[24] on agricultural business and to get medical attention for a heart condition. He was a local entrepreneur who had used political contacts and local position to achieve an improved standard of living for his family, in the process generating resentment within the community. His success—relative to the local context—can be traced partly to his participation in the agrarian reform movement. The redistribution of land provided the facilitating circumstances for his economic advancement.

Domínguez's family had worked on various haciendas owned by the Rincón Gallardo family for at least four generations. He began to work when he was 6, helping to bring cow dung from the hills for use as fuel.

---

[24]El Puesto has closer political and economic relations with Aguascalientes than with Lagos. To get to Lagos, residents must walk 16 kilometers to the nearest milk-route stop, whereas one of El Puesto's residents operates a bus which makes a daily trip to Aguascalientes.

By the time he was 11, he had joined his uncles and grandfather in sharecropping and other paid labor on the hacienda in order to augment the family income and maize ration. He recalled that he would look at the results of his family's sharecropping labor:

> I could see stacks of maize that we would harvest. And with any little debt that my grandparents owed, [the hacienda] would take it all, nothing would be left. Those granaries would be filled to the top with maize. And when they shelled the corn, 25 mule-carts with large steel wheels would leave, and they would take them, laden, daily to Aguascalientes. . . . I would see all that they took from us, and we had nothing left even to purchase [necessities] with.

These observations left him anxious to figure out some way to retain more of what he and his family harvested. With the Revolution came new experiences and ideas. In 1916, when revolutionaries (apparently Villistas) came through El Puesto, they opened the granaries and distributed corn to all of the peons. But when that had been consumed, the residents had no grain left to eat or plant; for three months they were reduced to a diet of cactus and cow's milk, and many died of hunger. At the same time, Domínguez began to hear about Emiliano Zapata and the revolutionary goal of redistributing land.

Domínguez had his first political experience in about 1918. An older friend in El Puesto knew one José Cuéllar, who was campaigning (either for himself or someone else) for the municipio presidency in Lagos. A small group of men (and the precocious Domínguez) met Cuéllar secretly in the hills above the hacienda, and pledged him their support.

Domínguez recalled that he and another resident of El Puesto petitioned for ejido land, representing themselves and eight other interested men, in the early 1920s. The petition never reached Guadalajara, however.[25] Subsequently, Domínguez' name allegedly appeared on a Cristero "hit list" of agraristas. Not finding him, the Cristeros moved on to attack the agraristas in the nearby village of Tecuán, where they hanged the

[25]The first petition for land recorded in the expediente ejidal for El Puesto (ASRA) is dated November 1939. No mention is made of a lost, earlier petition. However, it is possible that the earlier plea was rejected because peones acasillados were ineligible to petition for ejido land until the Agrarian Reform Law was revised in 1934 and expanded under President Cárdenas (see Chevalier, 1967: 165). Because the reform movement in Lagos was quiescent during the Cristiada—and Lagos is, in any case, far from El Puesto—the petitioners might not have been informed that their petition had been rejected. Domínguez believed that someone was bribed to prevent the petition from ever being submitted.

father of the ejido leader in that community. Domínguez believed that he was denounced by the hacienda administrator and community residents who opposed reform. Facing such local opposition, and with no knowledge of the fate of his petition, the 20-year-old Domínguez went to the U.S. for 11 months in 1924–25. (He returned to the U.S. under the bracero program in 1945 for six months.) During this sojourn he began the effort to become literate, building on the few letters he knew already. He was married upon his return to El Puesto in 1925.

In the years that followed, Víctor Reyes, Macedonio Ayala, José Romero, and others tried to convince other residents in El Puesto to push for land reform, but only Domínguez and two others were willing to take up the struggle. Macedonio Ayala had loaned Domínguez a book by the Flores Magón brothers, and he liked their ideas about "the social issues, especially the distribution of land, improving life for the [poor] families." He explained that although his wife and his father at first opposed his agrarista activities and threatened to abandon him, he persisted,

> so that all of us poor people could get out of the miserable poverty in which we found ourselves. My family was without any sandals, pants, or hats, because I had nothing with which to buy them.

For three years after Domínguez' return from the U.S., the hacienda administrator would not employ him on the hacienda, so Domínguez lived by selling onions. It paid little, and he was always in debt. When a friend became manager of the hacienda, he was finally granted lands to sharecrop for four or five years. Then, in an effort to avoid expropriation, the hacienda owner began to sell off portions of land of varying size. His plan was to divide a large part of his land into "*colono*" plots, enabling interested (and solvent) peones to purchase through contracts and installments the land they had been sharecropping. Under this plan, the peones would have become small private landowners. Domínguez arranged to pay for two small plots totaling 16 hectares. However, after three years, the contracts were canceled by the hacienda owner. When Domínguez and others appealed to the Agrarian Department for redress, they were told that the only recourse was to become ejidatarios, because the Department had not authorized the creation of a colono community.[26]

---

[26]This account is drawn from my interviews with Domínguez, but it is substantiated by evidence in the expediente ejidal (ASRA). These records show that the contracts were signed in March 1936 (one Nicolás Domínguez signed his in January 1937). The contracts,

Domínguez would have preferred to be a private landowner rather than an ejidatario, but "it couldn't be or shouldn't be done, because then the people with money would monopolize the land again, because others [smallholders] would sell it [to them]. That happened in many places, even right here." Given the alternatives, he chose to pursue ejido land. In the course of petitioning for an ejido, Domínguez and a friend from El Puesto went to the presidential residence in Mexico City to seek help from President Cárdenas. They were received as part of a larger group of agrarian petitioners, and the President ordered that they be given money to help defray their travel expenses. In January 1940, they also wrote letters to the state governor and to the head of the Mixed Agrarian Commission in Guadalajara pleading their case. These letters, signed by Domínguez and two other residents, are now in the files of the Agrarian Reform Ministry. They read in part:

> Tell us that we are not entitled to what we seek within our country, perhaps because it might be that we are not Mexicans, or workers, or revolutionaries (so many have been the alleged difficulties and pretexts that they give us); or, worse, because in this case the interests of Money in the hands of the eternal and disguised enemies of the Revolution and of our Institutions, those who have impeded [reform], have bribed the lower authorities of the Supreme Government, so that we have not been properly or satisfactorily treated.
>
> . . . We ask that our problem be quickly and definitively resolved, because we have for so long worked to organize ourselves; and if we haven't succeeded, it has been because of the maneuvers of the rich people, who, in collaboration with the reactionaries and the priests, say that all those who take land in the ejido are damned.

Local resistance to land redistribution in Domínguez's community was manifested in many ways. Community residents refused to accept arms offered by the government to agraristas, or to accept involvement in petitioning for an ejido. After the presidential decree creating an ejido for El Puesto was signed in October 1943, only 10 people accepted the first ejido plots.

During the Cárdenas administration, Domínguez and a handful of other family heads in El Puesto sent their children to the local federal school, despite opposition from priests and other residents. All of his

---

which peones regarded as purchase agreements, could also have been interpreted by their language as rental contracts. They were canceled in 1939.

children finished primary school (three years); through contacts, he was able to send one daughter to a teachers' school in Guadalajara, and a son to an agricultural school. All of his sons are now ejidatarios.

Until recent years, Domínguez remained involved in politics as a local political broker. After 12 years as a leader of the land reform drive, he served an equal number of years as *delegado municipal*, an office which can be profitable for its occupant.[27] He participated in attempts to secure local improvements from government agencies, such as the building of schools and dams and installation of electricity and potable water. He served for many years as a representative of the official party at polling places—in which capacity he said that they used to have to do "some crooked things" in order to get the official party votes to outnumber PAN (opposition party) votes. Domínguez twice sought nomination as the campesino-sector representative on the Lagos ayuntamiento, but was defeated both times at the sector convention in Lagos by residents of other communities. He often used to go to election rallies when busloads of campesinos were taken into Lagos town, but he gave that up in his later years.

One of the most remarkable qualities about Nicolás Domínguez is his pride—his articulate sense of worth as a human being. One can imagine that this quality may have contributed to a strong, assertive, perhaps authoritarian leadership style. As Domínguez observed in one interview,

> I have never wanted to work with a boss. Even though I am poor, [I believe that we are] equal—I mean, not equal in circumstances, like equal in wealth and that, no. That's impossible. But equal in life, in body, yes. The man who is a millionaire, he is different because of his millions, and his schooling, and perhaps also because of his talent. [But] if I had been educated in some school, even though I might not have been as great, I would not have been so dumb either, right? I would be something else. But I was unable; in those days, there was nothing.

In another interview session, he was angry about a radio commentator he had heard a few days earlier criticizing the laziness and low productivity of Mexican campesinos:

[27]*Delegados* are representatives of the municipio government in each of the 6 administrative districts (*delegaciones*) into which the municipio of Lagos de Moreno is divided. They are responsible for registering births, deaths, and marriages, and for taking preliminary testimony in criminal cases. They can also be paid to overlook local illegalities such as the unauthorized sale, transportation, and slaughter of cattle and pigs.

That's not true. If he would come to the countryside, I would show him. I'd bring him a team of horses, and then I'd tell him, "You take that team for a week, or a year, and you drive them and do all you can, as you expressed it on thus-and-such a day [on the radio], and produce. If it doesn't rain, produce. And if it rains too much, drive through the mud. Those words you said, that's fine . . . just because you think so. But you don't know what a campesino suffers."

Domínguez also expressed his anger that campesinos are blamed for not fully using government agricultural aid, such as extension agents, when these employees are not conscientious about their jobs:

An extension agent came here, and he promised to come often, every two weeks, to give us explanations and to tell us how [to do things]. So then one day, I told him, "We are already experimenting with all of those techniques you are talking about. We are already doing that. So you promise to come every week, and you don't. And out there the politicians are saying that there are extension agents and that they are showing the campesinos and telling them what the techniques are and what they should do. And you don't show your face. And if you come, you come here, to the meeting hall, to the meetings, but you don't go to the fields. Then they blame us." So he said, "Well, I'll tell you, I don't come because I've found a better job." "Ah," I said, "that's fine. What difference does it make to you?"

Domínguez felt envied, resented, and shunned by his own community:

The people hated us [at the time of the land reform]. They still do, even more now, with all the envy. . . . They pushed us old ejidatarios aside. What they don't know! If they had suffered what we did for the whole village, for everyone. And now, some consider us bandits. . . . There is hatred, envy, because we were once something, even if we aren't now. We did participate.

Reflections of the Old Guard

The old guard of agraristas in Lagos came of age politically during a period of sweeping change within the Mexican political system, change marked by greater accessibility of the federal government to the demands of campesinos and urban laborers, and by more open expression of radical political ideologies in the national political arena than during any previous or subsequent period. Most members of the old guard had extensive exposure to the workings of the political system, at local, state, and even national levels. Following their participation in the agrarian reform movement, they observed or participated in numerous electoral campaigns and represented their ejido communities in a wide variety of encounters with government agencies, seeking benefits ranging from ejido expansions to the provision of agricultural and "urban" services.

Given this wealth of political experiences, and the circumstances under which they became agrarian activists, the old guard's assessment of current political practices and government performance in Mexico is of particular interest. My interviews with them included questions on three broad topics: contemporary politics and government in Mexico, current problems of ejido communities, and the fate of agraristas after the land redistribution was completed. Their responses are summarized in this concluding section.

Support for the System

In general, I found that the first agraristas, having opted to work within the established rules of the political game during their time of greatest political activism, continued to be system loyalists. They still voted for the official party and believed that their rights were properly protected under the Constitution and the Agrarian Reform Law. They *were* willing to criticize the way the system sometimes functions. Some resented the way they had been taken for granted by politicians and the way they were often treated by government bureaucrats. There was sometimes anger in their recitals of government benefits meted out only to those who could pay for them. They were even willing to comment negatively on the way the campesino sector has been ignored by most administrations since Cárdenas. However, these things were generally described as shortcomings of the incumbents, rather than basic flaws in the system of governance.[28]

All of the first agraristas became affiliated with the official party when they received ejido land—some even earlier, during Cárdenas' campaign for the presidency. As ejidatarios, they were automatically members of the CNC, the campesino sector of the official party. They served as the party's representatives at polling places. They regarded their ties to the PNR, and its successor, the PRI, as an affiliation of convenience, not of

[28]In this respect, the old guard conformed to patterns of political attitudes found commonly among campesinos and urban workers in Mexico today. See Craig and Cornelius (1980: 371–378) for a review of these research findings.

conviction. "If one doesn't belong to the PRI, one can't accomplish anything."

The agraristas did not have much day-to-day contact with the PRI superstructure. They dealt, instead, primarily with the CNC, either directly or through the regional CNC representative (in the Comité Regional Agrario) or through the Vieja Guardia. They were recruited by the local representatives of the CNC to attend political campaign rallies. Most important, they often worked through attorneys and bureaucrats of the CNC in Guadalajara and Mexico City when dealing with the Agrarian Reform Ministry on community or individual problems related to their ejido.

Although aware of the existence of other opposition parties, the agraristas viewed political opposition as synonymous with support for the Partido de Acción Nacional (PAN). Despite dissatisfaction with government service-delivery, none would consider joining forces with PAN, because it would be an alliance with old enemies. They regarded supporters of PAN and of the right-wing Sinarquista movement as one and the same: conservative individuals, closely tied to the Catholic Church, and opposed to agrarian reform. In any case, they saw the opposition parties as performing strictly symbolic functions, with no real power ceded to them by the regime.

They also regarded political campaigns as symbolic acts. They regretted that none of the political candidates (particularly for the ayuntamiento) would genuinely represent the interests of campesinos. In part, they attributed this to the way in which political candidates for offices at all levels are selected. Nominees are announced, and the agraristas are simply expected to endorse, rally, and vote. Ernesto Rodríguez summed up the agraristas' view of the party nominating conventions: "There are no debates, nothing. . . . This isn't a democracy, it is rule by designation." ('*Aquí no es democracia, es dedocracia.*')

The agraristas unanimously described how candidates—regardless of the office to which they aspire—come to the campesinos for their vote and then ignore them once they are in office. "Just let us give them the election, and that's as far as it goes. They just don't acknowledge us after that, not for anything. They talk very pretty to us, but later they forget."

Although they themselves have participated in campaign rallies, where campesino supporters are often bussed in by the PRI, the agraristas criticized the motives of campaign participants. They contended that the people who work on campaigns do so only to secure favors and jobs, and that those who go to the rallies do so with no real interest in the election. Campaign rallies are held in the main plaza in Lagos, but as Juan Oliva explained, "There are sweet rolls, and people who clap, without knowing what for. It's a bad comparison, but they do what the monkeys do—one goes, and they all follow."

Because of the way elected officials have behaved, courting the campesinos at election time and ignoring them later, the agraristas did not respect them. They have grown weary of promises and rhetoric, and view politicians as totally self-interested opportunists. Nicolás Domínguez charged that politicians, enriched by their positions, "have taken the money from Mexico to enjoy in other countries, to make other countries rich. And Mexico continues to sleep the eternal slumber." When Arcadio Amézquita was asked to describe his experiences with politicians, he recalled the one time his support for a candidate yielded any post-election benefit for him:

> Once one Urbano [Esparza], who was a member of the agrarian community of Moya, was a candidate. He was a compañero, because we had struggled through the cause together. [He came to me, saying]: "I come to ask you a favor, to see if you will give me your support." [I answered]: "The only thing I ask is that whenever you come to Lagos, you remember us." From the others we got nothing, but from him we did. I would get tequila to drink each time he came, and the others would get a pail of popsicles.

On Government Responsiveness

Ejido communities in Mexico today are almost exclusively dependent for external assistance upon the government, whether local, state, or federal. All problems relating to individual and community land-tenure rights which cannot be handled within the community are referred to the Agrarian Reform Ministry. Ejidatarios rely increasingly on the government for fertilizer, and on government banks for loans to purchase machinery or livestock. Access roads, irrigation systems, potable water, and electricity are installed by the government. Only for the sale of their crops, livestock, and labor can ejidatarios turn to the private sector.

As a result, ejido communities and their leaders have built up long histories of petitioning for government services—and waiting. All levels of government in Mexico postpone (rather than deny) many more requests for aid and services than they grant. As the old-guard agraristas whom I interviewed explained, the government seldom says outright that it will not grant the aid they seek. "They don't pay attention. They don't treat one badly, true, but it's just 'Come back tomorrow,' and time passes and nothing is fixed." As a result of these delays and the small amount of resources allocated for public projects in the Los Altos region,[29] the only government benefits which most of the ejidos in Lagos de Moreno have received are the original grants of land and (for some of them) access to irrigation water, either through the central irrigation system fed by the Cuarenta dam or (most commonly) small earthen dams.

Despite this treatment, the agraristas' strongest feelings were of annoyance or resentment rather than anger. In part, they blamed themselves and their fellow ejidatarios for not being persistent enough in nagging the authorities. In part, they felt that they simply had not struck the right formula for capitalizing on the capriciousness with which benefits are granted. Commenting on the recent good fortune of the ejido at El Puesto, which had received some attention from the state government then in office, Nicolás Domínguez observed:

> This [state] government has been very good to us. Never seen the likes of it. But who knows but what it's due to a reception they gave [the Governor] on a visit he made here. They received him very nicely, and he went away very grateful; and due to that, well, he is responding a bit.

The agraristas also knew that money is critical in the allocation of government benefits at the local level. Ever since they began with the reform movement, the agraristas have watched money change hands as a means of delaying, accelerating, redirecting, or securing government attention. All of them spoke about their experiences or the experiences of friends with Agrarian Department engineers who were paid off by landowners to deny ejido petitions, to limit the size of land grants, to select which lands would be surveyed as ejido land, or to alter preliminary census results. In later years, they observed the selectivity with which laws governing grazing rights and minor criminal offenses have been enforced. Finally, they reported providing small gratuities themselves when they had to transact ejido or personal business with government functionaries, especially in Mexico City. As a result of all these experiences, they were well aware that money buys justice and attention, or can just as easily thwart justice. Again, they blamed not the laws, but

---

[29]It was not until the 1970s that the state and federal governments began to develop a comprehensive public-investment strategy for Los Altos de Jalisco (Departamento de Economía, Estado de Jalisco, 1973).

government functionaries. "It's just that here the strongest one dominates the weakest. That's the way it has always been."

The Presidency

As viewed by the agraristas, the key to equitable treatment by the government is in the tone set by national political leaders, especially the
President. It is in the agraristas' evaluation of past presidents that we see
most clearly the influence of their experiences in the agrarian reform
movement. When asked what they knew about President Cárdenas and
his ideals, they uniformly replied with general references to his program
of land redistribution and his nationalization of the petroleum industry
in 1938. Echoing sentiments expressed by the others, Víctor Reyes explained,

> General Cárdenas was the [president] we admired a lot, the one
> who gave the most. Because no other government has given as
> much [ejido] land. All have given, but not as much.[30] The
> [bureaucratic] processes were easier, faster, and everything.

Several of the agraristas described how Cárdenas showed his interest in
the general welfare of the poor, giving much personal attention to the
individual problems of the campesinos and requiring the same of his
subordinates. Reyes recalled:

> [If] there was a problem to solve in the farthest part of any
> region, they would write to him or complain to him; and to inform
> himself, he would personally go to see. We would see him pho-
> tographed, drinking water from a pottery jug or a gourd.

Not surprisingly, the presidents who followed Cárdenas were not held
in equal esteem by the agraristas. In several different contexts, they
would describe Cárdenas, and then report a vacuum of leadership, respect, or assistance from the federal government—until the administration of Luis Echeverría (1970–76). Amézquita reflected the sentiments of
other agraristas when he observed that of the best presidents he had
seen, "the first was Lázaro Cárdenas, and now this one. The others have

---

[30]By 1940, Cárdenas had redistributed more land to more campesinos than all of his
predecessors combined. He granted 10,651 ejidos (out of a total of 13,091 granted from
1915 through 1940), with a total of 18,352,275 hectares, benefiting 1,020,594 campesinos
(out of 1,442,895 benefited by all presidential decrees through 1940).

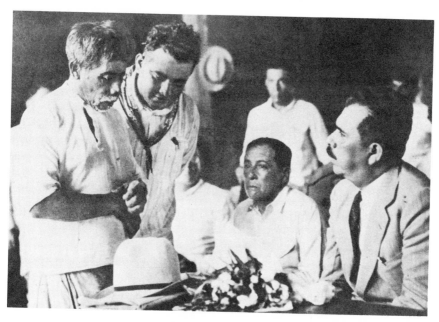

President Lázaro Cárdenas receiving petitions from campesinos in an unidentified village (ca. 1936). According to one tabulation, Cárdenas devoted 673 work
days—nearly one-third of his presidential term—to such community visits, re-
recording requests for land, minor village improvements, and other needs, and
issuing work orders to local officials. The visits were always unannounced.

been good, not bad; they all work. But only these two with earnestness
and a desire to see their country blossom."

Under Echeverría, the agraristas benefited directly from the first national increase in the officially guaranteed price of corn in ten years.
Some of the ejido communities in Lagos also benefited from small
earthen dams built under the Echeverría administration's Plan Benito
Juárez. However, in many cases, the agraristas' admiration for Echeverría stemmed not from direct benefits personally received, but from
the increased attention reputedly accorded by his administration to
agrarian problems in other parts of the country, coming after a long
period of government neglect.[31]

[31]Among a random sample of male family heads in nine rural communities in and
around the municipio of Lagos, interviewed in July–August 1976, only 16% believed that
they had benefited personally from any of the Echeverría administration's policies or
programs affecting the agrarian sector (Cornelius, 1978). At the time of the survey, Echeverría had been in office for 5 1/2 years.

An ejidatario's dwelling in the ejido community of Dieciocho de Marzo, near Lagos town, in 1976. All dwellings in the community are of adobe construction with dirt floors. The community still lacks electricity, piped water, and other basic services.

Ejido Communities

Among those members of the old guard who became ejidatarios, participation in the formation of agrarian communities seems to have influenced their ideas about how such communities *ought* to work. In general, they agreed that ejidatarios should be willing to cooperate at least in communal tasks such as the conservation of grazing lands, repairing fences and watering-holes, and maintaining cattle-guards and dams. They lamented the fact that today such cooperation must be demanded by ejido officials rather than being voluntarily given.

This belief in the desirability of voluntary cooperation for occasional communal tasks did not extend, however, to support for the collective organization of ejidos, nor even to much enthusiasm for cooperative credit societies within ejidos. While my fieldwork was in progress, the government of President Luis Echeverría was attempting to impose a gradual collectivization of some ejidos, establishing cooperative credit societies in others. Regional representatives of the government's ejido bank and of the ministries of Agrarian Reform and Agriculture encountered strong resistance from ejidatarios of all ages in their efforts to implement the government's policy.

Asked why there were no collective ejidos nor many ejido credit societies in Lagos, the old guard's replies reflected their own desires for independence in their work and finances, and their lack of trust in the good faith or fair contribution of fellow ejidatarios. Most endorsed cooperation or collective organization only to achieve objectives that could not be attained through individual action.[32] In general, they agreed that collective organization of ejidos requires good, strong leadership—a degree of leadership control they neither chose to exercise nor would be willing to accept themselves. The following comments illustrate their views:

> [We don't work collectively] because then everyone has to work together and to divide among everyone all that is produced. Then, some have one or two sons, and they all have to work, but only the head of the house is recognized to receive a share of what is produced. . . . This fellow can work more, or less; another arrives early or late, and then they don't get along.

> They want us to work collectively, but we need them to send us a man from outside who will come to take charge of one, two, or three communities.

The old guard were distressed by the factionalism they perceived in their ejidos. They saw divided communities composed of a group of older, early leaders who petitioned for land or were among the first recipients, set against another group consisting of latecomers and religious "fanatics." As they described their conflicts with "*los nuevos*" (with its dual meaning of "the new ones" and "the youngsters"), there seemed to be two underlying sources of tension. First, there was the competition between the old and the young for ejido leadership and limited land. Second, there was the residue of resentment against people whose timidity or religious devotion caused physical and emotional hardships for the early agraristas, and may have delayed the redistribution of land.

Four specific types of conflicts between the old guard and other segments of their ejido communities surfaced frequently in the interviews: (1) conflicts with the latecomers who "arrived at the feast after the table was set"; (2) with new leadership which was regarded as insufficiently

---

[32]Relatively low levels of interpersonal trust and a generalized preference for individualistic rather than collective strategies of goal attainment are characteristic of the bulk of the Mexican population, both rural and urban (see Craig and Cornelius, 1980: 350, 372-373).

assertive or diligent in petitioning for new government services to the community; (3) with younger people who have less love for the land and value a regular wage above tilling the soil; and (4) with ejidatarios, younger than themselves, who try to force the older agraristas to relinquish their ejido plots and leadership positions. Although these sentiments were echoed in varying degree by all of the old ejidatarios, those whose comments follow were the most vocal and bitter.

We took direct action, without fear of anything, with the necessary courage. Now, whatever the problem, we see in some that, well, they don't boldly join in the affair; sometimes it's like they get stuck, like they don't want to succeed. I don't know what causes it. Why now, it's even less dangerous than it was then!

I see that young people no longer aspire to do [agricultural] work. Now what they want is to learn a little mechanics and to know enough to scribble a little so that they can earn a living more easily. But it is not possible for all of us to have that calling. The land must be made to bloom. If not, people cannot live. If there is no agriculture, there is no life.

I left the community in good shape—everything well documented, even up to the first [ejido parcel] titles. Now these [ejido officials], what do they do? It is a right, and a duty, of the [ejido] representatives to tell the [Agrarian Reform] Ministry, "What happened to the titles of So-and-So and Such-and-Such?" They don't do the negotiating.

The Fate of Agraristas

Except for José Romero, and Francisco Navia to a more limited degree, none of the first agraristas mentioned increased political participation among their objectives or ideals when they first joined the reform movement. However, in time they came to regard their participation in ejido or municipio politics as either a civic obligation or a source of personal or class advantage. Often they suggested that agraristas in political office might be less corrupt than the rich. Moreover, they believed that an agrarista would be more inclined to protect and promote the collective welfare of the poor, and especially of campesinos. With this in mind, I asked how agraristas in general had fared in politics since the redistribution of land.

Their assessment was unanimous: agraristas or representatives from campesino groups who have held political office at the local or state levels have had no appreciable political power since the Cárdenas era. They noted that, first, few such individuals have been chosen. Second, when they have been designated, they have occupied only "puppet" roles in the government. The following comments are typical:

> Why, since [José] Romero [was municipio president] there haven't been any supporters [of the workers]—not real supporters—in the government. They just say this and that. There isn't even a Conciliation and Arbitration Board here. Nothing.

> There have been some who have served [on the ayuntamiento]. But it is like someone who brings along a dog that one speaks to, and that's all. That's how they behave.

> We elected a campesino to the state legislature, Urbano Esparza. And since we were very close friends, I would occasionally visit him in Guadalajara. I told him, "Okay, I think it's about time you take the lead for us and take a stand in favor of your people." And he told me, "No, I have to attend all of the congressional sessions, but they regard me like something that—they don't even see me. They won't let me participate in the sessions. Nothing. I want to say something and no, 'Wait, So-and-So has the floor.' They won't let me speak. What can I do on behalf [of the campesinos]?"

The state legislature is the highest level of government in which the old-guard agraristas ever expected that they or their designated representatives might play a part. More commonly, they aspired to a position in the local municipio government. Even there, however, they became disillusioned with the role assigned to ejidatarios. Moreover, they saw that the top administrative posts always went to men from or allied with prominent families in Lagos town. During my fieldwork, the municipio president was Jorge Sanromán Quiñones, grand-nephew of Manuel Sanromán, formerly one of the largest landowners in Lagos, who was commonly believed to have played a major role in the local opposition to land redistribution in the 1920s and 1930s. As one of the agraristas explained, "We have had municipio presidents with whom we couldn't even speak, much less transact any business. El capital—the rich—they still control that situation."

I wanted to know whether these members of the old guard believed that their sacrifices and labors had yielded any enduring benefits, any positive changes in their lives or in their communities. Did they feel it was worth it? Overwhelmingly, the answer was "Yes!" They had no illusions about the way they still lived. They had done hard, physical labor most of their lives, yet very few had been able to move out of adobe houses with dirt floors. What money they have made, they have invested in their land, in a few cases in farm machinery (especially diesel well pumps) or in livestock. Some of them spent their money on liquor. There was scant evidence of nonessential consumption in household goods or clothing. Despite their low standard of living, they were pleased by what they had accomplished and satisfied with many aspects of their lives. They enjoyed the fresh air and the healthy country living. They took pride in what they had accomplished with their ejido plots, whether in providing for their families, in improving crop yields, or in educating their children. Above all, they came back to the reasons for which they joined the agrarian reform movement: to possess the fruits of their labors and to work independently, without accountability to a supervisor or landowner:

> The improvement here is that we share with no one what the Lord gives us; instead, we bring it home. Second, each of us works as much as he wants, without anyone bossing. One lives more agreeably. [Third], we have, we feel, rights before the government for schools and all, and it is up to us to make petitions, because for everything one must suffer.

> Now we live, well, eating in our way, poorly, but 'til we're full. Everything changed radically, because the grants of lands took from us many hardships—that is, all of us who set ourselves to work. Many of us were corrupted, because we took to drink, to spending wildly, to dishonoring the family, and all of that, and everything was wasted for several. You can say that about 80 percent [worked], and the remainder have been corrupted.

> Right now, many ejidatarios have sons who are engineers, physicians, teachers. . . . A campesino who works faithfully, who loves his work, and who takes care, has opportunities to have many resources.

> I suffered greatly at the hands of the rich, earning so little money, and wasting away. And aside from that, well, to have a free life. Now there is no oppressor who says: "This crop is harvested; let's get to planting [the next one] right away."

> We are better off. Don't you see, many—not just I—many have bought trucks; some, two or three tractors. And before, there was

nothing. Nothing even to till the soil. I am not rich in anything, but I live happily. Eating beans or sometimes soup, like that. But it is very different now. Since we began to farm the land as our own, we have enough to buy a pair of pants, a hat, shoes, and often enough to buy things to eat that one hungers for. The whole village is that way now. If you had seen it before—it was a shame.

The agraristas who became ejidatarios believed, then, that their own circumstances had changed for the better since they began to farm their own land. However, they worried about their sons and other men in the ejido communities today who do not have ejido land because there is not enough to go around. They commented on the large numbers of men now working as day laborers for private landowners, at salaries below the official minimum wage,[33] and especially on how many were leaving the rural communities to work in urban areas or in the United States. Some lamented the fact that local agricultural workers did not even lodge formal complaints about minimum-wage violations by rich employers. Thus for many old-guard agraristas, their own sense of accomplishment is offset by concern for others whose situation appears to be the contemporary equivalent of their own circumstances before the land reform. Cipriano Barbosa may have spoken for many others when he observed:

Year after year they raise the taxes, and still we can say that we ejidatarios are in paradise. But what about the poor agricultural day laborer, who has to pay the high cost of living? Take, for example, my son-in-law [who was paid 200 pesos per week]. They make him work from 5 in the morning until 10 at night when he returns home. No, we are worse off than in the times of Don Porfirio Díaz.

[33]In 1976, the official minimum wage for agricultural workers in Lagos de Moreno was 33 pesos per day (U.S. $2.64, at the pre-December 1976 exchange rate; U.S. $1.32, at the 1981 exchange rate). According to the 1970 general population census (Dirección General de Estadística, 1971: Table 29, p. 616), 90% of the agricultural laborers in the municipio of Lagos had incomes of fewer than 500 pesos per month (U.S. $40, at the pre-December 1976 exchange rate; U.S. $20, at the 1981 exchange rate).

7

Conclusion:
The Legacy of
Agrarismo

The chapter of agrarian activism in Lagos de Moreno's history ended, relatively quietly, in 1940. A decade and a half of turmoil had begun when a small group of rural dwellers, urban laborers, and tradesmen banded together to provide each other with protection and support in an effort to secure benefits guaranteed to them by law. Their organization was neither a revolutionary movement mobilized in violent opposition to the government, nor yet a handmaiden to it. Their struggle for "land and liberty" was conducted in the face of strong local opposition, and, at least at the outset, with vacillating support from non-local officials. This study has shown that the achievement of land redistribution in the municipio of Lagos de Moreno involved much more than is suggested by the procedural guidelines established in the Agrarian Reform Law, more than has been captured by official ejido archives, and more than national-level histories have suggested. Here we take a final, retrospective glance at the reform movement of the 1930s and its leaders, with a brief look at a later generation's experience with some of the same problems which the agrarista movement hoped to resolve.

The Genesis of Reform

In an area which lacked nationally prominent reform leaders, how did the communities and individuals who petitioned for ejido lands become caught up in the struggle for land reform? The Revolution of 1910–17 brought to Lagos a federal army garrison and new political authorities nominally loyal to Francisco Madero, as well as recurrent invasions by revolutionary peasant armies. Still, the Revolution was not an immediate mobilizing force. In Lagos, the 1910 Revolution did not reflect local aspirations for land reform, nor did it spawn the leadership of the local reform movement. The Revolution weakened but did not destroy the local economy. Few Laguenses participated in the armed struggle, and the land-tenure pattern remained essentially unchanged. Nationally, however, the Revolution did lead to Constitutional changes which became the legal basis for land redistribution in the municipio, and which led to the inclusion of campesinos and laborers in the national political community. These changes represented the first opening toward a set of new political opportunities and reduced individual and collective risks.

After the Constitution of 1917 was promulgated, some Laguenses began to hear about land reform in other parts of Mexico. The decision to form a local reform movement grew out of the Laguenses' assessment of national politics, their calculation of the political, economic, social, and physical risks to participants, and the commitment of regional and community leaders to the ultimate goal of "land and liberty."

Based on Article 123 of the Constitution, and in the wake of increasing labor agitation under Presidents Obregón and Calles, there was some national support in the mid-1920s for the establishment of labor unions like the Unión de Obreros Libertarios in Lagos. Simultaneously, low wages and job insecurity brought on by a surplus of labor and frequent closings of the Fábrica La Victoria stimulated local labor organization. As an urban center at the intersection of important highways and railway lines, and with a local tradition of education, the town of Lagos nurtured some key local labor leaders—Nieves Ortiz, Aniceto Martínez, the Espinosas and Prados, and José Romero. The local potential for political organization was exploited by municipio authorities (Susano Castañeda and Clodoaldo Gómez) sent to Lagos by Governors José Guadalupe Zuno and Margarito Ramírez. Thus local aspirations for labor and land reform coincided with governmental efforts to encourage the formation of local reform organizations, as a means of implementing state and federal policies. Governors Zuno and Ramírez also used these organized local interest groups as political support bases, to counter the opposition to their social reform policies. However, in the late 1920s and early 1930s, when external support declined, local conditions became the primary factor sustaining the reform organization in Lagos.

The coalition of urban laborers and agraristas which guided the reform movement in Lagos has been observed elsewhere in Mexico, primarily in regions with a large wage-labor force involved in commercial or plantation agriculture.[1] In these cases, the laborer-campesino coalition is generally described as a local manifestation of national and regional organizing activities, or as an effort by agricultural wage-laborers to obtain higher wages and better working conditions by enlisting the support of organized labor in the cities.[2] This study has documented a case of locally led and locally sustained urban laborer-agrarista collaboration to achieve the redistribution of land—a case in which laborers joined campesinos in petitioning for the first ejidos, and helped to recruit other campesinos as participants in the reform movement. The coalition in Lagos was established at the initiative of urban labor. It was maintained because municipio-level leaders hoped it might provide a political power-base for social reform extending beyond the land-tenure issue. Rank-and-file members regarded the coalition as a mutually beneficial support group, in which the strength of unity might achieve more (higher wages for labor, land for agraristas) than each group could separately attain.

The first agraristas in Lagos were therefore both laborers and campesinos. The majority of the campesinos had been sharecroppers or wage-laborers on large and medium-sized landholdings. Only one had been a resident peon on an hacienda (a peón acasillado). Many had, in addition, very modest capital resources—their own very tiny plots of land, or homes, or livestock. They were not wealthy small farmers, but they were not among the poorest or the most exploited campesinos in the region. Nearly all of the earliest campesino community leaders, and many of the urban laborers, had also worked in the United States, where they were exposed to higher wage scales, better working conditions, and alternative religious belief and authority systems. In the U.S. they also developed basic literacy skills or strong aspirations for self-education. The municipio-level leaders of the movement in Lagos were all skilled craftsmen, urban laborers with some ties to rural communities, and white-collar workers.

In some ways, then, the first agraristas in Lagos resemble participants in other peasant movements described in previous studies. Such studies have found that the leadership of peasant movements in Mexico—at

[1] It also has parallels in the modern political history of several other Latin American countries, e.g., the campesino-laborer alliance strategy that the Chilean Left adopted from time to time during the period from 1932 to 1973 (see Drake, 1978; de Vylder, 1974; and Loveman, 1976).

[2] See Alcántara, 1977; Fowler, 1970; Restrepo and Eckstein, 1975; Restrepo and Sánchez, 1972; and Reyes Osorio et al., 1974.

least in the initial stages—was often not composed primarily of the poorest tillers of the soil.[3] Huizer and Stavenhagen (1974: 403–404) have written that peasant movements in Mexico and Bolivia took root in areas where modernization had begun; where urban living or working experiences and contact with an increasingly capitalist economy had begun to spread. Specifically, they note that

> Though poverty and oppression of peasants were common in all of these areas, these factors in themselves do not appear to have provoked automatically the formation of resistance or protest movements. It was rather the confrontations of their conditions with modernizing influences which led to an awakening of political consciousness.

Some of the specific modernizing influences which they cite are not relevant to the Lagos case, but it is certainly true that some participants in the movement were stimulated by what they read in books and newspapers, by what they saw and experienced outside of Lagos, and by what they learned about labor and campesino movements elsewhere in Mexico from individuals who were neither laborers nor campesinos. These experiences which awakened the political consciousness of the agraristas did not translate automatically into political action; they led instead to a redefinition of the problems which confronted them, and to a changed calculation of the risks they were likely to encounter on the road to resolution of the land-tenure problem.

The Ideology of Reform

What social, political, or economic arguments were used to justify land reform? How elaborate was the ideology, and how extensive were the participants' goals for reform? Why did campesinos and urban workers become agraristas?

Rank-and-file laborers in the Unión de Obreros Libertarios and the Sindicato de Oficios Varios joined these unions to insure a fair price for their services and to maintain that price through collective strength. They began organizing agrarian communities because some among them (Nieves Ortiz, the elder Francisco Navia, Aniceto Martínez, and later José Romero and Macedonio Ayala) believed in the social justice of land reform. They also hoped to strengthen their group politically by

[3]See, for example, Fowler 1970; [Fowler] Salamini, 1976, 1978; Friedrich, 1970; Reyes Osorio et al., 1974: 579–604; Womack, 1968.

forming an alliance with the largest population group in the area—the campesinos. Finally, they were encouraged by state government officials and other outsiders (for example, Captain José Vallarta, Roberto Calvo Ramirez) to move into the political arena of agrarian reform.

The campesinos joined the SOV-initiated petitions for land reform because they were unwilling to work for the wages and under the terms which prevailed in the municipio in the 1920s and 1930s. They wished to be their own bosses, accountable to no one else, and to have their families be the sole beneficiaries of the fruits of their labors. Their goals were "land and liberty."

The ideology and motivations of community-level leaders and rank-and-file union members were straightforward and relatively simple. Unlike some other peasant movements in Mexico and elsewhere, the movement in Lagos was not an attempt to restore rights that had been violated by landowners or the state. There had been no "golden age" when local campesinos owned their own lands. First individually and then collectively, the Laguenses settled on a definition of problems, objectives, and strategies through careful, rational calculation. Their goal was not simply economic improvement for the individual participant. In Lagos, the reform movement was also an attempt to introduce new ideas about the value of a man's labor and the conditions under which he had a right to work and support his family. The campesinos' ideology was uncomplicated and individualistic, but it had radical, far-reaching implications for traditional social and economic structures in the local area.

By contrast with rank-and-file campesinos and laborers, the municipio-level leaders in Lagos had been exposed to social and political theories in which land reform was only one of several changes which would lead to a new social and political order. Because José Romero was the only survivor among these leaders, any generalization beyond his particular case must be quite tentative. However, it appears that the principal leaders were not ideological purists. They used whatever organizational alliances and ideological perspectives offered (a) the prospect of some outside support useful in achieving the group's objectives, and (b) ideas which might strengthen the movement's philosophical base, illuminate new strategies, or build useful skills. Romero's own history, as well as the affiliations of the reform organizations in Lagos, reflect pragmatic eclecticism in this regard. We have noted influences from the anarcho-syndicalist Flores Magón brothers, their Liberal Party, and newspapers published by them and their followers; contacts with the Communist Party and its members; affiliations with the socialist founders of the peasant and labor movements based in Veracruz and Michoacán; and ties to state authorities (Margarito Ramírez, Saturnino Cedillo) affiliated with the official national party. Despite their diversity, these associations did share two general political objectives (at least in rhetoric): the redistribution of wealth ("socialization of the means of production," higher wages, collective bargaining, and land reform), and the expansion of political participation among workers.

Inhibiting and Facilitating Factors

What conditions permitted the formation of a local agrarian reform movement and land redistribution? The complicated and protracted procedures for obtaining a final presidential grant of ejido land are described in detail in Appendix A. We have seen how this process could be delayed or subverted by potentially affected landowners, local community residents opposed to or fearful of land reform, Agrarian Department engineers and other officials who succumbed to bribes or intimidation by the local elite, and half-hearted implementation of the laws by state and federal governments. Local opposition reduced the ranks of the first petitioners by murder, persecution, and employment boycotts. Disillusioned by delays and hardship, many of the first agraristas left Lagos. Fear generated by local landowners and the clergy dissuaded many communities and individual residents from joining the movement, at least until the last stages of land redistribution.

One of the most consistent patterns emerging from this research is the interdependence of local mobilization and external support. In the late 1920s and early 1930s, the strength of the local movement and its ability to secure favorable decisions on its behalf were severely limited by the absence of external support and protection. Subsequently, the support of *some* state and federal government officials for the local reform organization proved crucial to the group's survival and the achievement of its objectives.

While outside political figures (e.g., Governors Zuno and Ramírez, President Cárdenas) encouraged local reform movements and community petitions for ejidos, the redistribution of land in Lagos would have taken much longer, and might not have occurred at all, without the determined pursuit of redistribution by local-level reformers. Comparative studies (e.g., Tai, 1974) have argued that successful land reform depends upon having a national government that is independent of the landed elite—an independence sometimes achieved by stimulating demands for land reform and thus creating a mass support base for the reformist regime. But the case of Lagos suggests that the political independence of the central government and the strong commitment of national leaders to the goal of land reform may not be sufficient to achieve results without equally committed, persistent local mobilization to secure the implementation of laws originating at the national level.

The dependence of agrarian reform movements on the state to attain and protect land reform, and the pattern of campesino political participation which that dependence breeds, constitute one of the basic problems revealed by this and other studies of peasant movements. It bears directly upon the capacity of the state to control and subvert independent demand-making by peasants in the post-reform period. It is clear that governments (e.g., the Cárdenas administration) which seek to impose social changes that threaten powerful elites must build support bases among groups which favor the intended changes. In that way, supporters can be cited as the source of demands, and the strength of such groups as evidence of the need to implement reforms. Beneficiaries of the reforms can then be incorporated into the government and party structure, both because their participation may be consonant with the political philosophy underlying the reforms, and because such participation lends legitimacy to the changes. But the participation of benefited groups can often be manipulated to serve a variety of needs, including system stabilization and political cooptation.

In Lagos, political activism before and during the Cárdenas period was regarded by such leaders as José Romero as a means to work within the system to secure more extensive reforms and more effective representation of agrarista and labor interests in official circles. At the national level, similar reasons for political participation by workers and campesinos were articulated by Vicente Lombardo Toledano, Ursulo Galván, Adalberto Tejeda, and Cárdenas himself. However, to most of the community-level agrarista leaders in Lagos, and to ejidatarios nationally in the years following the Cárdenas administration, political participation was mainly an insurance policy to protect reforms already achieved. This sense of indebtedness to the national government among beneficiaries of land reform has allowed the regime to use this group as a support base to consolidate its control of national politics and to counter more radical demands from other quarters.

Numerous Mexicanists have criticized Cárdenas' policy of establishing a national peasant organization (the Confederación Nacional Campesina) which was incorporated into the official party structure.[4] They regard the CNC as the embodiment of heavy-handed federal control and cooptation of peasant movements—control which has led to an increasingly conservative campesino organization. In Lagos de Moreno, however, the precipitous decline in the strength and reformist fervor of the local agrarista organization can be attributed only in part to the establishment of the CNC. It is true that with the consolidation of state and federal control over the peasant sector, and its affiliation with the official party, the Liga Regional in Lagos was reduced to a role of political endorsement rather than initiation (although its power to initiate was always limited, relying as it did on outside actors for protection). However, in 1938—the same year that the national CNC was created—other government policies of equal or greater significance to the demobilization of the peasant movement were being implemented.

During his last two years in office, Cárdenas began to consolidate and strengthen the ejidos which had already been created during his Presidency, establishing ad hoc agencies designed to deal with the problems associated with the new land-tenure system (credit, supportive technical services, etc.). The number of new ejidos granted declined toward the end of his administration, and dropped still more during the two presidential regimes which followed. As federal government emphasis shifted from land redistribution to increasing agricultural production and building a physical infrastructure for industrial development, support for local land-reform initiatives also declined. Among the first indicators of this trend was the formation of a national association to protect the interests of "small" private landholders (the local branch of the Asociación de Pequeños Propietarios began to function in Lagos in 1942). This was followed by increases in the issuance of presidential "certificates of unaffectability," guaranteeing that certain landholdings could not be expropriated to form ejidos for at least 25 years.

Simultaneously, developments at the local level in Lagos also reduced the momentum of the local reform movement. With the grants of land, Lagos' agraristas turned their attention to problems of economic survival (obtaining tools, credit, and livestock), and to the internal governance of the ejido communities. The leaders who remained in Lagos became immersed in the immediate problems of community factionalism, challenges to individual ejidatarios' land-tenure rights, and needs

---

[4]See, for example, Cockcroft, 1974; Córdova, 1975a; Hamilton, 1975; L. Meyer, 1977.

for a variety of community services. Most of the incentives for collective organization—at both the municipio and community levels—had been removed. Moreover, the granting of ejidos effectively disintegrated the solidarity that had developed between campesinos and urban workers in the local reform movement. Except for electoral campaigns, there is no evidence of municipio-wide organizing efforts by the Lagos agraristas since 1940.

Persisting Problems

This study of the agrarian reform movement in Lagos has focused on the period between 1924 and 1940. During this period, most of the ejido land in the municipio was requested, the majority of the first basic ejido grants were awarded, and the militant phase of the agrarista organization ran its course. However, the problem of land tenure was not solved by the end of the Cárdenas administration, either locally or nationally. Since 1940, ejido communities have continued to submit petitions for expansion of their original land-grants to satisfy the needs of a rapidly growing population of eligible campesinos. The vast majority of these petitions have been denied or shelved. My informants could recall only two petitions that had been granted in Lagos during the past decade, and one of these involved land voluntarily surrendered by a landowner in response to a petition for ejido expansion.

Numerous problems affect the campesino sector in Lagos today, but the most important are insufficient arable land, a lack of steady employment for the landless population, inadequate credit and irrigation facilities for the ejidatarios who possess land, and insecurity of land tenure for ejidatarios and private landholders alike. Given the persistence and severity of these problems, one is compelled to ask: What difference has the agrarian reform made in the politics, society, and economy of Lagos and its residents?

One of the main reasons why the agraristas petitioned for land was to enable them to become their own bosses, no longer subject to wage exploitation and demeaning treatment by large landholders. Since the agrarian reform, the treatment of agricultural laborers and ejidatarios by members of the upper class in Lagos has improved in some respects. Wages have risen, although rarely to the official minimum-wage level. Housing conditions have improved for ejidatarios and for wage-laborers on small agricultural properties; but for the majority of rural dwellers in the municipio, housing remains a significant problem. The old agraristas continue to regard the rich as a source of exploitation—particularly in the marketing of agricultural produce—even if their relationships with selected members of that class may be personally beneficial or amicable. And the private landowners and relatives of former hacendados continue to resent the ejidatarios, whom they describe as shiftless and opportunistic.

The attitude of the upper class is tinged with fear—not so much of the ejidatarios and other poor rural-dwellers, whom they regard as incapable of doing much on their own, but of unscrupulous "others" (e.g., peasant organizers and government officials) who might use land hunger and the political dependence of ejidatarios to promote self-serving schemes in which the landed would once again be adversely affected. The sexennial change of Presidents, and the policy shifts usually associated with the transition of power at the national level, are sources of discomfort and insecurity for ejidatarios and private landholders alike. If present policies benefit either sector, there is always the possibility that these policies will be reversed by the next administration.

Politically, the ejidatarios remain a significant voting bloc. As ejidatarios, they are automatically members of the CNC sector of the official party (now called the Partido Revolucionario Institucional, PRI). Except for the small number of urban labor union members, they constitute the only organized political group in Lagos. As such, they are called upon to endorse party candidates and government policies. They are the backbone of the PRI, in a municipio which is otherwise politically apathetic, abstentionist, or supportive of the main opposition party (the Partido de Acción Nacional, PAN). As residents of rural communities, ejidatarios also participate to a limited degree in community petitioning for "urban" services (potable water, electricity, sewers, street paving, and road grading) and irrigation facilities.

But the participation of individual ejidatarios and ejido communities in the political process is intended to secure specific personal or community benefits—never class or sector advantages. Benefits to the ejidatarios as a group, or to the landless agricultural workers, are initiated and delivered from above. Ejidatarios have representatives on the ayuntamiento; but since the Cárdenas era ended, this representation has not yielded any significant benefit to rural communities. Scarce municipio resources continue to be spent overwhelmingly on local government employees' wages and on projects which are concentrated in Lagos town and its immediate vicinity. The ayuntamiento's occasional decisions to make expenditures in rural communities usually result from personalis-

A street in Azulitos, one of the largest ejido communities in the municipio of Lagos, in 1976. Azulítos is located in the northernmost portion of the municipio, near Aguascalientes. Despite its substantial population (over 1,600), the community lacks electricity, piped water, and an all-weather access road.

tic pressures (e.g., the relative of a council member owns a ranch nearby).

The agrarian reform has yielded significant benefits for the local economy, at least relative to the conditions which obtained before the reform. Land redistribution probably has helped to diminish what would otherwise have been disastrously high rates of unemployment and underemployment in a municipio characterized by large families and very limited capital investment which might generate new jobs. In addition to being employed part-time in wage-labor themselves, often in the United States, numerous ejidatarios now employ their own wage-laborers for some portion of the agricultural season. Because of the small size of the plots and the large families to be supported from them, ejido land cultivation tends to be more labor-intensive than farming on the private landholdings in the municipio.

In general, the municipio's private landowning class adapted smoothly to post-reform conditions. Most did not leave Lagos, and even today they or their descendants are the wealthiest people in the municipio. The reduced availability of cheap labor and the loss of substantial portions of their arable land due to the reform induced private land-owners to adopt more capital-intensive production methods and to convert much of their remaining land to cattle-raising. As a result, although Lagos' economy is still agriculturally based, it has been diversified to include small- and large-scale dairying and manufacturing of related products such as agricultural machinery, fodder for cattle, cheese, ice cream, and powdered baby formula.

Unemployment remains a problem, however, in most parts of the municipio. Petitions for ejido expansions are now justified in terms of unemployment rather than the reasons given by the agraristas in the 1930s to secure the original land-grants. In most ejido communities, the population of eligible landless young men and families equals or surpasses the number of ejidatarios. While campesinos still hope for more land, many of the expansion petitions have been pending for decades, and the landless have no real expectation that their requests will be granted.

What young men in Lagos speak about increasingly is the need for sources of non-agricultural employment in the countryside—small industries, public-works projects, and so forth. And most of them consider it the government's responsibility to provide these sources of employment. Indeed, in this respect, the old guard is right: the young are more interested in wage-labor and non-agricultural employment than the older generation. Apart from the fact that there are not enough agricultural jobs to go around, it is also clear that young Laguenses regard unmechanized subsistence agriculture as difficult and unrewarding work. These perceptions are frequently reinforced by short-term work experiences in Mexican towns and cities, and in the United States, usually as undocumented immigrants.

Since the 1910 Revolution, and particularly since the administration of Lázaro Cárdenas, Mexican Presidents have felt compelled to express their commitment to the continuation of agrarian reform as a symbol of the "institutionalized Revolution" in Mexico. Even chief executives such as Miguel Alemán and Adolfo Ruiz Cortines, who redistributed far less land than others, have bowed rhetorically to the need for maintaining the land reform program. When, as in the case of President Echeverría, the rhetoric was loudest, frequently repeated, and reinforced by presidential grants of land and other programs benefiting some ejidos, this advocacy of campesino interests paid off in heightened agrarista support for the regime.

President José López Portillo bluntly declared at the outset of his administration that the solution to the plight of the poor and landless campesino in Mexico "is not to divide up the land, but to multiply production. To bring justice to the campesino is not to give him land nor divide it up, but rather to create [larger] units of production, to increase efficiency, and to generate wealth."[5] This shift in emphasis from access to land to increased food production was also reflected in the López Portillo administration's Sistema Alimentario Mexicano.[6] Thus justice for the campesino sector is now redefined as increased income and agricultural productivity, rather than as land.

Increased income—for whom? There is much disbelief that the government's new policy will put more income into the pockets of impoverished campesinos rather than the commercial middlemen, local *caciques*, and large landholders who have reaped most of the financial rewards of previous government initiatives in the rural sector. As the generation of men who received land during the 1930s passes away, and as today's generation of landless campesinos confronts a highly uncertain economic future with no reasonable prospect of receiving land through governmental action, what kind of support can the Mexican state expect to elicit from this segment of the population?

It has often been observed that the Mexican regime utilizes its capacity to mobilize support among the lower classes as a bargaining chip in its dealings with more privileged groups. Since the end of the Cárdenas period, control over the rural workforce has enabled the government to make decisions that it considered politically necessary, even while such decisions were resisted by private business interests.[7] Accordingly, some analysts of Mexican politics have argued that a significant erosion of the government's campesino support-base—whether it occurs gradually or abruptly—may make it impossible for the state to counter the demands of property-owning elites.[8]

But there is considerable disagreement as to what, if anything, can be done at this point in Mexico's history about the increasing power of the

[5]Quoted in *The New York Times*, December 13, 1977.

[6]The Sistema Alimentario Mexicano (Mexican Food System) announced on March 18, 1980, was a major reformulation of policies and programs affecting the rural sector, the main objective of which was to boost the production of basic food staples by small farmers in the so-called "subsistence sector." This policy package, and shifts in Mexican rural-development policy leading up to it, are analyzed in Bailey and Link, 1981; Grindle, 1981; Redclift, 1981; and Schumacher, 1981. An official statement and defense of the plan can be found in Luiselli, 1982.

[7]See, for example, the case study presented in Purcell, 1981.

[8]This scenario and the evidence bearing on its plausibility are discussed in Whitehead, 1981.

private sector to mold Mexico's political and economic future. Some say that the government should respond by aggressively organizing more campesinos and urban workers, under the auspices of the CNC and other government-controlled mass organizations.[9] This was, of course, the strategy employed by the Cardenistas in the 1930s to counterbalance the strength of private economic elites. Realistically, however, the government's capacity to mobilize campesinos in times of political crisis has been eroding for many years. Too many promises have not been kept. Land redistribution has been reduced to a trickle, and hopes for major new redistributions in the future have been effectively dashed. The leadership of government-controlled mass organizations is old and burned out, and it has not been replaced by younger, more dynamic cadres. The masses—both rural and urban—are increasingly cynical and unwilling to follow cues from the government.[10] As Mexico settles into a period of oil-based economic development, concentrated primarily in the urban-industrial sector, it is entirely possible that the rural poor will lose more real income through inflation than they will gain from new government investments in the rural sector.

Landless and unemployed campesinos in municipios like Lagos de Moreno might try to organize themselves in order to maximize their benefits (if any) under the new national development strategy. It now appears doubtful, however, that political and economic elites will allow the campesinos the opportunity and support necessary for such efforts to succeed.

[9]Susan Kaufman Purcell, presentation to a colloquium on Mexican politics and development sponsored by the Latin American Program, Woodrow Wilson International Center for Scholars, Washington, D.C., September 13, 1979.

[10]See, for example, the evidence from three rural communities reported in Salinas de Gortari (1980, 1982), which indicates that government-sponsored development programs in such communities do not necessarily increase support for the political system among the "benefited" campesinos. Both the finding and the explanations given for it are of particular interest, since Salinas de Gortari was appointed to the key position of Minister of Planning and Budget in the cabinet of president Miguel de la Madrid (1982–1988).

The Legal Procedure
For Agrarian Reform

The Agrarian Reform Law[1] defines the steps which petitioners and government agencies must follow before ejido lands can be granted in response to a community's petition for the redistribution of lands. The law has been amended several times, changing some of the requirements for individual and community eligibility, but the process of petitioning has remained essentially the same. Between 1924 and 1940, when almost all of the petitions for initial land grants (and many of the requests for expansions of existing ejidos) were submitted by agrarian communities in Lagos de Moreno, the process of petitioning for an ejido was basically as described in the following pages. Illustrations are drawn from the expedientes ejidales (ASRA) for ejidos in the municipio of Lagos de Moreno, particularly for the ejido of Lagos, which was one of the most contested cases and has one of the most extensively documented files.

The Petition

The review process is initiated by the community's submission of a petition to the state governor requesting a grant of land. The petition specifies which of three kinds of land-grants is being sought: restitution, dotation, or expansion. Grants of restitution require proof of prior community title to the lands, and because such documentation was scarce (it usually required proof of Spanish royal land grants to Indian commu-

---

[1]The Agrarian Code of 1971, with amendments of 1972, is published in its entirety in Martínez Garza (1975). The complete Agrarian Code signed in 1934 by President Abelardo Rodríguez is reprinted in Simpson (1937: 759-808).

nities), few ejidos were granted on this basis. By 1966, only 222 presidential decrees had established new ejidos by restitution, and 689 decrees legalized existing communal landholdings (Reyes Osorio et al., 1974: 541). Only two of the agrarian communities in Lagos de Moreno (Buenavista and the *comunidad indígena* of La Laguna) petitioned for restitution of lands. By far the majority of the ejidos have received dotational grants, awarded initially to communities which were ineligible for restitution grants because they could not prove prior community title, and later to communities of landless agricultural laborers with no history of communal landownership. Expansion grants are awarded to communities which have an ejido but lack sufficient land to support the total number of eligible ejidatarios.

The petitions submitted by agrarian communities in Lagos de Moreno were sometimes typed or handwritten, occasionally improvised, often following a set format; a few were submitted on printed forms which only required filling in blanks. Uniformly, they refer to the land reform laws and to the community's urgent need for ejido land because the residents are landless agricultural workers, compelled to sell their labor at low prices and neglect the care of their families. Sometimes the petition refers to specific haciendas in the vicinity which could be expropriated. As an example, the text of the petition submitted by the agrarian community of Lagos de Moreno is reproduced in Chapter 3.

According to the Agrarian Reform Law, the state governor must forward the petition to the Comisión Agraria Mixta (CAM—or in earlier years, the Comisión Local Agraria) within ten days of receiving it. The CAM, a state branch of the national agency charged with administering the land reform law,[2] studies the community's petition and submits its recommendation to the governor. As soon as a community's petition is received, the CAM is responsible for publishing it in the state's official journal (in this case, the *Periódico Oficial del Gobierno, Estado de Jalisco*). The date of publication is the first of several critical dates in the evaluation procedure: subdivisions and sales of large landholdings which would alter their eligibility for expropriation under the land reform law have not been considered legal if they occurred after publication of the

---

[2]The national agency charged with administering the land reform law has changed names various times, upgrading its rank within the federal government bureaucracy. It has been, in sequence of its development, the National Agrarian Commission (Comisión Nacional Agraria), the Agrarian Department (Departamento Agrario), the Department of Agrarian Affairs and Colonization (Departamento de Asuntos Agrarios y Colonización), and now the Agrarian Reform Ministry (Secretaría de Reforma Agraria).

petition. There are often lags of months or years between the dates of submission on the petitions and their publication, as well as between the dates of gubernatorial or presidential decrees and their publication in the official records of government activities.

The CAM is the first agency to study the petition. Its reports, and every subsequent review of a community's petition, all address the following questions: whether the community is eligible for and needs ejido land; whether there are enough eligible petitioners in the community; and whether there are landholdings which meet the expropriation requirements. Criteria for eligibility in each of these areas are specified by the Agrarian Reform Law. They are described here in some detail because they later become the basis for claims and delaying tactics employed by the potentially affected landowners.

To be eligible for a dotation grant,[3] a community or village must have been in existence for at least six months prior to filing its petition, and at least 20 residents must be eligible to receive land. (In the case of urban centers with a population of 10,000 or more—such as Lagos de Moreno—the minimum number of eligible recipients is increased to 150.) *Individuals* are eligible to receive ejido land if they were born in Mexico, are at least 16 years old if they are single or any age if married, have resided in the community for at least six months prior to applying for the land, and make their living from agriculture ("work the land as a habitual occupation"). Women who apply as individuals must additionally be widows or the sole provider for the family. Petitioners cannot own amounts of land equal to or greater than the unit of land to be granted each ejidatario, and must not have capital investments in industry or commerce of 2,500 pesos or more, or in agriculture of 5,000 pesos or more. Peones acasillados were not generally eligible for ejido lands until the exclusionary provision was partially amended in 1934 and totally eliminated in 1937.[4]

---

[3]Hereafter referred to only as an ejido grant; but it should be understood that the eligibility criteria described here differ in some significant ways from the requirements for restitution and expansion grants.

[4]Peones acasillados were agricultural workers who resided in housing provided by the hacienda owner. Three explanations are offered for this exclusion of acasillados from the land redistribution program. Bazant (1977: 178) argues that peones acasillados were ineligible because if they were granted land, the reform would deprive the large landowners of their laborers as well as their land. Nathaniel and Sylvia Weyl (1939: 78–79) suggest that the acasillados were excluded because it was believed that they would remain subservient to their employers even if they were brought into the ejido, and would thus subvert the political purpose of the land-reform program. Finally, if eligible, peones

Land Requirements

The Agrarian Reform Law also specifies which landholdings can be expropriated. The property can be any public or private landholding within a 7-kilometer radius (originally limited to 5 kilometers) from the center of the petitioning community which measures (originally) more than 500 hectares (later, under certain conditions, more than 100 or 300 hectares). Landholdings can be exempted from expropriation by invoking a series of rules referring to the crop that is cultivated and the quality of the soil. Cultivators of cotton and other plantation crops as well as cattle ranchers could receive exemption concessions for 25 years, for farms ranging from 300 to 50,000 hectares, depending on the soil quality.

In general, acreages of irrigated land, seasonal (rainfall-dependent) cropland, pasture, and woodlands were regarded as equivalent in a ratio of 1:2:4:8. Thus, in determining the maximum permissible size of a landholding, 100 hectares of irrigated land was equivalent to 200 hectares of seasonal cropland, 400 hectares of pasture, or 800 hectares of woodlands. Theoretically (although this often was ignored in Lagos), after the grant of ejido lands the original landowner should be left only with the maximum allowable hectares of the mix of different kinds of lands which he chose to retain. He was also generally permitted to select which part of the original landholding he would retain, provided he did so within a fixed period of time. By law, the landowner could also apply for compensation within one year of the date that the presidential resolution was published in the *Diario Oficial*. This indemnity was payable in government bonds.

Thus, once it has been established that the community is eligible to become an ejido, and that it contains the minimum number of eligible recipients of ejido land, attention turns to assessing the expropriability of nearby landholdings. It must be shown by land surveys conducted by government engineers that there are haciendas within the legal radius from the petitioning community[5] which exceed the maximum permissible size, and which would yield sufficient land to supply the number of eligible beneficiaries and still leave the original landholder with his legal

---

acasillados would further swell the ranks of potential recipients of land. This would significantly increase the amount of land to be expropriated. Thus the elimination of acasillados allowed landowners to retain lands they would otherwise lose, and completely protected haciendas which relied exclusively on resident labor.

[5]Measurement of this distance was contested in cases where petitioning communities were dispersed settlements, or when landowners refused to accept the community boundary points used for measurement.

limit of land. Until 1943, this meant that the nearby landholdings taken together had to have enough surplus land to yield an ejido grant of 4 hectares of irrigated land or 8 hectares of seasonal cropland per beneficiary, plus an additional plot of the same size for the ejido school's farm, and in some cases for a new urban center, and usually pasture or woodlands to be shared by all the ejidatarios.[6] Failure to legally satisfy any of these conditions would constitute grounds for denying the community's petition.

Because there were a number of large landholdings in the municipio of Lagos de Moreno and often several potentially expropriable haciendas near each petitioning community, the number of individuals and their legal representatives involved in each ejido review was large. This complicated the legal proceedings, particularly when any single landowner or property could be affected by grants to each of several petitioning communities. In those cases, review of the petitions had to be coordinated so that the grants would not overlap, and also to prevent the original landowner from being left with less than the legal maximum landholding. Attacked on several fronts, landowners reacted forcefully.

One of the least violent delay tactics used by the landowners (aside from legal writs of protection and procedural objections) was the division of the largest landholdings into smaller property units. These property divisions would reduce or eliminate the expropriability of a landholding by reducing its size. Sometimes this was done by wills-in-life to several heirs, or by sharing title with them. In several instances (for example, the haciendas of San Cristóbal, La Troje, Cieneguilla, La Punta, and Betulia), hacienda land was sold off in lots of 10 to 100 hectares. Some of these were forthright sales, but others were legal ruses.

The Census

Eligibility studies carried out by the CAM—and often repeated by the national agency after the gubernatorial decree—are completed by CAM engineers assigned to study and report on specific communities. For the ejidos in Lagos de Moreno, the longest delays—often of many years— were associated with this period of state-level review of the petitions.

[6]Between 1943 and 1947, the grants were increased to 6 and 12 hectares per recipient of either irrigated or seasonal land; after 1947, the grants were increased again to 10 and 20 hectares each of irrigated or seasonal land. The larger plots are clearly more economically viable. But the changes also disqualified petitions, and protected haciendas, in cases where there was not sufficient expropriable land to meet the community's needs as defined by the increased ejido plot size.

During the 1920s and early 1930s, many petitions were simply not resolved at the state level, and were forwarded to Mexico City with a "tacit negative" gubernatorial decree.

The petitioning community and the potentially affected landowners are notified of each phase of the eligibility study and given legal deadlines by which representatives must be named, or objections filed, in response to petition procedures. An executive committee composed of 6 community residents represents the petitioning group in its dealings with the government during the review process.

One of the first steps in the review is the agrarian census of the petitioning community. This is conducted by a CAM engineer, in the presence of representatives of both the community and the landowners. The inclusiveness of these censuses varies, sometimes listing all of the residents and sometimes only the eligible recipients of ejido lands. In some cases, the census also makes note of livestock or land owned by community residents (which might limit or negate individual eligibility). David Ronfeldt (1973: 61) has written that "Evidently an agrarian census was as much a political as a technical undertaking." This was patently clear in the municipio of Lagos de Moreno. Whether conducted by state or federal employees, the census was often repeated or amended in response to objections filed by community or landowner representatives. The census was critical, because the grant or denial of the ejido, and the amount of land expropriated for each individual in it, would be determined in large part by the number of eligible recipients censused.

The censuses were not always conducted house to house, nor strictly in accordance with the law. One of the censuses for Lagos de Moreno was reportedly compiled in the town's official party headquarters with the "assistance" of the municipio president and party officials, at a time when these authorities opposed the agraristas. Sometimes the engineers reported that the census could not be completed because of intense community opposition or the danger posed by civil disorder. Names were allegedly added or removed at the insistence of the landowners or agraristas, with no proof of the presence, residence, or existence of the individuals whose names were so freely exchanged. Charges of corruption abounded on both sides.

Objections filed in response to the census results were another major delaying tactic in the review procedure. The most common objection filed by community representatives was that eligible residents had been forced out of the community or were away on the day of the census. In some cases the engineers filed reports alleging that the residents were no longer interested in receiving land, or that they were unable to secure cooperation from the community in order to conduct the census. Community representatives subsequently filed objections denying these reports and charging collusion between landowners and engineers. The landowners filed long lists of objections to disqualify specific individuals appearing on the census rosters.

According to a narrow interpretation of the law, only the persons whose names appear in the census used for the final presidential grant are eligible to receive ejido parcels when the land is distributed. Due to intense local opposition, and to delays in the review process resulting from objections such as those described above, there was a high rate of attrition among the first petitioners for ejidos in Lagos. In many instances, grants were based on censuses which were five to ten years old. This gave rise later to internal community conflicts, and to legal objections by landowners concerning the real number of eligible recipients in each community.

Reports and Recommendations

When a census is completed, the CAM engineer submits the final tally of eligible recipients along with a report which includes his recommendations for action on the ejido petition. In Lagos, these reports often included a statement on how people in the commmunity made their living, including wages received, treatment by the landowners, the price of staples or the value of goods produced, and the quality of the land in the area. Sometimes they included comments on general economic or social conditions in the community, or on the extent of interest in land reform. Finally, relying on local property tax records, the report included the names of the landowners whose properties were within a 7-kilometer radius of the petitioning community, the size and tax value of the properties, and recommendations on which of these landholdings should be affected and the amount of irrigated, seasonal, or grazing land which could be taken from each property while leaving each original landowner with the maximum amount of land permitted by the reform law.

Once again, these reports are targets for various objections, usually by the landowners and occasionally by the petitioning communities. In Lagos, it was often alleged that when the ineligible persons on the roster were eliminated, less than 20 eligible recipients resided in the community. In some cases, the landowners submitted documents signed by community residents in which they swore that they were not interested in receiving ejido lands, or that their names were falsified on the petition, or that their names were added to the census roster against their will.

During the 1920s, the political status of the community was an important factor. For years, the petition submitted by La Escondida in the municipio of Lagos was delayed because it was incorrectly identified (by the municipio president) as a community of peones acasillados. And a lengthy debate was conducted over whether Buenavista and Moya were separate rural communities or merely suburbs of the town of Lagos (thus making them ineligible for a separate ejido). In addition, landowners often objected to being designated as targets for expropriation. They charged that their landholdings were too small, or farther from the petitioning community than the distance specified by law. In some cases, where the landholding had been subdivided or where title was shared by multiple co-owners, they sought to have each share regarded as a separate property (and therefore ineligible for expropriation). In some cases where the land had been sold off, the new owners objected to the possibility of expropriation on the grounds that they were small landholders; but their objections were denied if the sales had occurred after publication of the community's petition.

On the basis of the engineer's report, the CAM submits its recommendation to the state governor, who reviews the report and makes his own decision. If he decides to grant the community's petition, the CAM is charged with provisional implementation of the grant. This means that the petitioners are granted provisional rights to cultivate land, pending a final decree by the President of the Republic. Often implementation of the provisional decree is delayed by writs of protection secured by landowners while their objections are being reviewed by the courts or by the federal government. For example, the governor of Jalisco granted land to the ejido of Moya in 1925, but two of the affected landowners interposed writs of protection, and the community did not receive provisional possession of the land until 1933. Sometimes the agrarian communities objected to the location of the land they were granted, because of the poor quality of the soil. In such cases they usually charged that the landowners had bribed the CAM engineer to give them inferior lands.

Meanwhile, the CAM forwards all of the documentation on the community's petition to the national Agrarian Department. There, an advisory board reviews the petition and documentation, repeats some of the studies (particularly the census and land surveys of expropriable holdings), and eventually submits its own recommendation to the President. During these deliberations, the same objections voiced in response to the CAM studies are often reiterated to the federal agents. Once the President signs his decree and it is published in the *Diario Oficial*, the Agrarian Department assigns an engineer to carry out the final implementation, in a ceremony granting definitive possession of the land to the ejido community. The land is not necessarily immediately available to the ejidatarios, however; depending on the season, the landowners are given grace periods to harvest already-planted crops and relocate livestock and machinery.

The Agrarian Department's recommendation to the President includes a proposal of the amount and location of the land to be taken from each of the affected landholdings. The presidential decree is based on this recommendation. However, in some Lagos communities, years of debate followed the presidential decrees granting ejidos. In several cases the ejidatarios charged that they had not been given all of the land specified in the decree, or that substitutions had been made (e.g., rain-fed lands substituted for irrigated lands). The landowner sometimes charged that the land was occupied by the ejido in amounts or locations which did not accord with the decree. Thus the debate among landowners, ejidatarios, and the government was not stilled even by the President's decision.

The Ejido Grant

The presidential decree grants land to the ejido community. As part of the ceremony in which definitive possession is awarded, the members of the ejido elect a governing council (now called the *comisariado ejidal*) and a review committee *(consejo de vigilancia)* to oversee the performance of the comisariado ejidal. The governing council is empowered to distribute land equitably among ejido members, reserving the pasture and forest lands for communal use. Allocation of land use rights by the ejido council (with the consent of the Agrarian Department's local representative) must be in accordance with a list of individual priority rights specified by law. Each ejidatario has usufructuary rights to his parcel. According to the Agrarian Law, he may neither sell, sharecrop (except in special circumstances), nor rent his land; and should he fail to work it for more than two consecutive years, he forfeits his right to the plot.

In short, ejidatarios do not become private landowners; and while their right to cultivate their parcel is protected by law if they follow the rules, community politics and arbitrary decisions by local bosses may still affect individual rights to ejido parcels. Some of this insecurity of tenure can be removed by *aparcelamiento*. This involves yet another procedure, after the definitive possession is granted. Ejidos can request—at their own expense—a land survey and delimitation of all of the ejido's arable land into specific, bounded parcels. Each ejidatario is then given legal usufruct title to his parcel, which he forfeits only if he violates strictures imposed by law. The title also lists successors with priority to the right to cultivate that particular parcel. Only a small fraction of the ejidos in the Republic or in Lagos de Moreno have been *"aparcelados"*; precise statistics are not made public.

Appendix B

Supplementary Tables

Table B-1

Land Distribution in Lagos de Moreno, 1900 and 1930

Size of Landholdings (in Hectares)	1900				1930			
	Cumulative Total Hectares[a]	Cumulative Percent Hectares	Cumulative Total Owners[b]	Cumulative Percent Owners	Cumulative Total Hectares[a]	Cumulative Percent Hectares	Cumulative Total Owners[b]	Cumulative Percent Owners
0–1	990	0.42%	1,981	56.45%	1,881	0.78%	3,763	60.01%
1.1–20	12,974	5.48	3,117	88.83	23,160	9.57	5,780	92.17
21–50	18,654	7.88	3,277	93.39	31,573	13.05	6,017	95.95
51–100	24,281	10.26	3,352	95.53	37,271	15.40	6,092	97.15
101–200	31,164	13.16	3,397	96.81	46,266	19.12	6,147	98.02
201–500	48,684	20.57	3,449	98.29	61,596	25.45	6,197	98.82
501–1,000	68,307	28.86	3,476	99.06	82,007	33.88	6,226	99.28
1,001–2,000	92,441	39.05	3,491	99.49	113,275	46.80	6,250	99.67
2,001–5,000	130,225	55.01	3,502	99.80	147,727	61.04	6,262	99.86
5,001–10,000	146,236	61.78	3,505	99.89	190,942	78.90	6,268	99.95
10,001–20,000	176,203	74.43	3,507	99.94	212,216	87.69	6,270	99.98
20,001–30,000	200,522	84.71	3,508	99.97	—	—	—	—
more than 30,000	236,721	100.00	3,509	100.00	242,017	100.00	6,271	100.00

Source: This table is based on data compiled from the property-tax records in the local branch of the state tax office (Delegación de Hacienda del Estado) in Lagos de Moreno. For 1900, the data were tallied from the *Manifestaciones Prediales de 1900*, and for 1930 from the *Catastro Antiguo, 1900–1947.*

[a]For landholdings registered as measuring 201 or more hectares, the cumulative total hectares represent the *exact* number of hectares registered for those properties. For all properties measuring less than 1 hectare to 200 hectares, the cumulative total hectares are based on an *estimate* calculated by the following formula:

(midpoint of the size category) × (total number of properties tallied for that size category)

The midpoints used in this formula were .5, 10.5, 35.5, 75.5, and 150.5. The size (in hectares) of landholdings registered with multiple co-owners was divided by the number of co-owners (when known) and tallied in the smaller size category (see note b).

[b]Each registered landholding is regarded as representing a single landowner. This overestimates the number of owners, especially of properties above 50 hectares in size, since there are numerous cases of individuals owning multiple landholdings. However, the similarity of names made it impossible to separately tally owners. On properties of over 150 hectares which were co-owned by several persons, the total property size was divided by the number of co-owners listed and tallied as separate landholdings. For example, in 1900, Moya, Castelhondo y Anexos (1,285 hectares) was co-owned by three individuals and has therefore been tallied as three properties of 428 hectares. This correction was introduced so that the figures might more accurately represent the distribution of wealth among landowners in the municipio. However, some of these landholdings may have been operated as single property units rather than as independent subunits.

Table B-2

Land Reform Performance of Governors of the State of Jalisco, January 15, 1915–December 31, 1935

Governor	Petitions Denied	Petitions Approved	Hectares Distributed	Campesinos Benefited	Period of Office
Manuel M. Diéguez	0	3	3,497	322	1-20-15–3-21-15
					7-11-17–9-30-17
Manuel Aguirre Berlanga	0	4	4,701	799	3-22-15–7-10-17
Emiliano Degollado	0	1	1,000	383	10-17–3-20-18
Manuel Bouquel, Jr.	0	18	30,831	4,803	3-21-18–2-28-19
Luis Castellanos y Tapia	0	1	579	113	3-1-19–5-7-20
Francisco Labastida Izquierdo	0	5	3,667	654	10-5-20–2-28-21
Basilio Vadillo	0	26	51,397	7,518	3-1-21–5-29-22
Antonio Valadez Ramírez	0	11	12,162	2,294	5-30-22–2-28-23
José Guadalupe Zuno	5	107	113,637	22,157	3-1-23–5-25-26
Clemente Sepúlveda	0	1	2,096	262	5-26-26–7-28-26
Silvano Barba González	6	3	4,530	456	7-30-25–8-2-26
					2-3-27–2-28-27
Enrique Cuervo	1	0	0	0	1-19-27–2-2-27
Margarito Ramírez	28	36	21,158	3,995	4-21-27–7-24-29,
					8-2-29–8-7-29
José María Cuéllar	1	10	4,281	881	8-8-29–7-11-30
Ruperto García de Alba	12	9	5,621	797	7-12-30–2-28-31
Saul Gómez Pezuela	2	5	2,611	545	9-9-31–9-11-31
Juan de Dios Robledo	3	4	1,366	300	9-12-31–3-31-32
Sebastián Allende	33	66	28,244	4,097	4-1-32–2-28-35
Everardo Topete	0	35	36,462	4,042	3-1-35–12-15-35
Totals	91	345	327,840	54,418	

Source: Document in private archives of José Romero Gómez, Mexico City (AJRG).

Table B-3

Presidential Decrees Granting Earliest and Principal Ejidos in the Municipio of Lagos de Moreno

Ejido Name	Date Requested[a]	Presidential Decree[b]	Number of Parcels[c]	Hectares Granted[d]
Bernalejo	5-4-31	6-17-36 by L. Cárdenas*	49	1,492
Buenavista	11-11-24	5-6-27 by P. E. Calles	149	934
La Cantera	8-1-36	7-21-37 by L. Cárdenas	78	1,228
Cantera de los Torres	11-3-37	7-5-39 by L. Cárdenas	21	378
Cañada de Ricos	7-20-25	5-14-35 by L. Cárdenas*	126	1,110
El Chipinque	7-37	4-24-40 by L. Cárdenas	35	450
Chupaderos (now Primero de Mayo)	3-14-35	4-21-37 by L. Cárdenas	48	961
Ciénega de Mata (Lic. Primo Verdad)	3-12-25	7-8-36 by L. Cárdenas*	141	2,000
Las Cruces (Francisco I. Madero)	11-15-30	4-29-36 by L. Cárdenas	108	1,415
Cuarenta (San Miguel de Cuarenta)	2-21-18	9-12-29 by E. Portes Gil	147	882
Cuarenta (expansion)	12-14-35	7-7-37 by L. Cárdenas	50	900
La Escondida	2-24-25	11-14-30 by P. Ortiz Rubio	29	259
La Escondida (expansion)	7-30-34	4-21-37 by L. Cárdenas	96	716
Lagos de Moreno	1-17-25	5-22-35 by L. Cárdenas*	313	2,466
Loma de Veloces	5-3-31	4-15-36 by L. Cárdenas*	47	470
El Maguey	1-28-35	5-20-36 by L. Cárdenas	54	744
La Merced	11-3-36	4-7-37 by L. Cárdenas	56	664
Miranda	10-16-38	7-31-40 by L. Cárdenas	49	882
Moya	4-2-25	5-14-35 by L. Cárdenas	130	1,290
El Ojuelo	9-21-36	4-21-37 by L. Cárdenas	59	798
Las Palomas (Palomas-Sauceda)	10-1-36	5-19-37 by L. Cárdenas	60	960
Potrerillos	2-10-35	1-31-40 by L. Cárdenas	50	950
Puerta de la Chiripa	2-12-36	10-6-37 by L. Cárdenas	25	375
El Puesto	11-31-39	10-20-43 by M. Ávila Camacho	96	1,384
La Punta (Los Azulitos)	10-28-34	4-21-37 by L. Cárdenas*	195	1,542
San Jorge (Macedonio Ayala)	5-25-31	5-14-35 by L. Cárdenas*	31	296
Santa Cruz (Dieciocho de Marzo)	8-16-36	4-21-37 by L. Cárdenas	86	1,432

La Sauceda (Palomas-Sauceda)	5-3-36	4-21-37 by L. Cárdenas	110	1,593
El Tepetatillo (Tacubaya)	9-5-34	5-19-37 by L. Cárdenas*	56	442
El Testerazo	11-26-31	7-1-36 by L. Cárdenas*	28	324
El Trinidad	5-11-31	7-8-36 by L. Cárdenas*	38	416
La Troje	9-23-36	9-22-37 by L. Cárdenas*	146	1,751

Source: Presidential decrees published in the *Diario Oficial* of Mexico.

[a] Refers to the date on the application for an ejido, directed to the Governor of Jalisco.

[b] Refers to the date on the presidential decree and to the President who signed it.

[c] Reflects the number of individuals in the community who qualified as beneficiaries of the ejido (ejidatarios), plus one additional plot in all decrees signed by Lázaro Cárdenas, designated for the rural school building and farmland.

[d] Refers to the total number of hectares granted, including land for cultivation and communal grazing lands.

*Designates all presidential decrees which reversed a negative gubernatorial decision (denying petitioners the right to an ejido) or a "tacit negative" decision, in which no gubernatorial decision was made during the time limit specified by law.

Table B-4

Landholders of 500 Hectares or More in the Municipio of Lagos de Moreno, 1900

Landholder[a]	Number of Properties Owned	Largest Properties	Total Number Hectares Owned	Total Tax-Assessed Value of Properties
José María de Alba	2	Santana, San Marcos	1,622	$(13,000)[b]
Perfecto Alba	4	Rancho Nuevo	681	7,701
Canónigo Pablo Anda	1	Las Cruces	2,693	12,000
José María Azuela	1	Sepúlveda, San Antonio, Chipinque	941	28,000
Mariano Azuela and brothers	3	Providencia, El Llano, El Muerto	675	8,189
Antonio Díaz Infante	1	San Cristóbal	135	2,994
Antonio Díaz Infante with Félix Díaz Infante	1	Las Cardonas	513	2,412
Félix Díaz Infante	1	El Sauz de Díaz	192	3,000
Manuel Díaz Infante	2	San José, La Esperanza	807	15,500
Benigno Estrada y Barajas (estate)	1	Sauceda y Anexos	3,934	26,900
Bernardo Flores	1	San Bernardo y Anexos	5,605	65,000
Juan Gallardo	1	Magueyes	3,174	38,000
Miguel Gallardo	1	La Troje	668	28,000
Faustina García v. de Gómez	2	Lobos y Soledad, Portugalejo	713	6,296
Juan Gómez	1	Santa Cruz	2,653	38,000
Manuel Y. Gómez Mendívil (estate)	1	San Fandilas	513	10,000
Luis Gómez Portugal	2	San Rafael, El Sauz	1,668	26,900
Paula Gómez Portugal with Antonio Gómez Portugal (estate)	1	Tlalixcoyán	1,284	24,600
Carlos María González	2	El Hallazgo, Venta del Ojo de Agua	526	7,300
José González	1	Laborcita de González	1,412	23,000
María P. González	2	Cieneguilla, Pedernal	2,199	35,000
Pánfila González v. de Zermeño	3	San Isidro, Potrerillo, Potrero de los Caños	833	8,010
Nicolás Gutiérrez	1	Jaramillo el Bajo	872	14,600

Owner		Property		
Alberto Hermosillo	1	Labor de Hermosillo	646	13,800
Alberto G. Hermosillo	1	Cieneguilla de Jácome	480	14,000
Cástulo López	1	Bellavista	571	4,100
Francisco de P. López (estate)	1	San Juan sin Agua	899	11,000
Ignacio Madrazo	1	La Punta	24,319	232,000
Juana Malacara v. de Castillo	4	Los Ranchos, Noche Buena y Tapias, Adjuntas		
Antonia Mitre v. de Briseño	1	Portezuelo de Briseño	1,971	22,357
José Cipriano Moreno	4	Granadillas, San Cayetano, Ladera	652	6,930
Bernardo Moreno y Oviedo	4	Ceja de Bolitas, La Cantera	1,911	36,500
Domingo Moreno y Oviedo	1	San Nicolás	1,615	20,528
Eugenio Moreno y Oviedo	4	Portezuelo, Altamira	899	10,275
Francisca Moreno y Oviedo	2	La Estanzuela	1,873	30,832
Wenceslao Oñate	2	Santiago	1,070	10,792
Lic. Conrado Pérez Anda and brothers	3	La Palma	1,375	13,950
Octavio Pérez Castro	3	El Zapote, Jonitas y Divisadero	529	7,000
Eduardo Rincón Gallardo	2	Cienega de Mata, El Tecuán	878	12,342
Gen. Pedro Rincón Gallardo	1	La Troje	36,199	265,000
Pedro Romo	1	Betulia	15,847	140,000
Pedro Rosas (estate)	1	San Isidro de Abajo	1,894	26,000
Ana Rosso v. de Rincón Gallardo	3	El Puesto, Ledesma, San Cristóbal	556	8,000
Francisca Sanromán (usufructuaria)	1	La Ordeña	14,120	149,500
Ignacia Sanromán with Margarita Sanromán	1		607	6,800
Lic. José María Sanromán	1	Salto de Zuritas	784	10,000
Juana Sanromán	2	Jaramillo el Alto, La Galera	5,111	68,000
Leonor Sanromán	1	Labor, San Agustín y Portugalejo	984	40,000
Manuela Sanromán	1	Lo de Avalos	2,671	29,000
María S. Sanromán	1	Lo de Avalos	882	15,000
Carlos Serrano	1	San Francisco y Rancho Seco	2,396	47,000
Pascasio Serrano (estate)	1	Coecillo	5,295	62,000
Celso Serrano Flores (Hermosillo?)	6	San Nicolás	4,975	52,500
		Las Cajas, San Pedro, Santa Emilia	4,296	85,930

Table B-4
(continued)

Landholder[a]	Number of Properties Owned	Largest Properties	Total Number Hectares Owned	Total Tax-Assessed Value of Properties
Celso Serrano Flores and children	1	San Joaquín	924	14,000
Enrique Serrano Flores	1	El Centro	4,415	50,000
Genaro Serrano Flores	1	La Merced	4,378	45,000
Primitivo Serrano Flores with Abraham Serrano Flores and estate of Manuel Serrano Flores and Delfina Anaya de Serrano	1	Moya, Castelhondo y Anexos	1,285	40,000
Ignacio Torres Gómez (estate)	3	San José del Potrero	1,420	20,950
Josefa Vega v. de Calvillo and children	1	El Sauz de Calvillo	1,498	11,900
Antonio Velázquez Espinosa	3	Nazas de Velázquez	948	17,250
Bernardo Villalobos	1	El Cajón	556	8,000
Librada Zamora v. de Pont	1	Llano del Crespo	1,883	17,000
Tomasa Zarate with Genoveva Bravo	2	El Terrero	582	7,630
Benjamin Zermeño		El Sauz	1,637	18,000
Totals	106		190,144	$2,111,068

Source: Manifestaciones Prediales de 1900 and Catastro Antiguo, 1900–1947, Delegación de Hacienda del Estado de Jalisco, Lagos de Moreno, Jalisco.

[a]Some names appear more than once in the table, when they were recorded as co-owners of a landholding in the records.

[b]Parentheses denote missing data on the tax-assessed value of one or more properties. In most cases, the missing data correspond to the value of a relatively small landholding. Total tax-assessed value of these properties would be slightly higher than the figure shown.

Table B-5

Landholders of 500 Hectares or More in the Municipio of Lagos de Moreno, 1930

Landholder[a]	Number of Properties Owned	Largest Properties	Total Number Hectares Owned	Total Tax-Assessed Value of Properties
Perfecto de Alba	39	La Ordeña, Nazas, Rancho Nuevo	1,718	$49,554
Teresa Antuñano v. de Antuñano with José Alfonso and María Teresa Antuñano	1	Providencia	524	18,400
Victor Ayquesparsse with María Rincón Gallardo de Ayquesparsse	1	San Cristóbal, La Troje y Anexos	12,144	125,000
Félix Azuela y Padilla with Luz Padilla v. de Azuela	25	Sepúlveda, San Antonio, Chipinque y Anexos, El Muerto	663	37,014
María Paz Barrón y Rincón Gallardo with Alfredo, Manuel, Carmen, Guadalupe, and Francisco Barrón y Rincón Gallardo	3	La Troje, Betulia	7,943	219,000
Genoveva Bravo	2	El Terrero	582	15,200
José María Calvillo Vega	6	El Sauz, El Sauz de Calvillo	2,453	51,870
Jesús O. Casillas	10	San Rafael, El Portezuelo, Ladera de Cantareras	881	19,088
María de la Luz Castillo	25	Noche Buena, Los Ranchos, El Cerro	3,444	77,980
Genaro Cortina Rincón	1	El Puesto	7,872	140,000
Benigno Estrada y Barajas	1	La Sauceda	501	5,220
Enriqueta Estrada y Barajas	1	El Roble	760	8,217
José Luis Estrada y Barajas	1	Palomas	471	8,840
María Guadalupe Estrada y Barajas	1	Noche Buena	902	8,840
Prisciliana Estrada y Barajas	1	Noche Buena	798	8,840

Table B-5
(continued)

Landholder[a]	Number of Properties Owned	Largest Properties	Total Number Hectares Owned	Total Tax-Assessed Value of Properties
Prisciliana Estrada y Barajas with María Guadalupe and José Luis Estrada y Barajas	1	Palomas y Anexos	274	8,790
Finca de la Federación	1	Las Cruces	2,693	98,000
Bernardo Flores Gallardo with Sara, Elena, and María del Refugio Flores Gallardo	1	San Bernardo	4,551	87,150
Rosa Gallardo v. de Azuela with María de los Dolores and María Luisa Azuela y Gallardo	2	Los Angeles, Santa Rosa	1,118	27,500
Elena Gómez de Anaya	2	Santa Cruz	630	17,705
Josefina Gómez de Díaz Infante	2	Santa Cruz	624	17,000
Carmen Gómez de González with María Zarate v. de Gómez	3	Santa Cruz	620	17,400
Dolores Gómez de Moreno	4	Santa Cruz	653	19,475
Ana María Gómez de Sanromán	2	Santa Cruz, Cardonas	591	7,350
Manuel Gómez Mendivil (estate)	1	San Fandilas	513	20,000
Sebastián Gómez Pérez	1	Portezuelo de Briseño	789	15,800
Luis Gómez Portugal	4	La Daga, San Rafael, La Virgen	897	31,868
Paula Gómez Portugal and co-owners	1	Tlalixcoyán	1,284	49,200
Mercedes Guerra y Serrano	1	Moya, Castelhondo y Anexos	738	39,200
Rosa López Alba	3	Media Luna, San Juan sin Agua	545	14,210
Manuel López Gutiérrez	1	Bellavista	702	9,500
Francisco and José Madrazo	1	La Punta	21,275	396,249
Nicolás Madrazo	1	Ledesma, Alamitos, La Troje	4,723	200,000
Vicente Márquez	9	Las Tapias, Sauz de Díaz, Bajio del Purgatorio	1,394	(21,042)[b]

Owner	No.	Property		Value
Cleofas Martín del Campo	3	Venta del Ojo de Agua, El Hallazgo	709	20,400
Antonio Moreno y Oviedo	3	Anonera, El Puerte, P. Nuevo	569	21,930
Bernardo Moreno y Oviedo	18	La Cantera, San Juanico	1,297	(32,551)
Bernardo Moreno y Oviedo with Eugenio, Domingo, and Antonio Moreno y Oviedo	3	Ceja de Bolitas, P. Virgen	887	21,370
Eugenio Moreno y Oviedo	47	Santa Rita, Portezuelo, El Fuerte, San Nicolás	3,861	140,513
Francisca Moreno y Oviedo	2	La Estanzuela, El Fuerte	1,211	27,500
Antonio Morfín Vargas	1	El Tecuán	4,500	150,000
Alfredo M. Padilla	3	San Isidro y Anexos, Cieneguilla, La Labor, Lagunita y Cuchilla	2,150	65,600
Octavio Pérez	2	Divisadero, El Zapote	782	21,900
María de Jesús Pont	1	Llano del Crespo	941	17,000
Pedro Pont	2	Llano del Crespo, El Sauz	2,019	40,212
Julia Quiroz de Pérez Anda with José and Benjamín Pérez Anda	1	La Palma	599	14,000
Sixta Rentería v. de Tovar with Enrique Serrano Flores, Raymundo and Adolfo Tovar, and María Dolores Tovar de Antuñano	1	Estancia Grande (Coecillo, El Centro)	6,922	175,000
J. Reyes Zambrano	4	El Refugio	519	8,760
Carlos Rincón Gallardo	1	Betulia	750	32,000
Pedro Rosas (estate)	1	San Isidro	556	10,000
Dolores Sanromán v. de Fuertes	1	Labor, San Agustín y Portugalejo	785	56,824
José María Sanromán	30	San Francisco y Rancho Seco, La Daga, Jaramillo el Alto, San Isidro de Arriba	8,654	260,145
Manuel Sanromán	2	Salto de Zurita	836	29,400
Manuel Sanromán with Dolores Sanromán v. de Fuertes	1	Labor, San Agustín y Portugalejo	743	56,824
María del Carmen Sanromán	1	Lo de Avalos	3,553	88,063
Genaro Serrano	3	La Merced, Cieneguilla, Pedregal	6,825	164,700
Pablo Serrano Guillermo (or Pablo and Guillermo Serrano?)	1	La Troje	693	57,000

Table B-5
(continued)

Landholder[a]	Number of Properties Owned	Largest Properties	Total Number Hectares Owned	Total Tax-Assessed Value of Properties
Refugio Serrano	1	Moya	804	50,000
María de los Dolores Serrano de Arnaud	3	Coccillo, San Nicolás	7,890	156,700
Oscar Serrano Estrada with Gustavo Serrano Estrada	5	Portezuelo, El Circo, La Iglesia, San Joaquín	2,433	46,928
Salvador Serrano Hermosillo	1	San Pedro	620	26,920
José Guadalupe Serrano y Serrano	1	Las Cajas	2,151	85,000
María Guadalupe Serrano y Serrano	3	Nazas de Moreno, Santa Emilia, San Joaquín	1,418	57,880
Refugio Terreros v. de Rincón Gallardo	1	Cienega de Mata	29,801	238,775
Ignacio Torres Lomelín with Otilia and Esperanza Torres y Nordensternan	1	San José del Potrero y San Juanico	554	13,570
Joaquín Villalobos	11	Providencia, El Cajón	811	20,833
Rafael Villalobos	3	Las Amarillas, Nazas	1,114	34,260
María Zarate v. de Gómez	1	San Juan	3,174	76,000
Totals	322		184,401	4,209,060

Source: Manifestaciones Prediales de 1900 and Catastro Antiguo, 1900–1947, Delegación de Hacienda del Estado de Jalisco, Lagos de Moreno, Jalisco.

[a]Some names appear more than once in the table when they were recorded as co-owners of a landholding in the records.

[b]Parentheses denote missing data on the tax-assessed value of one or more properties. In most cases, the missing data correspond to the value of a relatively small landholding. Total tax-assessed value of these properties would be slightly higher than the figure shown.

Local History
Source Materials

Oral History Interviews

I am often asked about the ease or difficulty of conducting taped interviews among campesinos. I found the men and women with whom I worked to be both receptive and eager to help with my research. My visits, queries, and work were treated with respect and serious interest. Agraristas were eager for the story of their movement to be told, and flattered that I was interested in their personal involvement in it.

My first interview with any person was always the most crucial and difficult. Language fluency, residence in the region, references from friends, and my willingness to travel to outlying communities helped to establish rapport in these initial encounters. I conducted all of the interviews using a tape recorder, most often in the homes, yards, or fields of the informants. Every attempt was made to discourage the presence or participation of other persons; this was usually but not always possible.

I found many advantages to taping interviews. Early in fieldwork, tapes are a useful means of catching interview errors and missed opportunities, of learning regional word usages and idioms, and of capturing inflection. The tape recorder is also the best possible tool for the researcher who may wish to quote extensively from interview responses yet prefers not to take notes frantically during an interview. In addition, having the tape recorder present is a useful way to indicate the data-gathering purpose of a visit while keeping the exchanges relatively informal.

Whatever the problems of its use with elites, I found the tape recorder extremely useful with aging campesinos. In a situation where people are semi-literate and writing is reserved for official communications, note-taking aroused more curiosity and discomfort than a running tape recorder. To reduce the machine's prominence in the interview situation, I relied exclusively on the built-in microphone. During the first interview I explained that I wanted to capture the informant's experiences and ideas exactly as he told them to me, to prevent error or confusion—an advantage they readily appreciated. More campesinos understood what a tape recorder is and how it works than I had expected. Several of them took care to silence children and pets, and to help me find quiet places to talk. One man even warned me that his false teeth might make it difficult for him to be understood on the tape.

Archives

Secretaría de Reforma Agraria

The most accessible and detailed collection of community-specific documentation on agrarian issues in Mexico is housed in the Secretaría de Reforma Agraria (SRA) in Mexico City. The SRA archives are open for public and research use. Indeed, one of the side benefits of consulting these archives is the opportunity to observe ejidatarios, comuneros, pequeños propietarios, and their representatives and advisors as they seek information in the files to resolve problems they confront. The weeks that I spent with the Reforma Agraria files further heightened my sensitivity to the dependence of campesinos on intermediaries, and the scores of these who cultivate that dependence for personal profit—financial or political.

The SRA archives are organized by community into expedientes (folios) on ejido lands, comunidades indígenas, and water rights. I studied the expedientes ejidales for twelve of the most important ejidos in Lagos, including all of the communities in which I collected case study interview materials. These files vary greatly in size and detail. They should contain copies of all correspondence between officials of each ejido and the Secretaría de Reforma Agraria (formerly the Departamento Agrario or the Departamento de Asuntos Agrarios y Colonización), and all official decisions and supportive documents and correspondence affecting or relating to the community. These documents date from the first request for ejido lands directed to the state governor, up to any pending requests for expansion (ampliaciones) of communal land rights and correspondence relating to any other current problems whose solution has been appealed to the federal government. In addition, related correspondence from local officials, political parties, and individual ejidatarios is sometimes included.

In the case of Lagos, the files are interesting as much for what they do not contain as for what is in them. The problems which are most resistant to local solution are those which are appealed to the authorities outside of the municipio. Aside from the election of the Comité Ejecutivo and the first Comité Administrativo—that is, the community-elected officials who represent ejido petitioners in the negotiations for land, and the elected officials who are the first administrators of the ejido once land is granted—there is no correspondence about ejido officials and only infrequent correspondence about conflicts over rights to individual parcels of land. The exceptions to this generalization (which are rare in the files I examined) are cases involving charges of corruption and favoritism.

The Reforma Agraria files are so detailed and intriguing that examination of them is very time-consuming. The background of a community's petition for an ejido, objections raised by landholders, size of expropriable landholdings, and the details of presidential decrees (whether granting or denying original land grant petitions or petitions for extensions of ejidos) can be obtained more readily—but in greatly reduced detail—from the *Diario Oficial*, the daily published record of actions by the federal executive of Mexico. The entire presidential decree for each ejido is published in the *Diario Oficial*; a copy of the decree is also included in each community's expediente ejidal.

Regional and Local Archives

Information about elections and turnover of ejido officials, the names of individual ejidatarios, titles to ejido plots, and conflicts arising over these matters is kept in the files of the regional offices of the Confederación Nacional Campesina (CNC) and the SRA located in Lagos and Guadalajara. When I sought access to these files, explaining my intention to study the history of the local agrarian reform movement, I was repeatedly told that local and state archives contain only the materials just cited, "which are of no historical interest," and that I would be better advised to consult the Mexico City archives. The Mexico City archives are undoubtedly more complete—and, certainly, more accessible. More to the point, however, local files contain information which could lead more readily to charges of favoritism, corruption, and irregularities in the current management of the ejidos (for example, violations of the laws prohibiting reelection of ejido officials and rental of ejido plots). Moreover, local officials are reluctant to accept the responsibility of allowing unauthorized persons to examine archives without permission from their superiors.

Documents on the history of the regional and state campesino organizations was frustratingly scarce. The files of the Liga Regional Campesina (the state branch of the CNC) in Guadalajara were of no use for this purpose. Their "archive" was a small and dusty room in which there were mops, brooms, and some grimy boxes containing newspapers and other publications of the CNC. Other scholars who have sought comparable materials for other state peasant organizations (Falcón, 1978; [Fowler] Salamini, 1978) have found the personal archives of peasant leaders to be the most valuable source of historical documents. Similarly, the only documentation I was able to locate concerning the Liga Regional Campesina in Lagos was correspondence kept by individuals I interviewed, or which forms part of the expedientes ejidales in the Secretaría de Reforma Agraria.

Private archives, such as the documentation and photographs conserved by José Romero Gómez, are invaluable for local political histories such as this one. They are seldom complete, often in disarray, and the documents preserved usually were not selected with the historical record in mind. Moreover, their availability to the researcher often depends on serendipity and trust. When they can be located and accessed, however, they can make a significant contribution toward corroborating information obtained from oral sources or other archives.

During my first period of fieldwork in Lagos de Moreno, I was granted permission to study the Libros de Gobierno in the local parochial Church archives. These volumes have been useful to other scholars engaged in local historical research elsewhere in Jalisco, particularly in recreating pre-twentieth century community histories. My interest was in examining the volumes for 1925–40. The Church notary explained that the books were not maintained during the Cristiada, and that there were no historical Church records for that period. The entries recorded from 1930 through 1933, which I reviewed, were confined to brief logs of communications between local and regional or state Church officials, including quarterly reports, records of changes in appointments of local priests, and brief recordings of inspection trips taken by the parish priest within his district and visits to the parish by Church officials. I concluded that these archives were of secondary importance to my research, and postponed a detailed review of them until the second period of fieldwork. At that time, the same parish priest who had earlier given me access to the records denied me permission to study the books, arguing that the *Libros de Gobierno* were useful only for historical research of centuries past when parish records were more detailed. He was intractable. I was unable to determine if his change of mind was due to a change in Church policy or to my interest in the agrarian reform movement.

The response to my request for permission to study some of the local government archives was a pleasant contrast to the experience with Church records. When I asked to review the *Libros de Actas* of the Lagos municipio government council (*ayuntamiento*), municipal officials were quite willing to grant permission—once they could locate and dust off the volumes. Many volumes were missing, including those for the critical years 1928–38, and most were obviously seldom used. I later examined one of the missing volumes, in the possession of a private citizen.

The Lagos *Libros de Actas* have little direct bearing on agrarian reform. They contain the written, approved minutes of formal meetings of the municipal council. As such, they relate only to matters decided and discussed in that forum—most often to council expenses and employee appointments. They are useful as records of municipal officials (both elected and appointed) and of the provision of urban services (street lighting and paving, water rights, and park, slaughterhouse, and hospital maintenance). The books provide further evidence of the urban bias of municipal government and expenditures. They make scant reference to political problems, issues of agrarian reform, or relations between the municipal capital (*cabecera municipal*), the rural areas of the municipio which it governs, and the state government on which it is politically and financially so dependent.

Property Tax Records

The most unusual written documentation presented in this study are the data in Chapter 3 on land tenure patterns in Lagos de Moreno in 1900 and 1930. No other regional or community study in Mexico presents the same data, although Gil (1975), González y González (1974), and Martínez Saldaña and Gándara Mendoza (1977) cite similar sources for information on land tenure in the municipios they studied. The data presented here were compiled from historical (not current) property tax records in the Delegación de Hacienda, the local branch office of the state Treasury Department. The data for 1900, recorded in the *Manifestaciones Prediales de 1900*, are the most detailed records. Similar records of landholdings were collected throughout Jalisco in that year under Gubernatorial Decree 605 of October 6, 1899, by which property owners were required to report their rural and urban properties to the Oficina de Rentas in Lagos de Moreno. The registration of properties would both legalize unregistered land titles and provide a basis for revising taxation policy.

For both rural and urban properties, the full name of the owner and any co-owners, the date and manner of acquisition (purchase, inheritance, marriage, adjudication, etc.) are recorded, as well as the name of the person from whom the property was acquired. In addition, records of rural properties (*fincas rústicas*), the only ones on which detailed information was gathered for this study, contain the following information for each finca rústica: location (distance and direction from Lagos town) and boundaries of the property; size of the landholding; the owner's estimate of the quality and value of the land; a declaration of the number of buildings and other structures on the property and an estimate of their value; a declaration of the number of animals kept on the property and an estimate of their value; and an estimate of the number and value of tools and machinery. Space is provided for the owner's comments, usually used for references to the poor quality of the soil, the decaying condition of the buildings, and the lamentable inadequacy of private water storage facilities such as dams and wells. Records of urban properties (*fincas urbanas*) contain, in addition to the information described earlier, the location and boundaries of the property (usually street or neighbors' names), the surface area in square meters, the number of rooms in the structure, and the rent charged its occupants (if applicable).

By approximately 1908–09, hearings had been held by the Junta Revisora del Catastro, and the validated or reassessed value for each property is also recorded in the files. This reassessed value was recorded in the *Libro de Catastro* (*Antiguo*), used between 1900 and 1947 as the official property tax record in the municipio, and was consequently the basis for tax collections. The data on land tenure in 1930 were compiled from the *Catastro Antiguo*.

The *Manifestaciones Prediales* consist of 14 volumes with approximately 500 individual *property* entries in each volume. They are bound and organized alphabetically by the name of the landowner. The *Catastro Antiguo* began as the direct transfer from them of summary information on urban and rural real estate for each property *owner*, based on the owner's declarations in 1900. As real estate transactions of each owner were recorded between 1900 and 1947, the original alphabetical system collapsed. The record of property transactions for any individual owner can extend across several volumes or back and forth within a single volume. This introduces a margin of error in compiling information on landholdings for a particular individual, or on transactions affecting a single piece of property. There are also more missing data in these records, where portions of volumes or parts of pages have been lost.

The *Catastro Antiguo* consists of approximately 30 volumes. The information, organized by the name of the property owner, includes the following: the date and manner of acquisition of each urban and rural property and the name of the person from whom it was acquired; date of sale or transfer of any fraction of the property and the name of the person to whom title was transferred; where applicable, the name of the landholding and sometimes the name of the community in which it is located; the date on which such transactions were recorded (often months later than the date on which they occurred); and any tax reassessment of property value after 1910. Data used in this study for 1930 were compiled by checking, tallying, and recording all property transactions which had occurred prior to December 30, 1930, for each property owner.

Particular caution should be exercised in evaluating the tax-assessed value of the landholdings as reported in this study. They should be regarded as underestimated approximations to market value. Even the manager of the Delegación de Hacienda advised me that these values, as well as the owners' declarations in 1900 concerning the size of animal herds, the state of repair and number of buildings and machinery, and the existence and extent of irrigation facilities and irrigated fields, should all be regarded with skepticism. Data on the size and number of properties are probably more accurate, because of the incentive that these records could also be used as proof of ownership. Delegación employees did admit, however, that they continue periodically to find *predios ocultos*, properties which do not appear in the records.

Despite these weaknesses in the data, these local records are probably more accurate than the decennial agriculture and population censuses which include figures on land tenure. In fact, there are substantial discrepancies among the different data sources on the number and size of landholdings. Noting these differences, Álvarez (1958: 9–10) attributed them to "deficiencies in the data gathering," referring to the censuses. As an example, he points out that in 1950, for 15 municipios in Los Altos, the census recorded 17,067 rural properties totaling 927,928 hectares. For the same year, the *Catastro del Estado* showed 81,129 properties totaling 1,224,900 hectares. The census underenumerates the smallest privately owned properties. Still, the overwhelming difference in the number of properties is probably due to reporting of total hectares as a single unit in the census, whereas the state tax records contain separate listings for each titled unit of property. For this reason, the tax records may be a more accurate indicator of the degree of fractionalization of property.

They are also a potential source of highly detailed data for reconstructing local economic histories. Only a fraction of the obtainable information has been tapped in this study. For example, one can observe the use of property, particularly the smaller units under 20 hectares, as collateral for securing loans and often as capital in debt repayment. One can begin to trace inheritance and investment patterns within families. Particularly for 1900, when a more or less exact location is recorded for each property, one could map urban and rural land values within the municipio. Again for 1900, it is possible to partially reconstruct the composition of the haciendas because each *finca rústica* records (with debatable accuracy) the number of granaries, peons' houses, animal corrals, stables, and the main house and chapel (*casco*). Similarly, one can trace up to the present the divisions of large landholdings into smaller ones, with the date, nature of the transaction, purchaser, and size and value of property division or augmentation.

Official Archives in the United States

There is some valuable information in the U.S. National Archives (consular and military intelligence sections) to document some events and general political and economic conditions in Guadalajara and Los Altos. The most useful information concentrates on political crises, particularly the Cristero rebellion (1925–29). That information has been ably utilized by David Bailey in his book *Viva Cristo Rey!* (1974). There is, however, only occasional reference in the U.S. Archives to areas other than the state capitals (except for the Cristero battles). These occur most frequently in consular reports. Unfortunately—from the scholar's perspective—consulates near Los Altos (those in in Guadalajara, San Luis Potosí, Aguascalientes, and Zacatecas) existed only intermittently after the Revolution. All of them had closed by 1938. Therefore, the National Archives were not a useful source of local history data for this study.

Newspapers

I selectively examined issues of *Excelsior*, Mexico's principal daily newspaper, for periods when important political events were occurring in Lagos or Guadalajara. The same issues, as well as a sampling of monthly volumes for 1929–38, were examined for the daily Guadalajara newspapers, *El Jaliscience* and *El Informador*. Informants mentioned several other newspapers as sources of ideas and information for the reform movement in Lagos. These included *El Machete, Regeneración,* and *Antorcha.* I studied these newspapers to identify any references to Lagos, as well as to familiarize myself with what my informants had been exposed to. *Sagitario* and *Espártaco* were also mentioned by José Romero as newspapers which he regularly received, but copies of these could not be located.

Sr. Alfredo Hernández Terrés, editor and publisher of *Provincia,* a regional weekly newspaper published in Lagos, owned the most complete set of newspapers and literary magazines that have been published in Lagos. I was permitted to review his collections of the following periodicals: *Ecos de Lagos, El Defensor del Pueblo, Notas y Letras,* and *Provincia.*

For the most part, all of the newspapers—local, state, and national—are useful sources for understanding the context in which the Lagos agrarian movement developed. However, specific data about local events relating to agrarian and labor reform are extremely rare in all of these publications.

Bibliography

Agraz García de Alba, Gabriel
  1958 "Jalisco," pp. 281–424 in *Ofrenda a México: Compendio de geografía, historia, y biografías mexicanas*, Vol. I. Guadalajara, Jal.: n.p.

Alcántara, Cynthia Hewitt de
  See Hewitt, 1976.

Alcántara, Sergio
  1977 "Collectivist Peasant Organization in La Laguna, Mexico: 1930–1970." Paper presented at the Seventh National Meeting of the Latin American Studies Association, Houston, Texas, November.

Alonso, Jorge, Alfonso Corcuera Garza, and Roberto Melville
  1974 *Los campesinos de la tierra de Zapata, II: Subsistencia y explotación*. México, D.F.: Centro de Investigaciones Superiores, Instituto Nacional de Antropología e Historia (Ediciones SEP-INAH).

Álvarez, José Rogelio
  1958 *Los Altos de Jalisco: Bases para un programa de rehabilitación*. Guadalajara, Jal.: n.p.
  1964 *Jalisco: Nueve ensayos*, esp. "La región de Los Altos: Una área por rehabilitar," pp. 99–134. Guadalajara, Jal.: Ediciones Tlacuilco.

Anguiano, Arturo, Guadalupe Pacheco, and Rogelio Vizcaino
  1975 *Cárdenas y la izquierda mexicana*. México, D.F.: Juan Pablos.

Anonymous [probably Dr. Agustín Rivera y Sanromán]
  1972 *Plan de los anales de Lagos, 1529–1863*. Lagos de Moreno, Jal.: privately published.

Azaola Garrido, Elena, and Estéban Krotz
  1976 *Los campesinos de la tierra de Zapata, III: Política y conflicto*. México, D.F.: Centro de Investigaciones Superiores, Instituto Nacional de Antropología e Historia (Ediciones SEP-INAH).

Azuela, Mariano
  1942 *El Padre Don Agustín Rivera*. México, D.F.: Ediciones Botas.
  1945 *Andrés Pérez, maderista*. México, D.F.: Ediciones Botas.
  1971 *Los de abajo*. Englewood Cliffs, N.J.: Prentice-Hall. (Originally published in 1915.)
  1974 *Páginas autobiográficas*. México, D.F.: Fondo de Cultura Económica.

Bailey, David C.
   1974 *Viva Cristo Rey!: The Cristero Rebellion and the Church-State Conflict in Mexico.* Austin: University of Texas Press.

Bailey, John J., and John E. Link
   1981 "Statecraft and Agriculture in Mexico, 1980–1982: Domestic and Foreign Policy Considerations." *Working Papers in U.S.-Mexican Studies,* no. 23. University of California, San Diego.

Bartra, Armando (ed.)
   1977 *Regeneración, 1900–1918: La corriente más radical de la revolución mexicana de 1910 a través de su periódico de combate.* México, D.F.: Ediciones Era.

Bazant, Jan
   1975 *Cinco haciendas mexicanas: Tres siglos de vida rural en San Luis Potosí, 1600–1910.* México, D.F.: El Colegio de México.
   1977 *A Concise History of Mexico, from Hidalgo to Cárdenas, 1805–1940.* New York: Cambridge University Press.

Berthe, Jean-Pierre
   1973 "Introducción a la historia de Guadalajara y su región," pp. 130–147 in Jean Piel et al. (eds.), *Regiones y ciudades en América Latina.* México, D.F.: Ediciones Sep-Setentas, no. 111.

Brading, D. A.
   1978 *Haciendas and Ranchos in the Mexican Bajío: León 1700- 1860.* Cambridge and New York: Cambridge University Press.

Brading, D. A. (ed.)
   1980 *Caudillo and Peasant in the Mexican Revolution.* Cambridge and New York: Cambridge University Press.

Brandenburg, Frank
   1964 *The Making of Modern Mexico.* Englewood Cliffs, N.J.: Prentice-Hall.

Brenner, Anita, and George R. Leighton
   1943 *The Wind That Swept Mexico: The History of the Mexican Revolution, 1910–1942.* New York: Harper.

Brown, Lyle C.
   1979 "Cárdenas: Creating a Campesino Power Base for Presidential Policy," pp. 102–136 in George Wolfskill and Douglas W. Richmond (eds.), *Essays on the Mexican Revolution: Revisionist Views of the Leaders.* Austin: University of Texas Press.

Calvert, Peter
   1973 *Mexico: Nation of the Modern World.* New York: Praeger.

Cardoso, Lawrence A.
   1980 *Mexican Emigration to the United States, 1897–1931.* Tucson: University of Arizona Press.

Carlos, Manuel
   1974 *Politics and Development in Rural Mexico.* New York: Praeger Special Studies.

Carreras de Velasco, Mercedes
1974 *Los mexicanos que devolvió la crisis, 1929-1932*. México, D.F.: Secretaría de Relaciones Exteriores, Colección del Archivo Histórico Diplomático Mexicano, Obras Monográficas no. 2.

Chevalier, François
1952 *La formation des grandes domaines au Méxique*. Paris: n.p. (English translation published as *Land and Society in Colonial Mexico: The Great Haciendas*. Berkeley and Los Angeles: University of California Press, 1963.)
1967 "The *Ejido* and Political Stability in Mexico," pp. 158-191 in Claudio Véliz (ed.), *The Politics of Conformity in Latin America*. London: Oxford University Press.

Clark, Marjorie R.
1934 *Organized Labor in Mexico*. Chapel Hill: University of North Carolina Press.

Cline, Howard F.
1963 *The United States and Mexico*. New York: Atheneum.

Cockcroft, James D.
1968 *Intellectual Precursors of the Mexican Revolution, 1900-1913*. Austin: University of Texas Press.
1974 "Mexico," in Ronald H. Chilcote and Joel Edelstein (eds.), *Latin America: The Struggle with Dependency and Beyond*. Cambridge, Mass.: Schenkman.

Córdova, Arnaldo
1975a *La ideología de la revolucion mexicana: La formación del nuevo régimen*. México, D.F.: Universidad Nacional Autónoma de México, Instituto de Investigaciones Sociales.
1975b "La filosofía de la revolución mexicana," *Cuadernos Políticos*, no. 5 (July-September): 94-103.

Cornelius, Wayne A.
1973 "Nation-Building, Participation, and Distribution: The Politics of Social Reform under Cárdenas," pp. 392-498 in Gabriel A. Almond et al. (eds.), *Crisis, Choice, and Change: Historical Studies of Political Development*. Boston: Little, Brown.
1975 *Politics and the Migrant Poor in Mexico City*. Stanford, Calif.: Stanford University Press.
1976 "Outmigration from Rural Mexican Communities," pp. 1-40 in *The Dynamics of Migration: International Migration*. Washington, D.C.: Interdisciplinary Communications Program, Smithsonian Institution, Occasional Monograph Series 2, no. 5.
1978 "The Role of the State in Latin American Urbanization: Policy Impacts on Rural Out-Migration." Paper presented at the first meeting of the Working Seminar on Latin American Urbanization, Joint Committee on Latin American Studies of the Social Science Research Council and the American Council of Learned Societies, London, February.

1981 *Mexican and Caribbean Migration to the United States: The State of Current Knowledge and Priorities for Future Research.* Monographs in U.S.-Mexican Studies, no. 1, University of California, San Diego.

Craig, Ann L., and Wayne A. Cornelius
1980 "Political Culture in Mexico: Continuities and Revisionist Interpretations," pp. 325–393 in Gabriel A. Almond and Sidney Verba (eds.), *The Civic Culture Revisited.* Boston: Little, Brown.

de Alba M., Alfonso
1957 *El alcalde de Lagos y otras consejas.* Guadalajara, Jal.: Biblioteca de Autores Jalisciences Modernos, no. 3.

de Anda, J. Guadalupe
1974 *Los Cristeros.* México, D.F.: Ediciones del Departamento de Bellas Artes. (Originally published in 1937.)

de Appendini, Kirsten A., and Vania Almeida Salles
1975 "Agricultura capitalista y agricultura campesina en México: Diferencias regionales en base al análisis de datos censales." *Cuadernos del Centro de Estudios Sociológicos*, no. 10, El Colegio de México.

deForest Woodbridge, Margaret
1973 "Fifty Years of Mexican Community Studies: Perspectives on Land Reform." M.A. thesis, University of California, Los Angeles.

de la Peña, Guillermo
1980 *Herederos de promesas: Agricultura, política y ritual en los altos de Morelos.* México, D.F.: Ediciones de la Casa Chata.

de Leonardo Ramírez, Patricia
1975 "El impacto del mercado en diferentes unidades de producción, en el municipio de Jalostotitlán, Jalisco." Licenciatura thesis, Universidad Iberoamericana, México, D.F.

del Castillo, Gustavo
1979 *Crisis y transformación de una sociedad tradicional.* México, D.F.: Centro de Investigaciones Superiores del INAH, Ediciones de La Casa Chata.

Demyck, Noëlle
1973 "Organisation de l'espace dans les Altos de Jalisco (Méxique)." *Cahiers des Amériques Latines*, no. 7 (1): 223–279.

Departamento de Economía, Estado de Jalisco
1973 *Jalisco: Estrategia de desarrollo: Programa subregional y municipal, subregión de Lagos.* Guadalajara, Jal.: Dept. Econ., Jal.

Departamento de la Estadística Nacional, Estados Unidos Mexicanos
1926 *Censo general de habitantes, Estado de Jalisco, 30 de noviembre de 1921.* México, D.F.: Dept. Estadística, Mex.

de Vylder, Stefan
1974 *Allende's Chile: The Political Economy of the Rise and Fall of the Unidad Popular.* Cambridge, England: Cambridge University Press.

Díaz, José, and Román Rodríguez
1979 *El Movimiento Cristero: Sociedad y conflicto en los Altos de Jalisco.* México, D.F.: Editorial Nueva Imagen.

Dirección General de Estadística, Estados Unidos Mexicanos
1905 *Censo general de la República Mexicana, Estado de Jalisco, 28 de octubre de 1900.* México, D.F.: Direcc. Grl. Estadística, Mex.
1935 *Primer censo ejidal, 1935: Resumen general.* México, D.F.: Direcc. Grl. Estadística, Mex.
1943 *Sexto censo de población, 1940: Estado de Jalisco.* México, D.F.: Direcc. Grl. Estadística, Mex.
1951 *Segundo censo agrícola-ganadero de los Estados Unidos Mexicanos, 1940: Resumen general.* México, D.F.: Direcc. Grl. Estadística, Mex.
1965 *IV Censo agrícola-ganadero y ejidal, 1960: Resumen general.* México, D.F.: Direcc. Grl. Estadística, Mex.
1970 *Noveno censo general de población, 1970: Resumen general.* México, D.F.: Direcc. Grl. Estadística, Mex.
1971 *IX Censo general de población, 1970: Estado del Jalisco.* México, D.F.: Direcc. Grl. Estadística, Mex.
1972 *Directorio de Ejidos y Comunidades Agrarias; V Censo Ejidal, 1970.* México, D.F.: Direcc. Grl. Estadística, Mex.

D.P.E.S. (Departamento de Planeación Económica y Social, Plan Lerma Asistencia Técnica)
1968 *Investigación directa, áreas rurales, áreas urbanas,* II: *Los Altos, Jalisco.* Guadalajara, Jal.: Plan Lerma.

Drake, Paul W.
1978 *Socialism and Populism in Chile, 1932–52.* Urbana: University of Illinois Press.

Dulles, John W.F.
1961 *Yesterday in Mexico: A Chronicle of the Revolution, 1919–1936.* Austin: University of Texas Press.

Eckstein, Salomón
1966 *El ejido colectivo en México.* México, D.F.: Fondo de Cultura Económica.

Elmendorf, Mary L.
1976 *Nine Mayan Women: A Village Faces Change.* Cambridge, Mass.: Schenkman.

Espín, Jaime, and Patricia de Leonardo
1978 *Economía y sociedad en los altos de Jalisco.* México, D.F.: Centro de Investigaciones Superiores del Instituto Nacional de Antropología e Historia, Editorial Nueva Imagen.

Fábregas, Andrés
1975 "Estudio de la estructura socio-económica de la región de Los Altos de Jalisco: Resumen general." (Mimeo.) México, D.F.: Centro de Investigaciones Superiores, Instituto Nacional de Antropología e Historia.

Fagen, Richard R., and William S. Tuohy
1972 *Politics and Privilege in a Mexican City*. Stanford, Calif.: Stanford University Press.

Falcón, Romana Gloria
1975 "La participación campesina y el cambio político en México: La influencia de los grupos agraristas en la postulación de la candidatura del General Lázaro Cárdenas, 1928–1934." Licenciatura thesis, Facultad de Ciencias Políticas y Sociales, Universidad Nacional Autónoma de México, México, D.F.

1977 *El agrarismo en Veracruz: La etapa radical, 1928–1935*. México, D.F.: El Colegio de México.

1978 "El surgimiento del agrarismo cardenista: Una revisión de las tesis populistas." *Historia Mexicana*, 27, no. 3 (January-March): 333–386.

Feder, Ernest
1970–1 "Social Opposition to Peasant Movements and Its Effects in Latin America." *Studies in Comparative International Development*, 6, no. 8.

1971 *The Rape of the Peasantry: Latin America's Landholding System*. New York: Doubleday-Anchor Books.

Fowler, Heather
1970 "The Agrarian Revolution in the State of Veracruz, 1920–1940: The Role of Peasant Organizations." Ph.D. dissertation, American University, Washington, D.C.

[Fowler] Salamini, Heather
1976 "Adalberto Tejeda and the Veracruz Peasant Movement," pp. 274–292 in James W. Wilkie, Michael C. Meyer, and Edna Monzón de Wilkie (eds.), *Contemporary Mexico: Papers of the Fourth International Congress of Mexican History*. Los Angeles, Calif., and México, D.F.: University of California Press and El Colegio de México.

1978 *Agrarian Radicalism in Veracruz, 1920–1938*. Lincoln: University of Nebraska Press.

1980 "Revolutionary Caudillos in the 1920s: Francisco Múgica and Adalberto Tejeda," pp. 169–192 in D. A. Brading (ed.), *Caudillo and Peasant in the Mexican Revolution*. Cambridge and New York: Cambridge University Press.

Friedrich, Paul
1970 *Agrarian Revolt in a Mexican Village*. Englewood Cliffs, N.J.: Prentice-Hall.

Gamio, Manuel
1930 *Mexican Immigration to the United States*. Chicago: University of Chicago Press. (Republished, New York: Dover, 1971.)

García y Griego, Larry Manuel
1973 "Los Primeros Pasos al Norte: Mexican Migration to the United States, 1848–1929." Senior thesis, Dept. of History, Princeton University, Princeton, N.J.

Gil, Carlos Brambila
1975 "Mascota: A Mexican World Left Behind." Ph.D. dissertation, Dept. of History, University of California, Los Angeles.

Glantz, Susana
1974 *El ejido colectivo de Nueva Italia*. México, D.F.: Centro de Investigaciones Superiores, Instituto Nacional de Antropología e Historia (Ediciones SEP-INAH).

Gómez Flores, José de Jesús
1973 *Azuela en 1910: Médico del pueblo*. Lagos de Moreno, Jal.: n.p.

Gómez-Jara, Francisco A.
1970 *El movimiento campesino en México*. México, D.F.: Editorial Campesino.

Gómez-Quiñones, Juan
1980 *Sembradores: Ricardo Flores Magón y El Partido Liberal Mexicano: A Eulogy and Critique*. Rev. ed., Monograph no. 5, Chicano Studies Research Center, University of California, Los Angeles.

González y González, Luis
1973 *Invitación a la microhistoria*. México, D.F.: Sep-Setentas, no. 72.
1974 *San José de Gracia: Mexican Village in Transition*. Trans. by John Upton. Austin: University of Texas Press.
1979 *Historia de la Revolución mexicana, período 1934–1940, XIV: Los artífices del cardenismo*. México, D.F.: El Colegio de México.

González Navarro, Moisés
1968 *La Confederación Nacional Campesina: Un grupo de presión en la reforma agraria mexicana*. México, D.F.: Costa-Amic.

Graham, Lawrence S.
1968 *Politics in a Mexican Community*. Latin American Monographs, series 1, no. 35. Gainesville: University of Florida Press.

Grindle, Merilee Serrill
1977 *Bureaucrats, Politicians, and Peasants in Mexico: A Case Study in Public Policy*. Berkeley: University of California Press.
1981 "Official Interpretations of Rural Underdevelopment: Mexico in the 1970s." *Working Papers in U.S.-Mexican Studies*, no. 20, Center for U.S.-Mexican Studies, University of California, San Diego.

Gruening, Ernest
1928 *Mexico and Its Heritage*. New York: Century.

Gutelman, Michel
1974 *Capitalismo y reforma agraria en México*. México, D.F.: Ediciones Era.

Hamilton, Nora L.
1975 "Mexico: The Limits of State Autonomy." *Latin American Perspectives*, 2, no. 2 (Summer): 81–108.

Hamon, James L., and Stephen R. Niblo
1975 *Precursores de la revolución agraria en México: Las obras de Wistano Luis Orozco y Andrés Molina Enríquez*. México, D.F.: Sep-Setentas.

Hart, John M.
  1978 *Anarchism and The Mexican Working Class, 1860-1931.* Austin, Tex.: University of Texas Press.

Hernández, Salvador
  1975 "El Magonismo en 1911: La otra revolución." *Cuadernos Políticos*, no. 4 (April-June): 26-42.

Hewitt de Alcántara, Cynthia
  1976 *Modernizing Mexican Agriculture: Socioeconomic Implications of Technological Change, 1940-1970.* Geneva, Switz.: United Nations Research Institute for Social Development.

Hoffman, Abraham
  1974 *Unwanted Mexican Americans in the Great Depression: Repatriation Pressures, 1929-1939.* Tucson: University of Arizona Press.

Horcasitas, Fernando
  1974 *De Porfirio Díaz a Zapata: Memoria Náhuatl de Milpa Alta.* México, D.F.: Instituto de Investigaciones Históricas, Universidad Nacional Autónoma de México.

Huizer, Gerrit
  1968-9 "Peasant Organization in the Process of Agrarian Reform in Mexico." *Studies in Comparative International Development*, 4, no. 6: 115-145.
  1970 "Emiliano Zapata and the Peasant Guerrillas in the Mexican Revolution," pp. 375-406 in Rodolfo Stavenhagen (ed.), *Agrarian Problems and Peasant Movements in Latin America.* New York: Doubleday-Anchor.
  1972 *The Revolutionary Potential of Peasants in Latin America.* Lexington, Mass.: Heath-Lexington.

Huizer, Gerrit, and Rodolfo Stavenhagen
  1974 "Peasant Movements and Land Reform in Latin America: Mexico and Bolivia," pp. 378-409 in Henry A. Landsberger (ed.), *Rural Protest: Peasant Movements and Social Change.* New York: Macmillan.

Institut des Hautes Études de l'Amérique Latine
  1973 *Regiones y ciudades en América Latina.* México, D.F.: Sep-Setentas.

Jones, Ricardo Lancaster
  1974 *Haciendas de Jalisco y aledaños, 1506-1821.* Guadalajara, Jal.: Financiera Aceptaciones.
  n.d. "La hacienda de Santa Ana de Apacueco." *Boletín de la Junta Auxiliar Jaliscience de la Sociedad Mexicana de Geografía y Economía* (Guadalajara, Jal.).

Karst, Kenneth L., and Norris C. Clement
  1969 "Legal Institutions and Development: Lessons from the Mexican *Ejido*," *UCLA Law Review*, 16, no. 2 (February): 281-303.

Kirk, Betty
  1942 *Covering the Mexican Front: The Battle of Europe vs. America.* Norman: University of Oklahoma Press.

Krauze, Enrique
1976 *Caudillos culturales en la revolución mexicana.* México, D.F.: Siglo Veintiuno.

Land Tenure Center Library Staff
1974 *Agrarian Reform in Latin America: An Annotated Bibliography.* 2 vols. Land Tenure Center and *Land Economics,* University of Wisconsin, Madison.

Landsberger, Henry A.
1969 "The Role of Peasant Movements and Revolts in Development," pp. 1–61 in Landsberger (ed.), *Latin American Peasant Movements.* Ithaca, N.Y.: Cornell University Press.
1974 "Peasant Unrest: Themes and Variations," pp. 1–64 in Landsberger (ed.), *Rural Protest: Peasant Movements and Social Change.* New York: Macmillan.

Landsberger, Henry A., and Cynthia N. Hewitt
1970 "Ten Sources of Weakness and Cleavage in Latin American Peasant Movements," pp. 559–583 in Rodolfo Stavenhagen (ed.), *Agrarian Problems and Peasant Movements in Latin America.* New York: Doubleday-Anchor.

Landsberger, Henry A., and Cynthia Hewitt de Alcántara
1973 "From Violence to Pressure-Group Politics and Cooperation: A Mexican Case Study," in P. M. Worsley (ed.), *Two Blades of Grass.* Manchester, Eng.: Manchester University Press.

Larin, Nicolás
1968 *La rebelión de los cristeros, 1926–1929.* México, D.F.: Ediciones Era.

Leal, Juan Felipe, and José Woldenberg
1976 "El sindicalismo mexicano: Aspectos organizativos." *Cuadernos Políticos,* no. 7 (January-March): 35–54.

Lewis, Oscar
1959 *Five Families: Mexican Case Studies in the Culture of Poverty.* New York: Basic Books.
1961 *The Children of Sánchez: Autobiography of a Mexican Family.* New York: Random House.
1964 *Pedro Martínez: A Mexican Peasant and His Family.* New York: Random House.
1974 *A Death in the Sánchez Family.* New York: Random House.

Loveman, Brian
1976 *Struggle in the Countryside: Politics and Rural Labor in Chile, 1919–1973.* Bloomington: Indiana University Press.

Luiselli, Cassio
1982 *The Sistema Alimentario Mexicano (SAM): Elements of a Program of Accelerated Production of Basic Foodstuffs in Mexico.* La Jolla, Calif.: Center for U.S.-Mexican Studies, University of California, San Diego, Research Report Series, no. 22.

Mannheim, Karl
  1952 "On The Problem of Generations." In Paul Keckskemeti (ed.), *Essays on the Sociology of Knowledge.* London: Routledge and Kegan Paul.

Mares, David
  1982 "The Politics of Export-Oriented Agricultural Development: Dependency, Corporatism, and Local Politics in Sinaloa." Ph.D. dissertation, Harvard University, Cambridge, Massachusetts.

Martínez Garza, Bertha Beatriz
  1975 *Evolución legislativa de la Ley Federal de Reforma Agraria.* México, D.F.: Textos Universitarios.

Martínez Ríos, Jorge
  1970 *Tenencia de la tierra y desarrollo agrario en México: Bibliografía selectiva y comentada, 1522–1968.* México, D.F.: Universidad Nacional Autónoma de Mexico, Instituto de Investigaciones Sociales.

Martínez Saldaña, Tomás
  1980 *El costo social de un éxito político: La política expansionista del estado mexicano en el agro lagunero.* Chapingo, México: Rama de Divulgación Agrícola del Colegio de Posgraduados de la Secretaría de Agricultura y Recursos Hidráulicos.

Martínez Saldaña, Tomás, and Leticia Gándara Mendoza
  1977 *Política y sociedad en México: El caso de Los Altos de Jalisco.* México, D.F.: Centro de Investigaciones Superiores, Instituto Nacional de Antropología e Historia (Ediciones SEP-INAH).

Meyer, Eugenia
  1977 "Hablan los Villistas: Análisis del Villismo como movimiento social integrado a la revolución mexicana, a través de los testimonios de historia oral." Paper presented at the Seventh National Meeting of the Latin American Studies Association, Houston Texas, November.

Meyer, Eugenia, and Alicia Olivera de Bonfil
  1971 "La historia oral: orígen, metodología, desarrollo y perspectivas." *Historia Mexicana,* 21: 372–387.

Meyer, Jean A.
  1971 "La Cristiada," pp. 225–240 in Centro de Estudios Históricos (ed.), *Extremos de México: Homenaje a don Daniel Cosio Villegas.* México, D.F.: El Colegio de México.
  1973a "Perspectiva de análisis sociohistórico de la influencia de Guadalajara sobre su región," pp. 148–168 in Jean Piel et al. (eds.), *Regiones y ciudades en América Latina.* México, D.F.: Sep-Setentas, no. 111.
  1973b *La Revolución Mejicana, 1910–1940.* Barcelona, Spain: Dopesa.
  1973–4 *La Cristiada.* 3 vols. México, D.F.: Siglo Veintiuno.
  1976 *The Cristero Rebellion: The Mexican People Between Church and State, 1926–1929.* Cambridge, Eng.: Cambridge University Press.

Meyer, Lorenzo
  1977 "La etapa formativa del estado mexicano contemporáneo, 1929–1940." *Foro Internacional,* 58, no. 4 (April-June): 453–476.

Migdal, Joel S.
1974 *Peasants, Politics, and Revolution: Pressures Towards Political and Social Change in the Third World.* Princeton, N.J.: Princeton University Press.

Miller, Simon
1977 "Agrarian Reform and Economic Development in Mexico." Unpublished paper, University of Leeds, Yorkshire, England.

Montes de Oca, Rosa Elena
1977 "The State and the Peasants," pp. 47–63 in José Luis Reyna and Richard S. Weinert (eds.), *Authoritarianism in Mexico.* Interamerican Politics Series, vol. 2. Philadelphia: Institute for the Study of Human Issues.

Moore, Barrington, Jr.
1966 *The Social Origins of Dictatorship and Democracy.* Boston: Beacon Press.

Moreno Ochoa, J. Angel
1959 *Diez años de agitación política en Jalisco, 1920–1930.* Guadalajara, Jal.: Galería de Escritores Revolucionarios Jalisciences.

Mundale, Charles I.
1971 "Local Politics, Integration, and National Stability in Mexico." Ph.D. dissertation, University of Minnesota.

Olivera de Bonfil, Alicia
1966 *El conflicto religioso de 1926 a 1929: Antecedentes y consecuencias.* México, D.F.: Instituto Nacional de Antropología e Historia.
1976 "La Iglesia en México, 1926–1970," pp. 295–316 in James W. Wilkie, Michael C. Meyer, and Edna Monzón de Wilkie (eds.), *Contemporary Mexico: Papers of the Fourth International Congress of Mexican History.* Los Angeles, Calif., and México, D.F.: University of California Press and El Colegio de México.

Osorio Marbán, Miguel
1970 *El Partido de la Revolución Mexicana: Ensayo,* vol. 1. México, D.F.: Impresora del Centro.

Paez Brotchie, Luis
1940 *Jalisco: Historia mínima.* Guadalajara, Jal.: Ricardo Delgado.

Paige, Jeffery M.
1975 *Agrarian Revolution: Social Movements and Export Agriculture in the Underdeveloped World.* New York: Free Press.

Pérez Moreno, José
1957 *El tercer canto del gallo.* México, D.F.: Aguilar.

Popkin, Samuel
1979 *The Rational Peasant.* Berkeley and Los Angeles: University of California Press.

Powell, John
1970 *The Political Mobilization of the Venezuelan Peasant.* Cambridge, Mass.: Harvard University Press.

Powell, T. G.
  1974 *El liberalismo y el campesinado en el centro de México, 1850–1876.* México, D.F.: Sep-Setentas.

Pozas Arciénega, Ricardo
  1968 *Juan Pérez Jolote: Biografía de un Tzotzil.* México, D.F.: Fondo de Cultura Económica. (Originally published in 1952.)

Purcell, Susan Kaufman
  1981 "Business-Government Relations in Mexico: The Case of the Sugar Industry." *Comparative Politics,* 13, no. 2 (January): 211–233.

Quirk, Robert E.
  1953 "Liberales y radicales en la revolución mexicana." *Historia Mexicana,* 2, no. 4 (April-June): 503–528.
  1973 *The Mexican Revolution and the Catholic Church, 1910–1929.* Bloomington: Indiana University Press.

Raby, David L.
  1973 *Educación y revolución social en México, 1921–1940.* México, D.F.: Sep-Setentas, no. 141.

Redclift, Michael R.
  1981 "Development Policymaking in Mexico: The Sistema Alimentario Mexicano (SAM)." *Working Papers in U.S.-Mexican Studies,* no. 24, Center for U.S-Mexican Studies, University of California, San Diego.

Reisler, Mark
  1976 *By the Sweat of Their Brow: Mexican Immigrant Labor in the United States, 1900–1940.* Westport, Conn.: Greenwood Press.

Restrepo, Iván, and Salomón Eckstein
  1975 *La agricultura colectiva en México: La experiencia de la Laguna.* México, D.F.: Siglo Veintiuno.

Restrepo, Iván, and José Sánchez Cortés
  1972 *La reforma agraria en cuatro regiones.* México, D.F.: Sep-Setentas.

Reyes Osorio, Sergio, et al.
  1974 *Estructura agraria y desarrollo agrícola en México: Estudio sobre las relaciones entre la tenencia y uso de la tierra y el desarrollo agrícola de México.* México, D.F.: Fondo de Cultura Económica.

Riviére d'Arc, Hélène
  1973a *Guadalajara y su región.* México, D.F.: Sep-Setentas, no. 106.
  1973b "Guadalajara y su región: Influencias y dificultades de una metrópoli mexicana," pp. 169–174 in Jean Piel, et al. (eds.), *Regiones y ciudades en América Latina.* México, D.F.: Sep-Setentas, no. 111.
  n.d. "Tepatitlán (Jalisco): Une terre d'émigration." Unpublished paper, Institut des Hautes Études d'Amérique Latine, Paris.

Robe, Stanley
  1970 *Mexican Tales and Legends from Los Altos.* Folklore Studies, no. 20. Los Angeles: University of California Press.

Ronfeldt, David
    1973 *Atencingo: The Politics of Agrarian Struggle in a Mexican Ejido*. Stanford, Calif.: Stanford University Press.

Ruiz, Ramón E.
    1963 *Mexico: The Challenge of Poverty and Illiteracy*. San Marino, Calif.: Huntington Library.
    1980 *The Great Rebellion: Mexico, 1905–1924*. New York: Norton.

Rulfo, Juan
    1973a *El llano en llamas*. México, D.F.: Fondo de Cultura Económica. (Originally published in 1953.)
    1973b *Pedro Páramo*. México, D.F.: Fondo de Cultura Económica. (Originally published in 1955.)

Salamini, Heather Fowler
    See Fowler, 1976, 1978, and 1980.

Salinas de Gortari, Carlos
    1980 *Producción y participación política en el campo*. México, D.F.: Universidad Nacional Autónoma de México.
    1982 *Political Participation, Public Investment, and Support for the System: A Comparative Study of Rural Communities in Mexico*. La Jolla, Calif.: Center for U.S.-Mexican Studies, University of California, San Diego, Research Report Series, no. 35.

Sanderson, Steven E.
    1981 *Agrarian Populism and the Mexican State: The Struggle for Land in Sonora*. Berkeley: University of California Press.

Schmitt, Karl M.
    1965 *Communism in Mexico: A Study in Frustration*. Austin: University of Texas Press.

Schryer, Frans J.
    1980 *The Rancheros of Pisaflores: The History of a Peasant Bourgeoisie in Twentieth-Century Mexico*. Toronto, Ont., Can.: University of Toronto Press.

Schumacher, August
    1981 "Agricultural Development and Rural Employment: A Mexican Dilemma." *Working Papers in U.S.-Mexican Studies*, no. 21, Center for U.S.-Mexican Studies, University of California, San Diego.

Scott, James C.
    1976 *The Moral Economy of the Peasant: Rebellion and Subsistence in Southeast Asia*. New Haven, Conn.: Yale University Press.

Senior, Clarence
    1940 *Democracy Comes to a Cotton Kingdom: The Story of Mexico's.: La Laguna*. México, D.F.: Centro de Estudios Pedagógicos e Hispano-Americanos.
    1958 *Land Reform and Democracy*. Gainesville: University of Florida Press.

Shulgovski, Anatol
  1968 *México en la encrucijada de su historia.* México, D.F.: Fondo de Cultura Popular.

Silva, José D.
  1969 *Evolución agraria en México.* México, D.F.: Costa-Amic.

Silva Herzog, Jesús
  1960 *Breve historia de la revolución mexicana.* 2 vols. México, D.F.: Fondo de Cultura Económica.

Simpson, Eyler
  1937 *The Ejido: Mexico's Way Out.* Chapel Hill: University of North Carolina Press.

Singleman, Peter
  1975 "The Closing Triangle: Critical Notes on a Model for Peasant Mobilization in Latin America." *Comparative Studies in Society and History*, 17: 389–409.

Stavenhagen, Rodolfo
  1970a *Agrarian Problems and Peasant Movements in Latin America.* (ed.) New York: Doubleday-Anchor.
  1970b "Social Aspects of Agrarian Structure in Mexico," pp. 225–270 in Stavenhagen (ed.), *Agrarian Problems and Peasant Movements in Latin America.* New York: Doubleday-Anchor.
  1975 "Collective Agriculture and Capitalism in Mexico: A Way Out or a Dead End?" *Latin American Perspectives*, 2, no. 2 (Summer): 146–163.
  1977 "El campesinado y las estrategias del desarrollo rural." *Cuadernos del Centro de Estudios Sociológicos*, no. 19, El Colegio de México.

Stavenhagen, Rodolfo, et al.
  1975 *Neolatifundismo y explotación: De Emiliano Zapata a Anderson Clayton and Co.* México, D.F.: Nuestro Tiempo.

Tai, Hung-chao
  1974 *Land Reform and Politics: A Comparative Analysis.* Berkeley: University of California Press.

Tannenbaum, Frank
  1956 *Mexico: The Struggle for Peace and Bread.* New York: Knopf.

Taylor, Paul S.
  1933 *A Spanish-Mexican Peasant Community: Arandas in Jalisco, México.* Berkeley: University of California Press.

Tello, Carlos
  1968 *La tenencia de la tierra en México.* México, D.F.: Instituto de Investigaciones Sociales, Universidad Nacional Autónoma de México.

Tuck, Jim
  1982 *The Holy War in Los Altos: A Regional Analysis of Mexico's Cristero Rebellion.* Tucson: University of Arizona Press.

Van Young, Eric
  1981 *Hacienda and Market in Eighteenth-Century Mexico: The Rural Economy*

of the Guadalajara Region, 1675-1820. Berkeley: University of California Press.

Vega Kegel, Moisés
n.d. *Lagos y sus hombres.* Lagos de Moreno, Jal.: Biblioteca de Autores Laguenses.

Velasco, Miguel Angel
1975 "El Partido Comunista durante el período de Cárdenas," pp. 27–47 in Gilberto Bosques, Miguel Angel Velasco, and Heberto Castillo, *Lázaro Cárdenas.* México, D.F.: Testimonios del Fondo de Cultura Económica.

Walton, John
1977 *Elites and Economic Development: Comparative Studies on the Political Economy of Latin American Cities.* Austin, Texas: Institute of Latin American Studies, University of Texas.

Warman, Arturo
1976 *Y venimos a contradecir: Los campesinos de Morelos y el estado nacional.* México, D.F.: Ediciones de la Casa Chata.
1980 *"We Come to Object": The Peasants of Morelos and the National State.* Trans. by Stephen K. Ault. Baltimore, Md.: Johns Hopkins University Press.

Waterbury, Ronald
1975 "Non-revolutionary Peasants: Oaxaca Compared to Morelos in the Mexican Revolution." *Comparative Studies in Society and History*, 17: 410–422.

Weyl, Nathaniel, and Sylvia Weyl
1939 *The Reconquest of Mexico: The Years of Lázaro Cárdenas.* New York: Oxford University Press.

Whetten, Nathan L.
1948 *Rural Mexico.* Chicago: University of Chicago Press.

White, Robert A.
1969 "Mexico: The Zapata Movement and the Revolution," pp. 101–169 in Henry A. Landsberger (ed.), *Latin American Peasant Movements.* Ithaca, N.Y.: Cornell University Press.

Whitehead, Laurence
1981 "On 'Governability' in Mexico." *Bulletin of Latin American Research* (Oxford), 1, no. 1 (October): 27–47.

Whiting, Van R., Jr.
1977 "The Collective Ejido and the State in Mexico." Paper presented at the Seventh National Meeting of the Latin American Studies Association, Houston, Texas, November.

Wilkie, James W.
1973 *Elitelore.* Latin American Center, University of California, Los Angeles.

Wilkie, James W., and Albert L. Michaels, eds.
1969 *Revolution in Mexico: The Years of Upheaval, 1910-1940.* New York: Knopf.

Wilkie, James W., and Edna Monzón de Wilkie
  1969 *México visto en el siglo XX: Entrevistas de historia oral.* México, D.F.: Instituto Mexicano de Investigaciones Económicas.

Wilkie, Raymond
  1971 *San Miguel: A Mexican Collective Ejido.* Stanford, Calif.: Stanford University Press.

Wolf, Eric R.
  1969 *Peasant Wars of the Twentieth Century.* New York: Harper & Row.
  1975 "Fases de la protesta rural en América Latina," pp. 260–274 in Ernest Feder (ed.), *La lucha de clases en el campo: Análisis estructural de la economía latinoamericana.* México, D.F.: Fondo de Cultura Económica.

Womack, John, Jr.
  1968 *Zapata and the Mexican Revolution.* New York: Random House-Vintage.

Yáñez, Agustín
  1975 *Las tierras flacas.* México, D.F.: Joaquín Mortiz. (Originally published in 1961.)

Yates, Paul Lamartine
  1981 *Mexico's Agricultural Dilemma.* Tucson: University of Arizona Press.

Zuno Hernández, José Guadalupe
  1964 *Historia de la revolución en el Estado de Jalisco.* México, D.F.: Biblioteca del Instituto Nacional de Estudios Históricos de la Revolución Mexicana.
  1972 *Reminiscencias de una vida.* Guadalajara, Jal.: Biblioteca de Autores Jaliscienses Modernos, no. 4, El Diario. (Originally published in 1956.)

Archival Collections Cited

AJRG - Archivo de José Romero Gómez (in his possession, México, D.F.)

ASRA - Archivo de la Secretaría de Reforma Agraria (México, D.F.)

Libros de Actas - Archivo del Ayuntamiento (Lagos de Moreno, Jal.)

Libros de Catastro (*Manifestaciones Prediales de 1900*, and *Catastro Antiguo, 1900–1947*) - Archivo de la Delegación de la Secretaría de Hacienda del Estado (Lagos de Moreno, Jal.)

Libros de Gobierno - Archivo de la Parroquia (Lagos de Moreno, Jal.)

Newspapers Cited

Antorcha (Puebla, Mexico)

El Defensor del Pueblo (Lagos de Moreno)

Diario Oficial (México, D.F.)

Ecos de Lagos (Lagos de Moreno)

Espártaco (place of publication unknown)

Excélsior (México, D.F.)

El Informador (Guadalajara)

El Jaliscience (Guadalajara)

Labor (Lagos de Moreno)

El Machete (México, D.F.)

Notas y Letras (Lagos de Moreno)

La Palabra (Lagos de Moreno)

Periódico Oficial del Gobierno, Estado de Jalisco (Guadalajara)

Provincia (Lagos de Moreno)

Regeneración (various localities in the U.S. and Mexico, published intermittently from 1900 to 1918 by Enrique and Ricardo Flores Magón)

Regeneración (tercera etapa) (México, D.F., official newspaper of the Federación Anarquista Mexicana, 1961–70)

Sagitario (Tampico, Veracruz)

Vértice (Lagos de Moreno)

Index

Designer: Laurie Anderson
Compositor: Computer Typesetting Services, Inc.
Printer: Thomson-Shore, Inc.
Binder: John H. Dekker & Sons
Text: 10/13 Aster
Display: Aster